Behavior Management in K-6 Classrooms

NEA
EARLY CHILDHOOD
EDUCATION SERIES

Behavior Management in K-6 Classrooms

Karen Malm

A NATIONAL EDUCATION ASSOCIATION
PUBLICATION

Printing History
First Printing: February 1992

Note

The opinions expressed in this publication should not be construed as representing the policy or position of the National Education Association. Materials published by the NEA Professional Library are intended to be discussion documents for educators who are concerned with specialized interests of the profession.

Library of Congress Cataloging-in-Publication Data

Malm, Karen
Behavior management in K-6 classrooms / Karen Malm.
p. cm — (NEA Early childhood education series)
Includes bibliographical references.
ISBN 0-8106-0365-9
1. Classroom management — United States. 2. Children — United States — Conduct of life. I. Title. II. Series: Early childhood education series (Washington, D.C.)
LB3013.M322 1991
372.11'024—dc20 91-23797
CIP

CONTENTS

The Author

Karen Malm is a School Psychologist in the Granite Headstart Program, Salt Lake City, Utah.

The Advisory Panel

Geraldine Doswell, Elementary School Counselor, Lawrenceville, New Jersey

Jack Kramer, Associate Professor of Educational Psychology, University of Nebraska-Lincoln

Annamarie Lavieri, Second Grade Teacher, Bainbridge Island School District, Washington

Sharon Morgan, Kindergarten Teacher, Raymond Gabaldon Elementary School, Las Lunas, New Mexico

Richard J. Morris, Professor of Educational Psychology, and Director, School Psychology Program, University of Arizona, Tucson

Barbara Jean Penrod, Teacher of the Gifted, Meadowvale Elementary School, Johnstown, Pennsylvania

Diann Poston, Third Grade Teacher, Rickman, Tennessee

Donald K. Pumroy, Professor of Education and Psychology, and Director of School Psychology Program, College of Education, University of Maryland, College Park

Mary Regas, First Grade Teacher, Brunswick, Ohio

INTRODUCTION

The purpose of this book is to present a system of proactive classroom management for use in elementary classrooms. Proactive classroom management is a relatively new concept in classroom behavior management strategies. Gettinger (1)* described three characteristics of proactive classroom management. The first characteristic deals with the "proactive" concept, which is to prevent behavior problems rather than react to them. In this way, proactive management involves planning ahead to avoid a problem. The second characteristic considers the total process of the classroom, including ways not only to facilitate appropriate classroom behavior but also ways to facilitate achievement. Traditional methods of classroom management treat the instructional realm separately from behavior management. Finally, proactive classroom management deals with the entire class rather than with individual student behavior. It is a group approach in that if the group functions well, then the individual will follow the group. Sanford, Emmer, and Clements (2) summarized the concept of proactive classroom management to include "all the things teachers must do to foster student involvement and cooperation in classroom activities and to establish a productive working environment" (p. 56).

What then is behavior management? When teachers were asked what it meant to them, answers varied from a way to control children in the classroom to the use of time-out for misbehaviors. Behavior theory, in general, has been misconceived by the general public for a variety of reasons. Initially, the science of behaviorism meant to many people the training of rats to run mazes or the teaching of pigeons to peck at a disc for food. The very thought that people were controlled in some way or that we could understand human behavior through scientific methods seemed foreign. The public protested that we were "free" and

*Numbers in parentheses appearing in the text refer to the references at the end of the chapters.

that we were not controlled like some rats in a cage. As behavior theory became applied more to real-life settings and, as we now apply it to classrooms and classroom management, behavioral techniques still do not get a fair shake. Some teachers are heard to say, "Oh, I tried that behavior management stuff we learned in class. Some of it works, but I don't buy it entirely." Or, teachers are tired of the same old material presented over and over. "Use positive reinforcement to get children motivated. Have consequences for misbehaviors." The teaching community can become saturated with this material. So, why more material on behavior management? Because the material presented here puts behavior management into action, it is designed to be *useful* to the classroom teacher—not theoretical. One of the problems with much of the behavior management material presented to teachers is that techniques are taught in isolation. A teacher then tries to implement a technique separately from the entire classroom as a system that must be worked within its entirety. This book defines behavior management as an entire system, not an isolated technique.

Behavior management involves a system designed to effectively manage and control students in the classroom using the principles of behavior theory. Behavior management is not a singular technique such as positive reinforcement or time-out. It is not that simple. Instead, we need to understand behavior, understand what makes children behave and misbehave, and then use that knowledge to develop a positive learning environment and a pleasant experience for the teacher and the students. When we use a system, it makes sense that there should be a rhyme and a reason to implementing that system. To that purpose, the system presented here is a hierarchy.

The hierarchy of behavior management in the classroom allows for a look at the classroom system in terms of levels of impact. We begin with a broad perspective of the classroom. We will look at the classroom environment and how we can use that environment as part of our behavior management system. We will look at the cues the children receive from their environment

Figure 1
The Behavior Management Hierarchy[a]

Classroom environment	Least intensive (broad base to build upon)
Scheduling	
Classroom rules	
Reinforcement procedures	
Parental involvement	
Consequating behaviors	Most intensive

[a]The hierarchy builds one step upon another. One level must be stable before moving on to the next.

and how that affects their behavior. Next, we will look at scheduling concerns and how these can impact the learning experience. With effective use of scheduling, we can improve upon the teaching lesson and the children's willingness to learn. Classroom rules are an inevitable part of any behavior management system, and by learning appropriate rule setting we can maximize the effects of those rules. Reinforcement is a standard within any classroom system; but, again, the appropriate use of those reinforcers makes the difference. Parental involvement is key to an effective management system. Enlisting parental support will strengthen the behavior system in the class. When we have misbehaviors, we also need appropriate methods for consequating behaviors. We place consequences at the most intense level because it is more favorable to use positives first and then only afterwards to resort to consequences. Figure 1 outlines the six levels presented in this book.

An advantage of the hierarchical system is that it gives the classroom teacher a starting point. The task of setting up an effective behavior management system can be overwhelming, but the hierarchy gives us a place to begin. We also can use the hierarchy for troubleshooting what may be going wrong in an established system. We can examine each level to determine where the system is breaking down. We can check to determine that we have covered our bases and that we understand how each level impacts another. If our classroom environment is chaotic, then our reinforcers will not work. If our schedule does not allow children to work when they have the most energy, then our classroom rules may not be effective in handling behaviors. Each level must be under control before we move to the next level. This behavior management hierarchy is truly a system, a system that will break down if one of the parts is dysfunctional.

The intent of this book is first to give an overview of behavioral principles that will give teachers a broad-based understanding of why children behave and misbehave. Then, using this knowledge, we will build a classroom management system based on behavioral principles. By the end of the book, the reader should be able to identify behavior problems or classroom problems, analyze why they are occurring, and apply the behavior management hierarchy to find a solution. Remember that the keys to proactive classroom management are to plan ahead, to consider the total process of the classroom, and to manage the group instead of individuals.

REFERENCES

1. Gettinger, Maribeth. "Methods of Proactive Classroom Management." *School Psychology Review* 17, no. 2 (1988):227–42.
2. Sanford, Julie P.; Emmer, Edmund T.; and Clements, Barbara S. "Improving Classroom Management." *Educational Leadership* 40 (1983):56-60.

Chapter 1

THE BEHAVIOR MANAGEMENT HIERARCHY

UNDERSTANDING BEHAVIOR: A–B–C ASSESSMENT

Before we can begin to put together our behavior management system, we must understand the basic principles upon which behavior management is built—the science of behavior. In order to understand behavior, we will use the A–B–C assessment approach: *A*ntecedent–*B*ehavior–*C*onsequence. Although other approaches have been developed, this is the most simple and most applicable for our purposes.

Defining Behavior

We begin with defining behavior because this is the target of our management system and of our interventions. Behavior is something we can see; we can measure it; we can agree on the words to describe it; and it is something we can count or time. Behavior is *not* feelings, thoughts, or intentions—things that have different interpretations to different people. It is this point that gave behaviorism its bad name or the belief that "behaviorists don't believe people have feelings." Of course, people do have feelings. We just cannot see them; we cannot know if we are effectively changing feelings because we cannot count or measure a feeling of happiness or sadness. When we ask, "What is happiness?" to a room of fifteen adults, we get fifteen different answers. Feelings are personal and individual; thus, we cannot define as our goal "I want my students to be happy" because we will never know if we have met our goal. What we *can* do is to agree on which behaviors are manifestations of happiness, and then we can count those behaviors. In that way we will know if we are really making our children happier. We can count the number of positive comments made by the students, and we can count the number of times a child smiles when he/she is in the classroom. Figure 1–1 shows examples and nonexamples of behaviors we can use for behavior management purposes.

Defining Antecedents

Once we have defined the behavior, we can begin to analyze the chain of events that occurs around that behavior in order to help us to understand why children behave in a certain way; then, we can work to change or enhance the behavior. Let's look at the "A" in our A–B–C assessment that stands for antecedent. An antecedent is *anything* that occurs *before* a behavior happens. An antecedent can be a person, place, time, event, object, or even another behavior. Figure 1–2 gives examples of what could serve as antecedents to a behavior. Antecedents are important because once we see what occurs before to signal a behavior, we can stop that signal and cease the chain of events. We also can manipulate antecedents to promote an appropriate behavior. Antecedents may be difficult to pinpoint. Careful observation is necessary to try to uncover the event that happens before the behavior occurs; for example, the

Figure 1-1
Examples and Nonexamples of Targets of Intervention in Behavior Management

Nonexamples	*Examples*
Learning	Length of time working on an assignment
Being good	Sitting quietly while teacher talks
Having fun	Laughing during an activity
Making progress	Raising a letter grade

scenario presented in Figure 1–2 of Bob's mother getting ready for work and Bob wetting his pants. Initially, Bob's mother thought that the wet pants were a product of too many fluids for breakfast and a weak bladder. However, closer examination revealed that Bob never wet his pants on the days his mother did not go to work; thus, it appeared that the event of his mother going to work always preceded the behavior. To fully understand why the behavior occurs, we also must examine consequences.

Figure 1-2
Examples of Antecedents

Example of PERSON serving as an antecedent:
Antecedent: Sally's mother walks into the classroom.
Behavior: Sally cries in the classroom.

Example of PLACE serving as an antecedent:
Antecedent: Joe and his father arrive at the doctor's office.
Behavior: Joe has a tantrum.

Example of TIME serving as an antecedent:
Antecedent: It is 3:00 p.m., school is out at 3:15 p.m.
Behavior: The children become restless, misbehaviors increase.

Example of EVENT serving as an antecedent:
Antecedent: Bob's mother is getting ready for work.
Behavior: Bob wets his pants.

Example of OBJECT serving as an antecedent:
Antecedent: Ginger's sister takes out her favorite doll.
Behavior: Ginger and her sister get in a fight.

Example of BEHAVIOR serving as an antecedent:
Antecedent: Jerrad fights on the playground.
Behavior: Jerrad is distracted during seatwork and does not work.

Defining Consequences

A consequence is *anything* that occurs *after* the behavior. A consequence can be a person, place, object, event, or another behavior. Figure 1–3 gives the consequences for the chain of behaviors that occurred in Figure 1–2. Consequences can be easier to spot because once the behavior has occurred we can observe what happens immediately following that behavior. In order to put the final piece of our A–B–C assessment together, we need to understand consequences more in-depth.

Consequences can do three things to a behavior: (a) maintain, (b) increase, or (c) decrease. Consequences that increase or maintain a behavior are called "reinforcers"; those that decrease a behavior are called "punishers." There are two kinds of reinforcers: (a) positive reinforcement, and (b) negative reinforcement. Positive reinforcement is giving something positive such as food, attention, kind words, or money—anything that is perceived to be positive by the receiver. Negative reinforcement is more difficult to understand. Many teachers believe wrongly that negative reinforcement either is doing something negative to a child to get him/her to stop misbehaving or is reinforcing a child by something negative. Negative reinforcement actually is the *removal* of something negative following the behavior that, in turn, *increases* that behavior. In practice, the negative stimulus occurs, and then we must do something to stop the negative stimulus. Whatever we do to make it stop is the behavior that increases. We are reinforced by not having the negative stimulus occur. The behavior that made it stop happens sooner, more quickly, and with more intensity as we learn that our behavior changes the negative stimulus. A few examples will help clarify the concept:

1. A loud buzzer goes off in a classroom whenever children are not working. The buzzer goes off when children get back to work. The negative stimulus, the buzzer, is removed after the appropriate behavior—

working—occurs. Over time, the working behavior increases as the children try to avoid the negative stimulus.

2. A child wants the teacher to come over to his/her desk and he/she waves his/her hand and yells, "Teacher!

Figure 1-3
Examples of Consequences

Example of PERSON serving as a consequence:

Antecedent: Joe and his father arrive at the doctor's office.
Behavior: Joe has a tantrum.
Consequence: Joe's mother is called, and she comes to comfort him.

Example of PLACE serving as a consequence:

Antecedent: Joe fights on the playground.
Behavior: Joe is distracted during seatwork and does not work.
Consequence: Joe has to sit in the hall.

Example of OBJECT serving as a consequence:

Antecedent: Ginger's sister takes out her doll.
Behavior: Ginger and her sister get in a fight.
Consequence: Ginger's mother tells sister to let Ginger play with the doll.

Example of EVENT serving as a consequence:

Antecedent: Bob's mother is getting ready for work.
Behavior: Bob wets his pants.
Consequence: Bob's mother delays going to work to change Bob's pants.

Example of BEHAVIOR serving as a consequence:

Antecedent: It is 3:00 p.m., school gets out at 3:15 p.m.
Behavior: Children become restless, misbehaviors increase.
Consequence: Teacher sends children out to the playground to run around.

Teacher!" The teacher attends to him/her in order to stop the negative stimulus.

The teacher will respond more quickly and more often (the behavior increases) so that she can stop the negative stimulus. The concept of negative reinforcement will be important when we discuss how many misbehaviors are maintained.

Punishment, by definition, decreases behavior. There are two types of punishers: (a) application of an aversive, or (b) withdrawal of a positive. When we apply something negative immediately following a behavior, we see a decrease in the rate of the behavior over time. For example, we may put a check next to a name, demand extra work, or ask for a chore such as sweeping the floor. We also can remove something positive immediately following the behavior. For example, we can take away a favorite toy, move a close friend away from the misbehaving child, or take away a privilege. The key to punishment is to remember that it is punishment only if we see a decrease in the target behavior. Thus, if we remove a child from a positive experience and place him or her in time-out, and the behavior does *not* decrease, then, by definition, it is not a punisher.

WHY CHILDREN MISBEHAVE

Now, as we look at behaviors, we can pinpoint and identify a behavior; we can examine what happens before the behavior (i.e., what signals that the behavior is going to occur); and then we can see what the consequence of the behavior is. One piece of our puzzle is still missing; we have not uncovered why children misbehave. There are two basic reasons for misbehavior: (a) either the child is being reinforced for the misbehavior, or (b) the child does not possess the necessary skill. If the child is getting reinforcement for the behavior, then the behavior will be maintained or will increase. The child may know the correct behavior, but does not perform appropriately because the reinforcement for misbehaving is stronger than the reinforcement for appropriate behavior. For example, the class clown gets a lot of positive reinforcement from the laughter of his/her classmates. This reinforcement from peers is stronger than either the reinforcement for behaving appropriately or the threat of punishment. This phenomenon may be difficult to observe. For example, from using the scenario presented in the examples involving Joe and his inability to work following a fight on the playground (Fig. 1–3), we can see that the consequence for Joe's inability to concentrate is to sit in the hall. The teacher assumes this is a punishment. However, when Joe is in the hall, he gets to watch other children go by, he can ask a passerby for help with his assignment, and the pressure is off to conform to classroom standards of behavior. In other words, he is actually enjoying the time in the hall and is getting reinforced. As we look at other scenarios, we can see the reinforcing component presented in other misbehaviors in our examples. Jerrad's tantrum is reinforced by his mother's comfort. The classroom's restlessness and misbehavior are reinforced by getting to play outside. Bob's wetting accident is reinforced by getting to spend a few more minutes with his mother while she changes his pants. These hidden reinforcers are the key to understanding children's misbehaviors.

The other reason children might misbehave is because of a skill deficit. A skill deficit is present when the child does not possess the skills to behave appropriately. The child might never have been taught one skill or might never have been exposed to conditions that would warrant use of the skill. The term *skill deficit* is not intended to fault the child but merely expresses the absence of a skill. For example, a kindergarten student who has never attended preschool usually does not have the skills to sit at a desk for long periods of time. In this regard, he or she has a skill deficit. This may be exhibited in several misbehaviors such as jumping out of the chair, talking to neighbors, or calling out to the teacher. Another example is the child who has never been taught what "no" means and may come from an overindulged family life. Because the child does not understand what "no" means, he/she cannot respond appropriately to this as a command. For young children, skill deficits can be a major factor in understanding their misbehavior—a reason that is often overlooked by teachers.

A–B–C ASSESSMENT CHECKLIST

In order to make sense of A-B-C assessment and its impact for behavior management, the following checklist will be helpful. When you look at the misbehaviors in your class, examine the behavior carefully and methodically.

1. Define the behavior problem: Is it measurable? Observable?
2. Antecedents: What happens immediately *before* the behavior occurs?
3. Consequences: What happens immediately *after* the behavior occurs?
4. Does the child possess the skill or is there a skill deficit?
5. Is the child being reinforced for the misbehavior?

Using this checklist, you can complete your assessment of behavior that is key to targeting behaviors for interventions and using the appropriate method to deal with the behavior problem. The following case study highlights the use of behavioral assessment to deal with classroom misbehaviors.

CASE STUDY

Mr. Terrell teaches third grade at Grantview Elementary. He has twenty-six students this year, eighteen of them boys! He has heard that the boys can be difficult to handle, so he plans ahead with strict guidelines for appropriate behavior in class, along with well-outlined consequences. The children begin the year without incident, and Mr. Terrell thinks he has the problem licked; then one day, while the students are completing their seatwork, Mark decides he's had enough of this seatwork. He lets out a loud yawn, which is greeted by giggles from his classmates. Mr. Terrell scans the class to see who made the noise, but he is unsure. He decides to ignore the behavior, thinking that to attend to it may be to reinforce it. He had been taught in his behavior management series at the university to ignore some misbehaviors. Mark has been quietly looking at his paper; as he looks up, he notices a few classmates smiling at him. He lets out another loud yawn, which is greeted by even louder laughter from his classmates. Mr. Terrell clears his throat and tells the class to settle down. By now, a few more classmates look challengingly at Mark. He obliges, and lets out another loud yawn that breaks up the entire class—leaving Mr. Terrell to yell for silence.

1. What is the behavior?
   Mark yawns out loud.
2. What happens directly before the behavior?
   The first time the behavior occurred, we might suggest that it was the result of boredom. However, the next several times Mark yawns, he knew the consequence of his first yawn and was then challenged to yawn again. The antecedent in this chain is the students' challenging looks at Mark.
3. What happens directly after the behavior?
   The students laugh with Mark.
4. Is there a skill deficit?
   Probably not. Mark knows the class rules and has demonstrated previously that he was able to follow them initially.
5. Is the behavior getting reinforced?
   Most certainly. Mark is getting positively reinforced by the laughter of his classmates.

RESOURCES

General Classroom Management

1. Brophy, Jere. "Classroom Management Techniques." *Education and Urban Society* 18, no. 2 (1986):182–94.
2. Cheesman, Peter, and Watts, Phil. *Positive Behavior Management: A Manual for Teachers.* New York: Nichols Publishing Co., 1985.
3. Duke, Daniel, ed. *Helping Teachers Manage Classrooms.* Alexandria, Va.: Association for Supervision and Curriculum Development, 1982.
4. Evertson, Carolyn M.; Emmer, Edmund T.; Clements, Barbara S.; Sanford, Julie P.; and Worsham, Murray E. *Classroom Management for Elementary Teachers.* Englewood Cliffs, N.J.: Prentice-Hall, 1989.
5. Fromberg, Doris P., and Driscoll, M. *The Successful Classroom: Management Strategies for Regular and Special Education Teachers.* New York: Teachers College Press, 1985.
6. Jones, Vernon F., and Jones, Louise S. *Comprehensive Classroom Management: Creating Positive Learning Environments.* 2d ed. Boston: Allyn & Bacon, 1986.
7. Kuder, S. Jay. "An Ounce of Prevention. . . ." *Academic Therapy* 21, no. 4 (1986):531–36.
8. Maurer, Richard E. *Elementary Discipline Handbook: Solutions for the K–8 Teacher.* West Nyack, N.Y.: Center for Applied Research in Education, 1985.
9. Moorman, Chick, and Dishon, Dee. *Our Classroom: We Can Learn Together.* Englewood Cliffs, N.J.: Prentice-Hall, 1983.
10. Williamson, Bonnie. *H.I.P. Tips: How to Organize and Run a Successful Classroom: A Guide for Elementary Teachers.* Rancho Cordova, Calif.: Dynamic Teaching Co., 1986.
11. Shepardson, Richard D. *Elementary Teacher's Discipline Desk Book.* West Nyack, N.Y.: Parker Publishing Co., 1980.

Behavior Modification

1. Hersen, Michael, and Bellack, Alan S. *Behavioral Assessment: A Practical Handbook.* New York: Pergamon Press, 1985.
2. Kazdin, Alan E. *Behavior Modification in Applied Settings.* Chicago, Ill.: Dorsey Press, 1980.

Chapter 2

CLASSROOM ENVIRONMENT

The first place to begin a comprehensive behavior management system is with the physical space—the empty classroom. While few of us have a choice in the space given to us, it is what we do with that space that makes the difference. The classroom environment allows the teacher not only to represent his/her personality, but also it can set up parameters that govern children's behavior. Walking through schools, one can see extremes in different classrooms—from a classroom decorated simply with few wall hangings and neat rows of desks, to classrooms filled with colorful wall hangings and clusters of desks. Before we condemn the simple classroom completely, we should ask whether the other kind of classroom presents too many distractors to make learning and behavior management feasible. A careful balance can enhance the classroom environment and meet the needs of the child and the teacher. Planning for an effective classroom environment begins before the children enter the classroom.

DESK AND TABLE ARRANGEMENTS

Through the years children have been arranged in the classroom on benches, at tables, in desks, in rows, in circles, and in clusters. Teachers experiment with different arrangements continually, but is there any real research to support one arrangement over another? The answer ends up to be not as simple as we might think; in fact, the desk arrangement's impact on performance may depend more on the task than on the arrangement.

Several studies have demonstrated the effectiveness of using rows of desks rather than tables. Axelrod, Hall, and Tams (1) demonstrated that traditional seating in rows increases on-task behavior, while it decreases disruptions. Wheldall and

Lam (6) compared rows of desks with table formation and found that in the desk formation, on-task behaviors doubled. Class disruptions tripled in the table formation. Teachers' positive comments on academic behavior also were affected by the formations, with higher rates of positive comments during the desk formation.

Rosenfield, Lambert, and Black (4) compared rows, circles, and clusters in their study of desk arrangement and found more on-task behavior with circles and clusters than with rows. However, the task observed was a brainstorming session for a writing assignment. The students were expected to collaborate and make suggestions for ideas on the assignment. The circle arrangement seemed to be helpful for facilitating pupil interaction during discussions where active student participation was the goal. There were no differential effects found for disruptive behaviors. The circle arrangement does not necessarily mean a disruptive class. The students made more out-of-turn comments, but the comments were task-relevant. The students showed more withdrawn behavior in the rows. There was more hand-raising in the clusters, which the authors suggested was because the students had to get the teacher's attention—more so than in the circles.

Overall, it would seem that the best desk arrangement for everyday learning in the classroom is rows of desks. There appears to be more on-task behavior and less disruptions than with other arrangements. If there is room for space between the students, this may further decrease disruptions as students can keep their hands to themselves and their eyes on their own paper. For creative projects, group discussions, and activities where the goal is active student participation, either clusters or a circle is the arrangement of choice. Students seem to engage more freely in these arrangements and, if other behavioral techniques are in play, disruptions do not have to increase.

ENVIRONMENT

A classroom that is brightly decorated is a cheerful workplace; however, the teacher also must use caution that he/she is not creating distractions in the workplace. Children can be easily distracted; and, if the calendar reminding them that Halloween or Valentine's Day is coming soon, their minds may wander toward candy rather than toward their lessons. Overly decorated walls might make a room appear chaotic, and children might have difficulty concentrating as well. Classroom walls can be incorporated into instruction and behavior management.

Creekmore (2) developed a helpful organization for the effective use of classroom walls that is based on learning theory as well as on research. He used two basic principles of learning theory: (a) For children to learn, there must be an interaction between the material being taught and the student; and (b) students must be on-task or focused if new and/or complicated material is to be acquired and maintained by the student. There are three basic activities that occur in the learning environment: (a) acquisition of material, (b) maintenance of material, and (c) generalization of material to new situations. Creekmore took these tasks and utilized the classroom walls to enhance these learning activities. He called one wall the "acquisition wall," which includes the chalkboard and at least one bulletin board. The acquisition wall is used to teach new concepts to the class or to reintroduce material that the students have had difficulty learning. The wall should contain only those materials to be used in your teaching lesson and these should be removed following the end of the lesson. The idea is to not have any competing materials on the wall; thus, the child's attention is focused on the lesson currently being taught.

Following a lesson, material can be placed on a "maintenance wall." This wall is to the right or left of the acquisition wall. The materials on this wall review or reorient children to the material. The maintenance wall also is a good place for any concept support materials, such as number lines and alphabet letters. Creekmore pointed out that a good reason not to put these "help" items on the acquisition wall is that children can rely on them too easily as a visual aid rather than depending on cognitive processes to remember these items. The maintenance wall helps to strengthen the material learned in the lesson because students can refer to the concepts taught in the lesson and can review the material again.

The "dynamic wall" shows materials that can be found on typical elementary school walls such as theme materials (e.g., ghosts, Santa Claus, hearts, Easter bunnies) and calendars. The wall can be either a side wall or the back wall. It is called "dynamic" because the materials should be changed and should not be on permanent display. The dynamic wall can be used for children's work, notices, and so forth. Items that are not particularly related to the teaching lessons but add to the classroom environment are put on the dynamic wall.

Research has demonstrated that a substantially higher percentage of acquisition and generalizations are reached in the acquisition wall classroom than in a traditional classroom (2). More research is needed to further validate the use of the acquisition wall, but it appears that this classroom setup helps children to focus on the task by eliminating distractors and setting predictable parameters where learning material is presented. The maintenance wall is helpful for children who need more review and more help in preparing seatwork based on a new concept. This could help to free a teacher's time because the children can refer to the maintenance wall.

Another way to use one of the classroom walls is to develop a system of public posting of academic progress and/or behavioral goals. Displaying a student's progress in academics or behaviors can provide motivation and improve performance. Research has demonstrated the positive effects of public posting on both high- and low-ability learners, with low-ability learners improving the most (5). There are several key elements to setting up a public-posting system. First, there must be a visual display that is prominently displayed so that children can see the posting.

The display gives visual feedback to the students and should be used frequently as well as immediately to help children see their daily progress. For example, immediately after a child finishes a reading unit, he or she could check off that unit or move his or her marker one unit forward. In this way, the children see immediate results. Second, public posting should be a positive measure and should reflect success of the individual. The students should not be pitted one against the other or ranked, but the individual should work toward his/her own progress. The child's point of reference for success should be his/her own work. To illustrate, if a child finishes fifteen math problems one day, then he or she can set a goal to try to finish sixteen the next day. The child then feels success measured by his/her own progress rather than by being compared to the students who can finish thirty problems a day.

For the public-posting system to be most effective, there must be a built-in system for positive praise and reinforcement. The teacher should comment on individual and class improvement. Comments to individual students should be made privately or in a small group; thus, those students who are having difficulty do not feel left out. Group comments can include such remarks as the number of students who beat their old scores or who achieved a goal. In this way, even the low-ability students can enjoy the group praise. For added impact, you can ask the principal or other visitors to comment on the board. Children also can be taught to reinforce each other. This peer reinforcement can be very helpful. To add even more powerful reinforcement, tangible reinforcers such as prizes or privileges can be incorporated into the system.

Public posting also can affect behavior problems. Goals can be made for the class to reflect a group goal to achieve a behavioral objective. For example, the class might try to increase on-task performance by working for five minutes without an interruption. There might be a class objective to be more polite, and the children could try to say "please" and "thank you" five times a day. A group reward could be administered following achievement of a goal. Sometimes it is not necessary to have behavioral objectives as the focus of the public posting system because just the posting of academic success can have an effect on behavior problems. One study used public posting to advise daily quiz results and found a large reduction in behavioral disruptions (3). Children who are on-task do not have time to be disruptive! Remember to keep the public posting dynamic, visible, immediate, positive, and individually referenced. Figure 2–1 shows a few examples of public-posting systems. By using your imagination and grading scores, your public-posting system can reflect a motivating, dynamic part of your classroom environment.

CLASSROOM FLOW

In assessing the classroom, it is important to look at the traffic patterns in the room. Sit in the empty classroom and imagine the traffic flow during the day. Begin with the children entering the room. They will need adequate space to hang their coats and belongings and to find their seat. Obstructing coat racks with garbage cans on the floor, boxes of supplies, desks, and the like will create chaos and clutter in an area that can already be busy. Keep floor space clear, and allow several feet around this area so that children are not tripping over each other. Labeling coat racks or cubby holes can help ease the chaos. Children will learn where their space is, and this can cut down on confusion when hanging up materials. Using a color system for names or other differential labeling (e.g., shapes, animals, etc.) can be helpful at the end of the day. The teacher can call out for different groups to gather their belongings: "All children whose names are on red circles can get their coats." The experience can then be part of learning as well.

During the day, children will be involved in seatwork, groups, and independent play activities. Ask yourself whether children can move about the room with the minimal amount of disruption to others. Areas of congestion include the drinking

Figure 2-1
Examples of Public-Posting Systems

Reading - Story #	104	105	106	107	108	109	110
Sarah M.	✔	✔	✔				
Janet R.	✔						
David P.	✔	✔	✔	✔	✔		
Jacob K.	✔	✔					

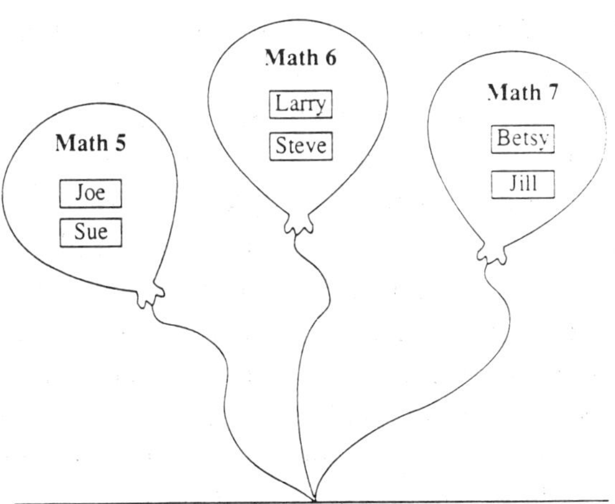

fountain, teacher's desk, central areas for turning in papers, the pencil sharpener, garbage can, classroom door, and any other central locations for supplies and books. There are several ways to handle these congestions. One way is to structure the environment by allowing more space in heavily trafficked areas. Allow wide alleys between desks and traffic areas, and move equipment such as TV monitors to corners where they will not get in the way. Another way to handle congestion is to limit access by way of classroom rules. For example, only one child can be at the pencil sharpener or drinking fountain at a time. Routines can be made to avoid congestion by having children hand out supplies such as scissors and glue or by having children collect papers. In this way, central locations can be minimized. The most helpful way to determine the traffic needs in your classroom is to walk through the day to determine where traffic flow is greatest. Make a sketch of the classroom layout and play with different arrangements before you actually move furniture!

WORK STATIONS

One way to enhance the traffic flow and to decrease behavior problems is to develop work stations or areas where students can find their own materials, organize their materials, and begin to work. This can develop independent work habits that are important skills and building blocks for later schooling. Children should know where to find supplies as needed and where to go after an activity is completed. Remember that your desk also can be considered a work station and can serve an important function in traffic flow and behavior management. Your desk should be where you can easily see all children. It should not obstruct traffic flow within the classroom, and you also should consider how much you use your desk. During class time, do you like to sit at your desk and grade papers? If yes, then your desk should be in a location to facilitate children visiting you there. Or, do you rarely sit at your desk, except after the students are gone? If yes, then your desk can be placed out of the way where it is not cluttering the classroom.

By developing work areas, the room becomes less congested and the children are able to move about freely. Furthermore, children can learn to discriminate what is appropriate behavior for different activities and different parts of the room. The book-and-puzzle corner is a place for quiet voices. The free-play table or toy table is for louder voices. Children can be self-directed, moving from one activity to the next, and having little idle time to get into trouble. When children finish work early, they can move to another activity and not bother their peers. Again, the use of a sketch of your classroom will help you to organize both traffic flow and work stations and also help you to visualize how to maximize your classroom space for better behavior management.

CASE STUDY

Ms. Morehouse entered her new classroom and groaned at the small and poorly organized space. She walked around the room and inventoried her equipment—student desks and chairs, a large round table without accompanying chairs, a teacher's desk and chair, a TV monitor, bookshelves, and a waste basket. She drew an approximation of the space and the permanent fixtures in the room (see Figure 2–2). She immediately saw that with the pencil sharpener near the door it would probably be best to limit access to it by making a rule that only one person could be at the sharpener at a time. The same was true of the sink, which, stuck in a corner, could cause congestion as children went to get a drink. One solution would be to allow only one child at a time to get a drink, or to allow the class to get drinks only at certain times during the day. As a group, the class could line up along one wall, and children could exit to one side of the sink. With only one blackboard, there was no choice as to where the teaching wall would be. The bulletin board adjacent to this wall could be the maintenance wall, as well as where the public-posting system could go. This wall is in view of all students and could be posted with an alphabet and number line. A daily posting of progress could be viewed by all children from their desks. The back wall would be a good place for decorations and seasonal wall hangings. Children's artwork could go on this wall or above the coat rack.

The next problem was the position of furniture. With such a small classroom and twenty-two desks, it was not possible to have all desks separated. Ms. Morehouse decided to compromise and place desks in pairs. This would allow for an

Figure 2-2
Model of Classroom

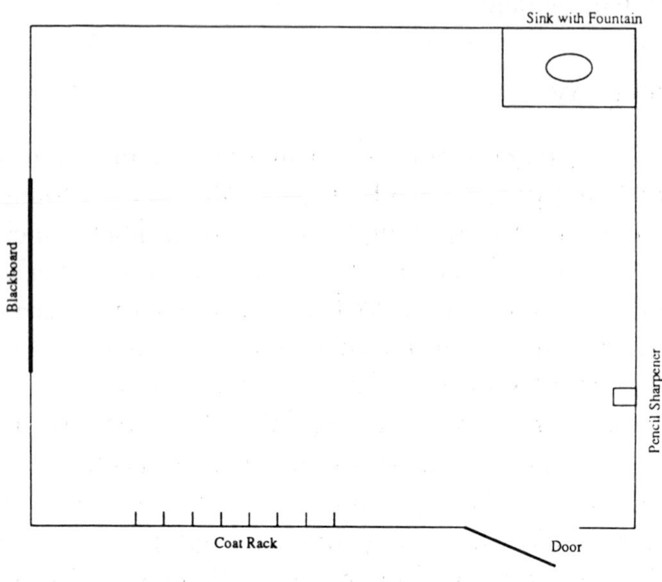

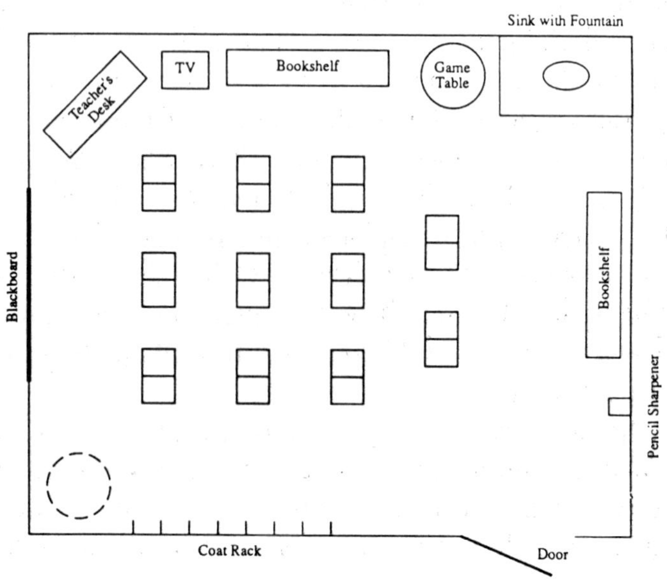

easy separation of troublesome pairs and have the least amount of contact possible to decrease distractions. Ms. Morehouse conducted reading groups by using a small circle of chairs. She decided to make space at the front of the classroom so that she could scan it for problems during the group time. Since she does not use her desk during the school day, she moved it to one side, out of the way, but convenient enough to put papers on it and check her schedule. The TV monitor also was moved to the side wall where it could be moved easily to the front of the class where all students could view it.

Work stations were then established such that children could move to new activities once they were finished with work. The round table became a game table, placed in the back of the room where it would not distract children who were still working. The large space in the back of the class allowed easy access to the work stations in the bookshelves. The bookshelves in the rear of the class contained work supplies and baskets for turning in and picking up papers. Reading and math books were placed in the other bookcase, and were passed out by class helpers as needed. Finally, Ms. Morehouse took the time to sit at each pupil's desk to see what the child would see. This allowed her to visualize all potential problems and distractions.

REFERENCES

1. Axelrod, Saul; Hall, R. Vance; and Tams, Ann. "Comparison of Two Common Classroom Seating Arrangements." *Academic Therapy* 15 (1979): 29–36.
2. Creekmore, W. N. (Skeet). "Effective Use of Classroom Walls." *Academic Therapy* 22, no. 4 (1987): 341–48.
3. Jones, David B., and Van Houten, Ron. "The Use of Daily Quizzes and Public Positives to Decrease the Disruptive Behavior of Secondary School Students." *Education and Treatment of Children* 8, no. 2 (1985): 91–106.

4. Rosenfield, Peter; Lambert, Nadine M.; and Black, Allen. "Desk Arrangement Effects on Pupil Classroom Behavior." *Journal of Educational Psychology* 77, no. 1 (1985): 101–8.
5. Van Houten, Ron. *Learning Through Feedback: A Systematic Approach for Improving Academic Performance.* New York: Human Services Press, 1980.
6. Wheldall, Kevin, and Lam, Yin Yuk. "Rows Versus Tables: The Effects of Two Classroom Seating Arrangements on Classroom Disruption Rate, On–Task Behavior, and Teacher Behavior in Three Special School Classes." *Educational Psychology* 7, no. 4 (1987): 303–12.

RESOURCES

Classroom Environment

1. Paine, Stan C.; Radicchi, JoAnn; Rosellini, Lynne C.; Deutchman, Leslie; and Darch, Craig B. *Structuring Your Classroom for Academic Success.* Champaign, Ill.: Research Press, 1983.

Public Posting

1. Van Houten, Ron. *Learning Through Feedback: A Systematic Approach for Improving Academic Performance.* New York: Human Sciences Press, 1980.

Classroom Arrangement/Work Stations

1. Hood-Smith, Nancy E., and Leffingwell, R. Jon. "The Impact of Physical Space Alteration on Disruptive Classroom Behavior: A Case Study." *Education* 104, no. 2 (1983): 224–30.
2. Lemlech, Johanna K. *Classroom Management.* New York: Harper & Row, 1979.
3. Malehorn, Hal. *Elementary Teacher's Classroom Management Handbook.* New York: Parker Publishing Co., 1984.

Chapter 3

SCHEDULING

Scheduling academics can affect behavior management in several ways. Children who have to work in long time frames get restless and bored, and will end up causing disruptions. Scheduling academics when a child is tired or wound up from outside activities likewise will cause problems. After recess, when children have been running around, it may be unrealistic to expect complete cooperation in the classroom. A "warm-down" activity such as listening to a story or quiet coloring can help set the mood of relaxation. Children have a short attention span for academics at this young age (only ten to twenty minutes), and it is helpful to change tasks frequently to maintain their attention. We also want to take time to think about our teaching priorities and how to make the most of the teaching day. Later, we can build on this academic time by increasing the amount of on-task time. Tuning the academics to the child's energy level will help lessen the amount of off-task behaviors in the classroom. If children are motivated, on-task, and the daily schedule runs smoothly, then the classroom will have fewer behavior problems.

SETTING UP A SCHEDULE

It is important to set your priorities before you make up your yearly schedule. This might include setting goals to help you to keep in mind what you expect your children to learn by the end of the school year. Setting goals will help you to stay on track throughout the year and also will help you to feel a sense of accomplishment during the year as you meet short-term goals. The first step in making a schedule is to list the subjects that you will be teaching. From this list, you should determine which subjects are taught on a daily basis (e.g., reading, math) and which subjects are taught less frequently (e.g., science). You also will need to determine how much time your reading groups will

Figure 3-1
Setting Up a Schedule:
Step-by-Step

---

1. List subjects that you teach.

2. Set your priorities for which subjects are most important in terms of academic progress. Set goals for what you expect the children to know by the end of the year.

3. List which subjects are taught daily, and which subjects are taught on a less regular basis.

4. Determine which subjects are taught in groups. Approximate the amount of time for a group and the number of groups.

5. Balance the day with a variety of teaching methods such as whole group, small group, structured activities, unstructured activities, and seatwork.

6. Plan for transitions between activities.

7. Review the schedule for balance and smooth transitions between activities.

---

take and how many groups you think you might have. This will help you to determine how much time during the day will be dedicated to groups and, in turn, how much seatwork the other students will need. Some districts have mandates regarding how much time should be spent on subjects; thus, you will need to consider this when you are deciding your time lines.

You will want to balance the amount of time spent in whole-group instruction, small-group instruction, independent seatwork, structured activities, and unstructured activities. It is through these different teaching methods that you can add variety to your class and keep your students' attention. Research indicates that children spend most of their academic day involved in independent seatwork, with less time spent in small-group and whole-group instruction (7). We also know that children achieve at higher rates when they are given more opportunities to respond (3). By breaking up the independent seatwork, not only can we keep variety, but we also can program in more chances for a child to respond and to practice skills. For example, seatwork can be difficult for young children; therefore, break it up by adding a peer-tutoring time when students can quiz each other. Group instruction can be varied by using either a straight lecture format or by rearranging desks for a more interactive approach. It is important to keep the day moving with a change at least every half hour; thus, young students will not become fatigued or bored with the activity, which often can lead to behavior problems.

Plan carefully for the first few days of school because these days will not follow your regular schedule. There will be administrative duties as well as getting-acquainted duties. Even though children may have gone through school together, they will need time to get acquainted with you and your classroom rules and procedures. We will discuss rules and routines in the next level of the hierarchy; however, now we will point out that the first few days of school is a good time to practice those routines. It is helpful to "get going" on your regular schedule by the third or fourth day. This will allow the children to get used to the daily routine more quickly.

The final word regarding scheduling concerns transitions between activities. It is important to allow time for these transitions so that, for example, thirty minutes for math does not whittle away to only twenty minutes. As students become accustomed to your schedule, the transitions will occur more quickly. Allow extra time in the beginning of the year to ensure that you are giving the amount of instruction you had intended. Figure 3–1 reviews the steps to set up your schedule.

AMOUNT OF TIME FOR LEARNING

When we talk about time spent learning, we are really

talking about several different variables. There is the amount of time we allocate to learning, for example, reading is from 9:00 to 9:30. This is the amount of time a teacher sets aside for teaching a given subject. Within that alloted time is a factor that we call the engagement rate, which is the percentage of the class that is engaged in the academic materials. At any point in which you are teaching, there will be children off-task. The engagement rate helps us to determine at any point during the day how many students are paying attention and how many are not. Each individual student spends a certain amount of time engaged as well, i.e., the student engagement time or time on-task. Finally, there is the academic learning time, defined as the amount of time a student spends attending to relevant academic tasks while performing with a high rate of success (4). In this way, we know not only that the children are engaged with academic material, but also that they actually are learning. Figure 3–2 summarizes these terms and their definitions.

Caldwell, Huitt, and Graeber (1) summarized the research in this area in an attempt to understand how achievement is related to time spent learning. For an average elementary school with a school year of 180 days, the average student attends 160 days, which includes subtracting days for illness, vacations, or skipping school. The average school day is five hours, which includes approximately two hours of reading/language arts instruction and approximately forty-five minutes of math instruction. Students are engaged approximately 60 percent of the allocated time, spending approximately seventy-two minutes on-task for reading/language arts and approximately twenty-seven minutes on-task for math. They are working successfully on relevant academic tasks for approximately half of this time, approximately thirty-six minutes each day for reading/language arts, and approximately fourteen minutes each day for math. When this time is averaged, the total number of hours of academic learning time is approximately ninety-six hours in reading/language arts and approximately thirty-seven hours in math!

Figure 3-2
Variables Used in the Concept of Time for Learning

Term	*Definition*
Allocated time	Amount of time a teacher sets aside for teaching a subject
Engagement rate	Percentage of class engaged in academic material
Student engaged time	Time on-task, or the amount of time the child is actively engaged in academic material
Academic learning time	Amount of time the student spends attending to relevant academic tasks while performing with a high rate of success

The key to academic achievement gains, then, is to increase the amount of time children are actively engaged in academic materials at a high success rate. We can reward children for outcome performance that will increase time on-task; however, for difficult tasks, research suggests that it is helpful to add a contingency for staying on-task (6). Praising children for working or using a token system for rewards, along with praise for academic performance (which can be tied into the public posting system) is helpful in increasing time on-task. It is important to note that merely praising children for staying on-task will decrease disruptive behaviors and increase attending, but this alone does not increase achievement (2). Reinforcement procedures as well as group contingencies for improving academic performance are discussed later in the hierarchy. At this point in our intervention hierarchy, it is important to be aware of the different variables involved in time spent learning. It has been demonstrated that making teachers aware of the literature on the relationship between student engagement time and achievement, along with being given feedback on their students' rate of engagement, can raise the level of engagement rate significantly (5). When we work on scheduling and finding time for academic achievement, we have to keep in mind the relationship between the time we allot to learning and the amount of time children actually spend on learning. Later on, we will discuss methods to increase the time on-task.

WHEN TO SCHEDULE ACADEMICS

When children first arrive at school, they are full of energy and might have difficulty settling into a task. Often they are bursting with information to tell you or their friends, or they may want to share something that happened on the way to school. We want to take this energy and enthusiasm and turn it into a useful activity. If we try to steer children into an activity that requires silent seatwork, we are setting ourselves up for frustration because it will take some time to reduce children's energy level. To use this energy, many teachers have found that a group discussion regarding the day ahead, a brief show and tell, and an "openings" routine help to settle down children. The "openings" is a routine in which helpers are chosen for the day, for example, the day of the week and month are presented, the weather may be discussed, and perhaps the Pledge of Allegiance is recited. Rather than seen only as a way to calm the children, learning is occurring as well. Children are learning (a) the days of the week; (b) about weather and how it impacts their day (e.g., discuss clothing to wear, whether they can play outside or not, etc.); and (c) to participate in a class discussion by sharing information. You can then end the openings discussion with a reminder of the schedule for the day, which should be posted where children can see it. The children have then had a chance to share, a chance to settle down, and will be ready for academics.

Morning is the best time for academics because children are fresh and ready to go. (Occasionally, you will have children who habitually have no energy and appear sleepy. These children might not have had breakfast or might have been kept up too late. At some point, it would be helpful to ask the child about breakfast and sleep times; if there appears to be a problem, ask the social worker or school psychologist, if you have one, to follow-up at home. You also may want to keep a few crackers in your cupboard to supplement the child's diet. Children's basic needs must be met before they are ready to learn.) It is helpful to begin the day with a group lesson. This will give children the independent seatwork that they will need to work on while you run your groups. Reading groups take up a large portion of your teaching morning and may need to be broken up into two separate times of the day. Remember that you cannot expect young students to sit at a desk for hours on end. A one-hour allotment for reading groups is plenty. If you have four reading groups and the groups tend to run twenty to twenty-five minutes, allowing for transition while groups trade, the class will be sitting for approximately two hours. If you break reading into two sessions, then only half of your class will be sitting for an hour. This hour can then be broken up by allowing children to participate in peer tutoring when their work is completed. For children who have finished seatwork, another option might be to have independent work stations with play activities. Do not be tempted to give more work to children who finish early. This will only serve to punish a child for getting his/her work done quickly. Instead, the child should be rewarded by getting to participate in other activities.

The afternoon is generally dedicated to other, less intensive, learning activities. The afternoon schedule will tend to change from day to day, with differing activities such as physical education, music, library, and so forth. Subjects such as science, health, and social studies are usually not taught every day; thus, these will rotate as well. The afternoon is a good time for interactive teaching; science experiments and health projects can be educational and entertaining. As the students' attention span and energy level wane, these fun activities can keep them involved. The end of the day can be used for art projects (e.g., making valentines, pumpkins, or shamrocks); finishing seatwork; and cashing in on reinforcers. The schedule presented in Figure 3–3 is an example of how to rotate activities, how to involve students in a variety of learning situations, and how to use their energy level to work for you.

Figure 3-3
Example of a Daily Schedule

Subjects taught:

Daily: Spelling, math, reading
Less than daily: Science, health, social studies
Nonacademic activities: Physical education, library, music, art

Reading groups: Four groups, twenty-five minutes each

Time	*Activity*	*Type of Learning Situation*
8:30	School begins	
8:30-8:50	Openings	Group activity—structured and unstructured
8:50-9:15	Group teaching: Spelling or math	Group activity—structured
9:15-10:15	Reading groups: 9:15-9:45 (Group A) 9:45-10:15 (Group B)	Small-group activity—structured
	Seatwork	Independent—structured
	Peer tutoring/work stations	Independent—unstructured
10:15-10:30	Recess	
10:30-11:00	Group Teaching: Spelling or math	Group activity—structured
11:00-12:00	Reading groups: 11:00-11:30 (Group C) 11:30-12:00 (Group D)	Small group—structured
	Seatwork	Independent—structured
	Peer tutoring/work stations	Independent—unstructured
12:00-12:10	Cleaning up: Bathroom, hand in papers, line up	
12:10-12:50	Lunch and recess	
12:50-1:05	Story time	Group activity—unstructured
1:05-1:30	Group lesson: Science Health Social studies	Group and/or small-group activity—structured and/or unstructured
1:30-2:00	Nonacademic activity: Physical education Library Music	Group activity—unstructured
2:00-2:30	Activity period Art work Finish seatwork	Group, small group and/or independent—structured or unstructured
2:30-2:45	Get ready to go home: Clean up class Turn in papers Fill in public posting Cash in reinforcers Pass out notes to go home	
2:45	End of school day	

REFERENCES

1. Caldwell, Janet H.; Huitt, William G.; and Graeber, Anna O. "Time Spent in Learning: Implications from Research." *Elementary School Journal* 82, no. 5 (1982):471–80.
2. Ferritor, Daniel E.; Buckholdt, D.; Hamblin, R. L.; and Smith, L. "The Noneffects of Contingent Reinforcement for Attending Behavior on Work Accomplished." *Journal of Applied Behavior Analysis* 5 (1972):7–17.
3. Fisher, Charles; Berlinger, David; Filby, Nikola; Marliave, Richard; Cahen, Leonard; and Dishaw, Marilyn. "Teaching Behaviors, Academic Learning Time and Student Achievement: An Overview." In *Time to Learn*, edited by Carolyn Denham and Ann Lieberman. Washington, D.C.: National Institute of Education, 1980.
4. Fisher, Charles W.; Filby, Nikola; Marliave, Richard; Cahen, Leonard S.; Dishaw, Marilyn M.; Moore, J. E.; and Berlinger, David C. *Teaching Behaviors, Academic Learning Time and Student Achievement: Final Report of Phase III-B, Beginning Teacher Evaluation Study in Beginning Teacher Evaluation Study Technical Report Series* (Technical Report V-1). San Francisco: Far West Laboratory for Educational Research and Development, 1978.
5. Leach, David J., and Nolan, Nigel K. "Helping Teachers Increase Student Academic Engagement Rate." *Behavior Modification* 9, no. 1 (1985):55–71.
6. Rosenberg, Michael S.; Sindelar, Paul T.; and Stedt, Joseph. "The Effects of Supplemental On-Task Contingencies on the Acquisition of Simple and Difficult Academic Tasks." *Journal of Special Education* 19, no. 2 (1985):189–203.
7. Rosenshine, Barak. "How Time Is Spent in Elementary Classrooms." In *Time To Learn*, edited by Carolyn Denham and Ann Lieberman. Washington, D.C.: National Institute of Education, 1980.

RESOURCES

Scheduling

1. Paine, Stan C.; Radicchi, JoAnn; Rosellini, Lynne C.; Deutchman, Leslie; and Darch, Craig B. *Structuring Your Classroom for Success.* Champaign, Ill.: Research Press, 1983.
2. Sprick, Randall. "Getting Started at the Beginning of the Year." In *The Solution Book: A Guide to Classroom Discipline,* edited by Randall Sprick. Champaign, Ill.: Research Press, 1981.

Chapter 4

AFFECTING ANTECEDENTS: RULES AND ROUTINES

We discussed antecedents in the A–B–C analysis of behavior (Chapter 1). You may recall that antecedents are *anything* that happens before a behavior occurs. They can serve as a discriminator for behavior. When we hear the five o'clock whistle, we know it is time to go home. When we see our children rub their eyes, it is time for them to go to sleep. Antecedents can govern our behavior or set the occasion for a behavior to occur. By manipulating antecedents, we can set the occasion for a specified desirable behavior to occur. The techniques we have discussed to this point affect antecedents. For example, the desk arrangement affects how children pay attention; in fact, we can manipulate on-task behaviors by changing the desk arrangement. With the scheduling concerns, we again are trying to set the occasion for positive behaviors. It is important to consider antecedents when developing an effective classroom management system. In a recent review of the effect of antecedents on behavior, one reviewer suggested antecedents "may exert just as powerful control over human behavior in developmental and educational contexts as do contingencies of reinforcement" (1, p. 215).

When we are trying to affect antecedents, we must spend some time thinking about the behaviors that we either want to avoid or want to elicit through our manipulations. When we are manipulating the classroom environment, we spend time anticipating problem areas in the room and then arranging the class to avoid the problem. When we discussed the reasons children misbehave, you may remember that one reason is that they do not have a necessary skill. They often do not know how to perform the appropriate behavior because they have not learned it. When we discuss antecedents, one of the important aspects is to teach the desired behavior. We can easily develop strategies to teach new behaviors to replace old behaviors, or to teach new skills that we want to elicit in class.

To develop a strategy using antecedents, write down the behavior that you wish to occur. In general, we can divide behaviors into those that we want to increase or maintain, and those that we wish to decrease or eliminate. By using antecedents, we can use a more positive approach to develop new behaviors. After we determine the desired behavior, we then must determine whether the child already has the ability to perform the behavior or whether he/she does not possess the skill. If the child does not possess the skill, then you will need to develop a teaching strategy to teach the desired skill. An example of this is teaching classroom routines. Children coming into your class for the first time have a skill deficit in knowing how to follow your classroom routines; thus, you must teach them. The same is true for your classroom rules. You must teach them what quiet is, teach them what sitting in their seats means, and teach them what to do when they want to ask a question. Children may have more pronounced skill deficits in areas such as social skills, including making friends, being polite, sharing, and helping others. If you have a school counselor, social worker, or school psychologist, they might be able to teach classroom units in these areas. Otherwise, you might need to teach these skills yourself. There are several good training packages available for social skills, a few of which are listed in the resources at the end of this chapter.

If you find that the children *do* know *how* to perform a skill, but do not perform it on a regular basis, then you need to manipulate the antecedents to elicit the behavior. Remember that an antecedent can be a person, place, time, event, object, or another behavior. Let's look at how we can use these different antecedents for our behavior management.

CATEGORIES OF ANTECEDENTS

Person

A person who serves as an effective antecedent for good behavior is usually the principal. Children often will behave appropriately when the principal comes to class. Visitors also often serve as antecedents to good behavior. This is particularly true if you have asked a professional to come to observe one of your difficult students! Just as the car never makes the strange noise when you bring it to the mechanic, your troublesome student will often behave like an angel once the school psychologist comes to observe! When we are training our students to recognize a person as an antecedent to good behavior, we also want to include ourselves. Since the teacher is in the class at all times and children cannot be expected to be on their best behavior at all times, we need to discriminate for the students when we mean business and when we do not. Nonverbal signals are one way to add this discrimination. The students see your hand raised; this signals them to quiet down and behave. You also might have a "look" the children recognize as the one that means "shape up!" However, remember that your discriminators will be more effective if you train your students to them. You may even let them know that when you fold your arms and have a stern look on your face, this means that they are too noisy.

Place

Places that become antecedents for good behavior are places such as the library or media center, the halls, the lunchroom, and any other public place where children are expected to behave in a certain way. Training is the most appropriate procedure here. You must outline the specific rules for behaving appropriately in specific places. You also can give children the freedom to have places where they can be wild, run around, and be more carefree. If children can learn to discriminate different behaviors for different places, it will be a benefit to managing your class—particularly on outings.

Time

Generally, we are all somewhat programmed by certain times of the day. We feel hungry at noon, and we are ready to go home at 4:00 or 5:00 p.m. Children fall into these schedules as well. They learn to anticipate events by following a general time schedule, even when they cannot tell time. Young children can tell you their daily schedule, reciting activity by activity, although they have no idea of the exact time things happen. To effectively use time as an antecedent means to have a schedule and to follow that schedule as closely as possible. When children have the predictability of their schedule, then they feel more secure and settled. When a teacher constantly changes schedules, then the children cannot predict their activities; they do not know what comes next. Children need the routine and predictability to help maintain their positive behaviors.

Event

Events can serve as antecedents, for example, a party that sets up behaviors to be less restrained or a test that serves to cause anxiety in many students. Typically, we use an event to avoid misbehaviors, for example, when a holiday is approaching. We know that children will have difficulty concentrating around holidays such as Christmas and Halloween; thus, we avoid the situation by engaging in tasks that require less structure. We do not need to totally avoid academics; rather, we should think of fun, yet educational, projects to help keep our students occupied.

Object

Objects can take on antecedent control if they are paired with the appropriate behaviors. For example, when the teacher has the reinforcer bean jar in front of the class, it signals to students that it is a time when they can earn beans as reinforcement for being quiet. Different colored flags can serve as discriminators for students to know that it is a quiet work time (red flag), a light talking time (yellow flag), or a time to move about the room (a green flag). In one school, a monitor was used to determine noise levels at lunch. When the noise level went above a specified level, then a buzzer went off that continued until the noise level dropped. The monitor became a discriminator for the students to remain quiet. Objects can serve as effective antecedents if students are trained to recognize the discriminator and if the object is used selectively—not all the time (then it loses its discriminating quality).

Behaviors

Behaviors can serve as antecedents as well. For example, when children appear to be restless and are having difficulty concentrating, then a series of relaxation exercises can serve as an antecedent to a more calm behavior. This type of exercise could be something simple such as stretching, for example, having students stand and reach for the ceiling and touch the floor while they take deep breaths. More formal relaxation programs that involve total body relaxation through tightening and releasing the muscles also are appropriate. The relaxation then serves as an antecedent to more calm behavior.

SETTING UP CLASSROOM RULES AND ROUTINES

One way to affect antecedents is through the use of classroom rules and routines. Every classroom has rules for the way things should be done, whether or not they are written. Children pick up many of the unwritten rules by observing, testing, or listening to previous students. "Never tell Mrs. Smith you *can't* do it; she'll say 'can't' is a word she doesn't know!" "It's okay to eat in Mr. Johnson's class, he never says anything." Unwritten rules obviously cause confusion and are ambiguous since not everyone may know them. Pity the new child who learns the hard way that Miss Crampton insists on using the word "please" in her class. Written rules are not automatically a solution to behavior management either. Too many rules or rules that are not clearly defined can be just as ineffective and confusing as unwritten rules. Once rules become well-established, they become habitual or routine. Routines include established, habitual rules but are also guidelines for appropriate procedures in class such as lining up at the door or going to the restroom. Routines also are important to help make classrooms run more smoothly. Again, it is important that students are clearly told what the routines will be, rather than having them piece together those expectations over the first months of class. The effective use of classroom rules includes setting up the appropriate number of rules, including student input in making rules, stating the rules positively, and then practicing the rules and routines.

GETTING READY FOR RULES

In the early grades of elementary school it is important to remember that children do not come to kindergarten knowing how to be students. The task demands of the students change over the first few years; thus, children must learn each year how to behave in class and what the expectations are for being a student. In these early years, it is important to keep in mind that the teacher's role is to instruct rather than to discipline the child for not behaving like a student. Before children start in your class, you should review what your expectations are for them and remember that those "angels" you had so well-trained at the end of last year are being replaced by children who are younger and who have not yet learned how to behave in your class. Your rules and expectations may change throughout the year as these children become more mature and socialized into the role of a student. For example, initially you might expect children to complete only short assignments that take ten minutes, while by the end of the year they can complete longer assignments. Their ability to complete independent seatwork might change as well.

They will become more independent and will be able to follow your instructions more readily.

Aside from concrete rules in class, there are routines that must be learned. Unlike rules, routines are expectations that you might have for how things should run in the class. Rather than posting routines, they are practiced to ensure that students know the procedures that make the classroom run smoothly. Examples of procedures include how to turn in assignments, how to line up for lunch, and what to do when you need the teacher's help. Since your scheduling has been determined, you can look at the day and decide which routines would make the class run more smoothly. Getting ready for classroom routines means examining which routines will enhance the traffic flow in the class, which routines will improve on your scheduling of daily events, and which will decrease classroom disruptions. Habitual rules also become incorporated into routines.

WRITING RULES FOR THE CLASS

Rules should be stated clearly and definitively, just as we discussed defining behaviors for behavior-management purposes. It is helpful to be as concrete as possible, especially when we are writing rules for young children. For example, a classroom rule might be, "Be helpful to others." However, if your six-year-old students do not know what is meant by the word "helpful," the rule is not going to be effective. Instead, we have to define the behavior we want, just as we discussed defining behaviors in the Introduction. By the time children reach the older grades, they will know these more ambiguous words; however, younger children need to be told exactly what the behavior means.

When making up classroom rules, it is helpful to examine the classroom needs. The basic needs that must be met are that children have to listen to the teacher and obey commands, that children do not hurt others or disturb others' property, and that children spend time learning. Your classroom rules should reflect these basic needs. Other behaviors often can be covered in your classroom procedures and expectations. For example, appropriate seat behavior can be covered in expectations. You can review with your class what is expected when they sit at their desks; for example, students should be seated, they should not talk out loud, and they should raise their hand when they need help. The reason we need to make these procedures and not rules, is tbat if we made a rule for all of our expectations, we would have hundreds of rules! It is generally believed that somewhere between three and eight rules are enough. If there are more than eight rules, children will forget them. It is helpful to begin with fewer rules, for example, three or four, and then add rules as problems arise. Giving yourself leeway will prove to be a benefit as the year progresses and as you learn the unique needs of your own class.

When you are making rules for your class, it is often helpful to have student input. In this way, the children will be actively involved in making their own rules rather than having someone else's rules told to them. This also will allow you to come to a group understanding of what the rules mean. If the children have helped you to choose the rules, then you can have a group discussion of what is meant by the rules. With your leadership, it will not be difficult for the discussion to end with the rules that you would have chosen anyway. Begin the rule-setting process before your group discussion. Make a list of the needs for your class and which rules would address those needs. Listed below are areas of need that typically are the basis for many rules:

1. *Safety:* Children should feel safe from physical harm from others. Their property should be safe from harm as well.

2. *Compliance:* Children should follow classroom rules, procedures, and teachers' directions.

3. *Maintaining a learning environment:* The classroom should be a place where learning can occur. Factors

that contribute to a learning environment include noise level, keeping materials where they belong, keeping the students' physical space (i.e., desks) in order, and following procedures in class.

4. *Achievement:* Children should achieve in academics and in emotional/social areas.

After you have established your classroom needs, jot down a list of rules that would meet those needs. It is imperative that the rules are clearly defined using concrete terms that your young students will understand. It is not uncommon to determine classroom rules such as, "Be polite to others"; "Always be courteous"; and "Respect your neighbor's property." Students will have difficulty with these rules. If we define the rules, then we can help the children understand whether they are following them. We can word them in the same way but add descriptors such as, "Be polite to others: Say 'thank you' and 'please.' " Especially with the young students, you must make the rules clear.

One last key to making rules is to state them positively. In terms of our behavior-management hierarchy, it is important to remember that we are trying to control behavior positively by dealing with the parameters of behavior before misbehavior occurs. When we state negative rules such as "no hitting, no talking, no running," we are setting up the children for a negative environment. Students are left with suppressing behaviors rather than learning new behaviors. Remember that your role should be teacher, not disciplinarian. By establishing positive rules, practicing the rules, and providing incentives to use the positive behaviors, you can cut down on your disciplinarian role. We can word almost any rule positively, although it is easier to make negative rules. Ask teachers what rules they need to control their class; most of the rules will be worded negatively. For every negative behavior, we can take the opportunity to teach a positive behavior. Figure 4–1 outlines the positive side of negative rules.

Figure 4-1
Making Positive Rules

Negative	*Positive*
No running in the classroom.	Walk in the classroom.
No talking during seatwork.	Keep a quiet mouth during seatwork.
No fighting.	Keep hands and feet to yourselves.
No swearing.	Keep a clean mouth and say what you really mean.
No talking when someone else is talking.	One person talks at a time.
No cheating.	Do your own work.
No stealing.	Respect other's property.

When you begin your class discussion of rules, ask the children what they think are important needs for the classroom. Prompt them with ideas, if needed, such as: "Do you think we should be nice to each other?" "Do you think we should do our own work?" Make a list of those needs on the board and have the children think of rules to go with those needs. For example, children might agree that they should be friendly to each other. Ask the children to suggest ideas about what "friendly" means, and how you can make a rule to go with being friendly. Children may respond with ideas such as sharing with others, saying nice things to each other, inviting others to play, and being polite. You may have an overall rule with the subparts that define the rule such as be friendly, share with others, say nice things to others, and invite others to play. You might want to work on just one rule a day for the first week of school. Children may get tired after brainstorming one idea. When you have finished one rule, post it where the class can see it. The rule also can be built into a positive social-skills training activity where children can earn reinforcers for exhibiting the prosocial behavior. For example, you might make a game of "Be Friendly to Your Neighbor Week." Children can keep track of the number of times they exhibit each behavior. In this manner, you are once again being a teacher rather than a disciplinarian.

PRACTICING ROUTINES

There are many daily routines that will be established in your classroom that will make behavior management easier. The routines are procedures that are similar to rules but are less rigid in the sense that there might not be consequences for breaking the procedure. Classroom routines include coming into the classroom in the morning, handing in work papers, getting the teacher's attention, going to the bathroom, and lining up for lunch. If you can plan in advance some of the routines that you would like to establish and write them down, you will be ahead of the game. We must always remember that young children do not come to school knowing how to be students, and that they must be taught everything. Older children may know what "get ready for lunch" or "line up at the door" means, but the little children do not know what is expected of them. We must teach them and then practice those routines with them.

The way to teach classroom routines is to define for the students all of the behavior components involved in the routine or procedure. You are letting the students know your expectations for that routine. Let's use the command "everyone line up at the door" as an example. If that command were given the first day of kindergarten, there would be general bedlam with children not knowing which door is meant, children pushing to be first, children yelling, and maybe even children crying as they are shoved. To teach "line up at the door," we begin with explaining which door we mean and when this command might be given. We then outline the behaviors such as:

Teacher: Line up at the door is something that I might ask you to do when? (Ask the class)
Responses: Library, recess, lunch, time to go home, assemblies.

Teacher: When we line up at the door, there are certain behaviors that make it easier for everyone to get there safer and more quickly and orderly. Can anyone tell me what those behaviors might be?
Responses: Walking, not pushing, quietly, one at a time.

Teacher: Those are all good ideas. We are going to pick some important behaviors that our class will follow when we line up. The first thing is that we will all walk to the door. The line leader gets to be first, so running will not get you there first for any reason. Second, we will keep hands folded so we are ready to walk down the halls with our arms folded. And we will keep our mouths quiet. Who can show me how to line up? (Children take turns lining up at the door exhibiting the correct behaviors).

Teacher: Everyone did a great job. Now, let's remember. When I say line up at the door, we will walk, keep arms folded, and keep a quiet mouth. Let's practice all together. Ready? Everyone line up at the door.

This teaching example was built on a discussion around the behaviors that make lining up easier. The children help to decide the procedure and thus can better understand what is needed for lining up. Children will be more invested if they help to decide rather than if they just are told what to do. It is helpful to practice all routines and review them as necessary. Students should be given corrective feedback in concrete terms such as "That's not walking," rather than, "You were terrible lining up." It also is important to praise them for completing procedures and to again give feedback in concrete terms: "Everyone did a great job turning in your papers today. You were quiet, you put them in the right basket, and you kept hands to yourself."

MAINTENANCE AND COMPLIANCE TO RULES AND ROUTINES

While initially working on establishing rules and routines in the classroom, usually we are aware of reminding students to follow the rules or of reinforcing compliance. However, once rules are established, we might forget about ongoing reinforcement of these rules. In order to maintain classroom rules and routines, it is important to remind pupils of what a good job they are doing following these rules and routines. Intermittent praise and reinforcement will increase the longevity of compliance to rules. A surprise party or special activity for "being good" and complying to rules can be an effective strategy for maintenance. Remember also that consistency among classroom personnel is the key. If a rule is a rule, it should be *a rule* for everyone all the time. If the teacher decides to skip the rule for today, the children will learn that it is okay for them to forget the rules on occasion as well.

OTHER TECHNIQUES USING ANTECEDENTS

Shaping

Most skills are taught through successive approximations to the final target response. Children or adults rarely perform a new skill perfectly the first time. Shaping involves the reinforcement of the small steps or the approximations of the final response. By reinforcing the small steps, we eventually reach our terminal objective. This is the process by which we learn to talk. Babies begin making babbling sounds, which we reinforce by either babbling or talking back. Slowly sounds begin to form and we repeat back the sounds such as "ba–ba–ba." Eventually, the toddler approximates words until, as a young child, he or she can talk. We can use the same principles in the classroom. We can shape students' behaviors by reinforcing the approximations to our terminal objective. For example, when we teach handraising, the terminal objective is for the child to quietly raise his/her hand when the teacher is needed. The child initially yells out. We teach handraising as a skill to obtain the teacher's attention. The child's first response likely is to yell, then raise a hand, perhaps while still yelling. We reinforce the hand raise, then add a new skill, raise the hand before yelling. Once this is mastered, we move to raise the hand without yelling. We successfully shape the behavior. In shaping, we are usually starting with a behavior that is already in the child's repertoire. Shaping is helpful when we have a child who we find to be difficult to reinforce. The child exhibits few behaviors that we find appropriate. However, through reinforcement of approximations, we reinforce the appropriate behaviors while ignoring the misbehaviors. For example, we want a child to sit in his/her seat during seatwork. Every time we see the child sitting, we say "nice sitting." The child might sit only for a few seconds and then is up again, but he/she is learning that sitting is the appropriate behavior. As we continue to reinforce these "small steps," eventually the child sits for increasing lengths of time. We shape the response we want by these successive approximations.

Modeling

The teacher or other children can serve as models of appropriate behavior for a child who does not perform a skill appropriately or who does not have the skill. In modeling, learning takes place through observation. By seeing others perform a skill as well as by seeing the consequences of the behavior, a child can learn a new skill. The teacher can present models by pointing out the appropriate behaviors: "I like the way that Sammy is sitting. He has his feet on the floor, his bottom on the seat, and his hands are on the table." The other children look at Sammy, see the model, and can then imitate this behavior. A distinction should be made between learning the appropriate response and actually performing it. While a child might "learn" the appropriate behavior, additional incentives may sometimes be necessary before the child performs the skill. In modeling, we assume that learning is taking place by the observation of an appropriate model. By pairing modeling with reinforcement, we can effectively teach new behaviors.

Prompting

To help initiate a response we can use a verbal prompt or cue. The prompt can be complex verbal instructions that tell the students what to do. For example, when we are teaching students what "get ready for lunch" means, we might initially give lengthy instructions. We might say, "Get ready for lunch, put your books away, wash your hands, and then line up at the door." Eventually we can fade our verbal instructions to a shorter and shorter set of instructions until the cue "get ready for lunch" elicits the desired response. At the beginning of the school year we are likely to use more verbal prompts and more complex directions as children attempt to learn our rules and routines in the classroom. By the end of the year, the sound of a bell may be the only cue needed to "get ready for lunch."

Nonverbal Signals

As a teacher, you know how tiring it is to talk for the entire school day. You get tired of asking children to be quiet, to listen to your announcement, to be attentive, and so forth. Nonverbal signals can be as effective as verbal prompts and can save your voice as well as your sanity. Nonverbal signals are signals or signs that require no verbal communication that you can give to your class that you have trained to elicit a certain response. We have all been trained in nonverbal signals. For example, when our parents wanted us to be quiet, they raised their index fingers to their lips. When we were coming close to a spanking for our misbehavior, we got a finger waved at us. In the classroom, we can develop signals as well. An arm raised by the teacher may mean that everyone is to be quiet and look at the teacher. The "index finger to the lips" can signal to be quiet. However, the children must be trained to understand the signals and the consequences for not following the signals must be clearly outlined. The standard index finger to the lips is used so frequently that it loses its message unless you train your students what it means in your class. For example, you may raise your finger to your lips and then start a countdown with your other fingers. Your students may have learned that if you get to five before they are quiet, then they lose a privilege that afternoon. Perhaps they miss two minutes of recess for every countdown to five you reach. Other teachers have made games out of being quiet. For example, the teacher begins a quiet "follow the leader": "If you can hear me, touch your nose; if you can hear me, touch your hair; if you can hear me, touch your elbow. . . ." As the class quiets, more and more children will participate. When they are quiet, you can make your announcement. These nonverbal signals save your voice, save your sanity, and they teach children to look for nonverbal communication signs to alter their behavior.

Precision Requests

Using antecedents and planning ahead for behavior problems are the essence of proactive behavior management. As you can see, we can manipulate antecedents to avoid many behavior problems. We also can use antecedents in our requests to students. We often can avoid behavior problems by using a planned sequence of commands, which also have planned consequences, to increase compliance to that command. Called "precision commands" or "requests" (2), these requests involve several key rules for improving compliance and can make a difference in the attitude your students have to your commands. One of the key components of precision requests is that they are just that, requests. We ask the children to do something and then add a "please." Adding the "please" seems to allow the children to comply because you are asking them to do something rather than commanding it. Also, when social skills are becoming more important in getting ahead in our society, using "please" serves as a model to our students. The request, then, sounds like this: "Johnny, come here, please"; or "Sally, come to my desk, please." When this request is made, it is important to try to establish eye contact with the student and to use a firm voice. A close proximity also helps to improve compliance, but may not always be possible in the classroom setting. Once the request is made, it is important to wait three to five seconds for compliance and then to follow-through with the request. In the classroom, two scenarios often happen: (a) either the teacher immediately issues another request, "Johnny, hurry up, I said to come here," or (b) the teacher gets distracted and forgets that the request was made. Then the students never learn that compliance is expected. This inconsistency on the part of the teacher may lead to a decrease in compliance as students take their chances on whether any consequence will occur from not following through. If the child complies with the first request, then he/she is reinforced and is told why he/she is getting the reinforcer: "Nice coming, Johnny, I liked the way you came promptly"; or "Thank you for coming to my desk, Sally. You listened well to my directions."

If the child does not respond in three to five seconds, then the command is reissued; however, this time the child is told that he/she "needs" to do the request. This added emphasis helps the child to realize that you are going to follow-through with the request, and it also serves as a discriminator for a consequence to follow if he/she does not comply. The request becomes: "Johnny, you need to come here"; or "Sally, you need to come to my desk."

If the child complies, then we again reinforce him/her with a social reinforcer for performing the request. If the child does not comply, we add a consequence. Consequences will be discussed in more depth in Chapter 5; however, at this point it is important to note that consequences that do not take a lot of time are most appropriate because requests are made frequently and the teacher cannot take a lot of time to perform elaborate consequences. For example, a mild aversive such as losing a point in the classroom management system might be appropriate.

What is important is that the consequence is preplanned so that both the teacher and students know what will happen. In times when the student is getting us angry and pushing our buttons, we can have that planned consequence to fall back on. If you can manage a calm voice (even though you may be boiling inside!), you will be able to be more effective and will not give the student the reinforcement of seeing you "lose it." Although precision requests seem awkward at first, as you use them they will become more natural and automatic, making your job a lot easier. You can directly affect your students' behavior by using predictable and preplanned requests and consequences. Antecedents are the key in making a positive classroom environment.

CASE STUDY

Mrs. McMillan greeted her first grade class the first day of school and realized that she had forgotten how small six-year-olds are. She knew that she had to get the classroom rules and procedures down the first week so that things would run more smoothly in the classroom. During a group discussion, she talked about rules and asked the students how they thought rules are helpful. Children responded that rules could be for safety, such as looking both ways before crossing the street. Mrs. McMillan listed "safety" on the board. The children then offered that rules could help you make friends, such as not grabbing toys and saying nice things to others. Mrs. McMillan added "being friendly" on the board. One child mentioned that rules help you know where to go and what to do. He said that his mother had been in a car accident because the other driver had not followed the rules. Mrs. McMillan wrote "appropriate behavior." She then focused on one area each day. She wrote the word "safety" and led a discussion about the importance of feeling safe at school. She asked the children what would make them feel safe at school. Replies included, "If nobody hits me"; "If I can tell on somebody that hurt me"; and "If my things don't get stolen." Mrs. McMillan offered, "If we made a rule that said 'everyone' keeps hands and feet to themselves, would that make school a safe place?" The children agreed and, therefore, she had rule number one.

The next day she wrote "being friendly" on the board. She asked the children what being friendly meant. Children said sharing, being nice, saying nice things to each other, helping each other with schoolwork, and giving candy to friends. Mrs. McMillan decided to choose more than one item for this general rule of being friendly; thus, she could use this rule for teaching social skills. Under the general rule of "being friendly," she listed the following: (a) share with others, (b) help others when they need it, and (c) give compliments to others.

Finally, on the third day, Mrs. McMillan wrote "appropriate behavior" on the board. She asked what the children thought appropriate behavior in the class meant. They responded "no running," "no yelling," "no cheating," "no goofing off," and "no hitting." Mrs. McMillan pointed out that they had all thought of things you should not do in class. What were things you could do? This was harder for the class. After much thinking, a few ideas were mentioned: (a) "Sit quietly at your desk"; (b) "Do your own work"; and (c) "Use inside voices." She listed these under the general heading of appropriate behavior and decided that these three general rules were enough for now. She posted the rules where the class could see them and planned to review them daily for the first week and then intermittently thereafter.

REFERENCES

1. Glynn, Ted. "Antecedent Control of Behavior in Educational Contexts." *Educational Psychology* 2 (1982):215–29.
2. Jenson, William R.; Malm, Karen W.; Loveless, Tony; and Hughes, Don. "Iron County School District Motivation Project." Typescript, Iron County Utah, 1990.

RESOURCES

Social Skills Training

1. Jackson, Nancy F.; Jackson, Donald A.; and Monroe, Cathy. *Getting Along with Others: Teaching Social Effectiveness to Children.* Champaign, Ill.: Research Press, 1983.
2. Likins, Marilyn; Morgan, Daniel P.; and Young, K. Richard. "Being Positive and Making Friends." In *Utah State University Social Skills Project.* Logan, Utah: Department of Special Education, Utah State University, 1984.
3. McGinnis, Ellen, and Goldstein, Arnold P. *Skillstreaming the Elementary School Child: A Guide to Teaching Prosocial Skills.* Champaign, Ill.: Research Press, 1984.
4. Morgan, Daniel P., and Young, K. Richard. "Teaching Social Skills: Assessment Procedures, Instructional Methods, and Behavior Management Techniques." In *Utah State University Social Skills Project.* Logan, Utah: Department of Special Education, Utah State University, 1984.
5. Peterson, T. J.; Young, K. Richard; and Morgan, Daniel P. "Talking with Others: Teaching Conversation Skills to Children and Adolescents." In *Utah State University Social Skills Project.* Logan, Utah: Department of Special Education, Utah State University, 1984.
6. Walker, Hill M.; McConnell, Scott; Holmes, Deborah; Todis, Bonnie; Walker, Jackie; and Golden, Nancy. *The Walker Social Skills Curriculum: The ACCEPTS Program.* Austin, Tex.: Pro-Ed, 1983.
7. Young, K. Richard; Morgan, Daniel; Cheney, Deb; Peterson, T. J.; and Likins, Marilyn. "Basic Social Interaction Skills." In *Utah State University Social Skills Project.* Logan, Utah: Department of Special Education, Utah State University, 1984.

Proactive Classroom Environment

1. Jones, Vernon F., and Jones, Louise S. *Comprehensive Classroom Management: Creating Positive Learning Environment.* Boston: Allyn & Bacon, 1986.
2. Swick, Kevin L. *A Proactive Approach to Discipline.* Washington, D.C.: National Education Association, 1985.

Chapter 5

REINFORCEMENT STRATEGIES

DEVELOPING A POSITIVE REINFORCEMENT SYSTEM

Types of Reinforcement

Positive reinforcers can increase achievement in class as well as decrease disruptive behaviors. A positive reinforcement system can involve many different systems of reinforcement. When we discuss positive reinforcers, remember that a positive reinforcer is defined as *anything* that increases or maintains the occurrence of a behavior. There are four general classes of reinforcers. They are listed here in order of the most basic, or the first reinforcers we learn, to the more complex. Social reinforcement takes learning for it to become a reinforcer, although it is the optimal reinforcer.

Edible Reinforcers

Food is one of the most basic reinforcers. It is the first reinforcer we learn as infants. Children and adults like to eat, and we can usually find some food that will be motivating for a person and that will be a reward. Some professionals have ethical problems using edible reinforcers in the classroom. They feel that when childhood obesity is on the rise and health problems related to "junk food" are increasing, we should find other rewards to use. However, one cannot argue about the highly reinforcing quality of edible reinforcers. We can use this reinforcer in combination with other reinforcers, for example, a party, to increase the rewarding value of the activity.

Material Reinforcers

Material reinforcers can include anything from pencils, stickers, and pictures to tokens that can be traded for other reinforcers. Children enjoy earning material goods for their activities, and this can offer a powerful motivator. Problems for teachers might arise with material reinforcers due to the costs involved; however, sometimes the school budget or the PTA will have the money to cover these kinds of materials. A token system can be less costly because material reinforcers can be handed out over longer periods of time or the tokens can be used to earn activities that do not cost anything.

Activity Reinforcers

Children can earn activities for good behavior. A creative teacher can use any fun activity such as playing board games, doing artwork, playing outside, or getting to be a class helper or line leader to reinforce children's behavior. The activity itself can be the reward, or children can earn points or tokens to trade for activity reinforcers. A caution with using activities as rewards is noted in that all activities should not become reinforcers since children who have difficulty earning these rewards may become discouraged because they never get to participate. Also, if a child never gets to play the board games, for example, they may not become reinforcing because he/she does not know that they are fun.

Social Reinforcers

A social reinforcer is a social gesture, verbal comment, or behavior that rewards or reinforces the child. This is the most important reinforcer because it will be generalized to adulthood, and, it is hoped, will continue to serve as a motivator throughout life. Examples of social reinforcers include a smile, a light touch on the arm or back, a positive comment such as "good job," or attention from the teacher. Social reinforcers are a key to any positive classroom and should be combined with all methods of reinforcement.

It is important for teachers to understand that providing rewards is *not* bribing. A bribe, according to *Merriam-Webster* (8), is "to corrupt or influence [one in a position of trust] by favors or gifts." There is a negative influence inferred from the notion of bribery. Positive reinforcement, on the other hand, rewards the student for appropriate behavior. A reward is "something given or offered for some service or attainment" (8). The positive reinforcer is a consequence of appropriate behavior rather than an enticement. It is important for teachers to realize that we all work for positive reinforcers. We work so that we can get paid, so that we can eat, and so that we can enjoy leisure activities. It is unfair to expect children to work for no reinforcement when we enjoy the fruits of our own labors.

When choosing reinforcers, it is important to remember that reinforcers differ from child to child. What is reinforcing to one child may be a punisher for another one. For example, teacher attention can be very rewarding for some students, while others try to avoid it. When implementing a classwide reinforcement system, it is important to have a variety of reinforcers available so that all students may find something they like. It also can be beneficial for students to help make up the classroom list of reinforcers. In this way you can be assured that the reinforcers are items that students will actually work for.

Delivering Reinforcers

The delivery of the reinforcer is as important as the reinforcer itself. For example, if you are given a watch for twenty years of service with the district, it will be more rewarding if it is given to you at a large banquet acknowledging your contribution to education rather than if it is left in your mailbox. We might bristle when someone tells us that we look nice, but they use a sour tone of voice. The same is true when we give reinforcers to our students. Following are several key factors involved in effectively giving reinforcers.

Immediacy

Feedback must be given immediately following the occurrence of the behavior. If a child follows directions, it is more effective to praise the child immediately following the behavior rather than to wait until another time. Social praise and tokens are easy methods for giving immediate feedback to students. You can easily note a student's behavior: "Betsy, nice working, give yourself a point." Correcting papers immediately, either by exchanging papers with peers or by having you grade the shorter assignments, will enable students to get feedback immediately; it also will cut down on your after-school grading. Children get immediate feedback in their learning if they are tested on the material frequently. After a day's lesson, children can get immediate feedback on the new material by taking a brief test and having their peers grade it.

Frequency

It is important to give feedback frequently to students. Some authors suggest that a child should receive a minimum of one reinforcer every fifteen minutes. It may be helpful to take a baseline on what your average rate of reinforcement is. Choose a one-hour block of time when you can count the number of positives you give to students. You can make a check on a paper or use a counter to determine your average rate of giving positives. If it is less than four an hour, you may need to do some work! Research has shown that during seatwork time, frequent and brief teacher contacts to students who are on-task can improve rates of on-task behavior (10).

Enthusiasm

When you deliver a reinforcer, it should be done in an enthusiastic manner. Sound like you really mean it! Young children especially enjoy an enthusiastic voice tone. You can add enthusiasm by having the entire class participate in cheering students' progress. At the end of the day, when the public posting is reviewed, you can have the entire class applaud for the general pool of students who have completed their goals. If you act excited, then your students will be excited too.

Eye Contact

Another important element of the delivery is to use eye

contact when you deliver the reinforcer. Think about how you feel when a compliment is given to you but the person does not look at you. While eye contact preferences differ across cultures, our culture invites eye contact. Lack of eye contact is often viewed with mistrust, suspicion, and deceit. When we look someone in the eyes, it denotes sincerity and honesty. The child also feels that the reinforcer was truly meant for him/her. When you give a classwide compliment, glance around the room and try to establish eye contact with as many students as possible.

Describe the Behavior

When you deliver a reinforcer, it is important to let the student know exactly what he/she is being reinforced for. *Describe exactly* what the student did that earned him/her the reinforcer. For example, "Good working," becomes, "Good working, everyone is keeping quiet and working on their own assignments." "Nice job," becomes, "Nice job, you wrote neatly and finished all of the sentences." Research has shown that giving specific praise for a student's behavior and describing the particular behavior are more potent in maintaining accuracy than general praise (2).

Variety

Use a variety of reinforcers. If you give the children the same reinforcers day after day, they lose their value as the students satiate on the reinforcer. Even a very highly valued reinforcer can lose its significance if it is given all the time. We can vary reinforcers by using a reinforcement menu or by using innovative techniques such as spinners and mystery motivators (discussed later).

Close Proximity

Close proximity can increase the value of a social reinforcer. It is more meaningful when you tell students that they are performing well if you are at their desks rather than across the room. Pairing the social reinforcer with a light touch can increase the strength of the reinforcement as well. An effective method of delivering reinforcers is to walk through your classroom from time to time and to praise students directly.

Personalize the Reward

You can personalize the reinforcer by using the student's name when you deliver the praise. This also can facilitate eye contact since most children will look when their name is called. Personalizing the reinforcer in a classroom system can include having children decorate their own point cards or write their own name on a public posting card. If the child feels that the reinforcer is meant for him/her specifically, it will increase the value of the reinforcer.

Remembering all of these factors may seem overwhelming at first; but with practice and use, they become more natural and sincere. Put together, the scenario may resemble the following:

> Jeremy approaches Mrs. Johnson's desk with his handwriting assignment completed. He hands in his assignment, and Mrs. Johnson reviews the work saying, "Jeremy, let's see how you did today on your handwriting. Look at what good work you did today! You remembered to cross all of your 't's' and you put a period at the end of every sentence!" She then looks him in the eyes, places a hand on his arm, and says, "I'm proud of your work today, Jeremy. You can give yourself a star."

INDIVIDUAL REWARD STRATEGIES

One method of setting up a reward system in the classroom is to have each child receive reinforcers for his/her work and to have an individual goal or tally sheet. There are several different ways to set up an individual system.

Self-Control/Self-Reinforcement

Children can give themselves a reinforcer for appropriate behavior, with contingencies for appropriate behavior either self-determined or determined by an external source such as the teacher. In one study with an eight-year-old boy, self-assessment of on-task behavior resulted in higher rates of on-task performance than when the teacher assessed on-task (3). Teaching children to monitor their own behavior can have long-lasting effects as they learn to take control of their own behaviors. Children as young as kindergarteners can learn to set goals and be rewarded for achieving their goals. The younger the child and the lower he/she is cognitively, the more concrete and the more simple the self-monitoring program should be. The simplest system used to develop a self-monitoring checklist is one that students check off as they complete each assignment. A square grid can be used for younger children; for nonreaders, symbols can replace words. Figure 5–1 gives an example of such a check-off system.

Children also can set goals to finish a certain number of problems each day. As the child works, he/she can cross off another problem being completed. A simple number line taped on a child's desk can serve as a monitoring device. The child can

Figure 5-1
Self-Monitoring System for Goal Setting

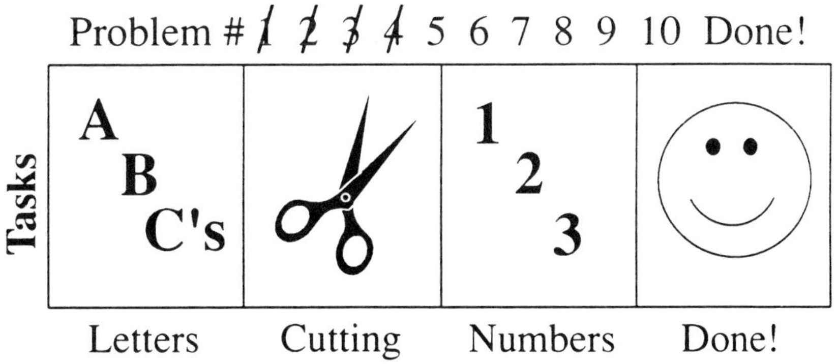

then reinforce himself/herself to complete each problem:

Goal: To finish ten problems today.

1 2 3 4 5 6 7 8 9 10 Done!!

Self-reinforcement also can be used to control behavior problems. Children can have set behaviors that they are working on such as "staying in seat" or "keeping hands to self." Following a work period, the teacher can remind students to check their behavior goals and to give themselves a check if they reached their goal. A spot-check by teachers will increase the reliability of the students' self-monitoring.

With any self-monitoring program, goals that are achieved can be tied into a larger reinforcement system since the mere checking-off of goals will lose its power of reinforcement after a period of time (remember variety?). Children who achieve their goals for the day can post their achievement on a public-posting system or can exchange goal sheets for activity or material reinforcers. A self-monitoring system allows for direct feedback following completion of the goal and also can help maintain a higher level reinforcement program through delaying the more time-consuming reinforcers. To set up a self-monitoring system, the following is suggested:

1. Discuss the self-monitoring system with the child. Have the child help by choosing goals or behaviors to work on. Then define the goal in concrete terms so that both you and the child understand the goal.
2. Determine the method of recording. A checklist on the child's desk is an easy method. Laminating daily goal sheets can help with keeping the system both easy and readily available; thus, you will not have to run off new goal sheets each week.
3. Determine the frequency of the monitoring. Deciding the frequency of the monitoring will partially depend on the goal. Remember that the more

immediate the feedback, the better; thus, for work completion, checking-off as soon as the work is done is best. For behaviors, time intervals are more appropriate. Natural breaks in the day can work as times for the child to self-monitor his/her behavior. For example, behavior can be assessed at first recess, lunch, second recess, and before going home. The child will need to be reminded to check his/her behavior that again can be matched to the teacher's observations. For a child with more severe behavior problems, the teacher may have to time shorter intervals, such as every ten to fifteen minutes.

4. Transfer daily data to a more permanent record such as a public posting system or a check in your roster book. In this way you can monitor a child's progress over time and determine whether changes need to be made in the self-monitoring program.
5. Determine whether stronger reinforcers are needed. If the child seems to work for a while on the self-monitoring system and then seems to lose interest, it may be that stronger reinforcers are needed. Tying into another reinforcement system may strengthen the self-monitoring system.

Individual Contracting

Sometimes it might be necessary to contract with a child on an individual basis to improve work completion or behaviors. In contracting, the teacher negotiates with the pupil on goals and then monitors the data to determine whether the child has achieved his/her goals. Contracting can be the first step to using a self-monitoring system as described above. Research has found that contracting is effective in increasing students' productivity (6). Some research even suggests that students attain more of their goals when they choose their own goals (4).

When setting up a contract, the teacher and child agree on a goal and on the reward for achieving that goal. The frequency of monitoring the goal can be variable as it was in self-monitoring; however, immediate feedback is often not possible since the teacher is the monitor. Often contracts are checked at intermittent times during the day or at the end of the day. During the closing activities, children can have their contracts checked and reinforcers dispersed. To set up a contract, the following is suggested:

1. The teacher and student decide on a goal and a reward for achieving the goal.
2. A monitoring system is devised. A paper-and-pencil checklist, similar to that used in self-monitoring, can be used. The child can keep the contract or the student can bring it to the teacher for the information to be recorded.
3. Frequency of data collection is determined.
4. The schedule for dispensing reinforcers is determined. For example, does the child receive a reward daily or at the end of the week? Is the reward contingent on perfect completion or partial completion? The teacher and the student can negotiate the terms of the reinforcement.
5. Adding a consequence for not meeting the contract can add to the strength of the contract. The teacher and the student can negotiate a consequence.
6. Adding a bonus for work completed above the contract standards can add additional motivation.
7. Information from the contract is transferred to a more permanent system for monitoring long-term gains.

Sample contracts are presented in Figure 5–2.

Token Economies

In a token economy system, students can receive tokens

Figure 5-2
Sample Contracts

Contract for: Dan Jones

Goals: 1. I will complete at least ten out of fifteen math problems daily.
2. I will finish handwriting assignments accurately and on time.

Reward: Five minutes free play with game of choice.

Bonus: Goal 1. If more than ten problems are completed, I get one extra minute for each problem over ten completed.
Goal 2. If I finish handwriting assignment before time is completed and the work is neat and accurate, I can color until the rest of the class is done.

Day of the week:	M	T	W	TH	F
Goal 1	10	10	11	10	12
Goal 2	No	Yes	Yes	Bonus	Yes

Contract for: Sarah Hillman

Goal: I will keep my hands to myself when in line at lunch daily.

Reward: Can sit with best friend Marsha at lunch.

Consequence: If I do not keep my hands to myself, I need to sit by myself.

Day of the week:	M	T	W	TH	F
9/16-9/20	Yes	No	No	Yes	No
9/23-9/27	No	Yes	Yes	Yes	Yes

for reinforcers and then turn in the tokens for more tangible reinforcers such as activities or material reinforcers. Token economies are useful because the reinforcement can be given immediately and then more potent reinforcers can be administered later. They have been shown to be successful in increasing on-task performance for even the most distractible children, including hyperactive children (1, 9). Tokens can be actual chips, or beads, or checks on a paper. Either the teacher or the child can keep track of the tokens. A large bead abacus can be used for dispensing reinforcers, especially during small-group activities. Names can be placed along the rows of beads, and as each child earns a token, the bead is slid over to denote that the child has earned a reinforcer. At the end of the group, the child can transfer the points earned over to a tally sheet. The child also can have a tally sheet on his/her desk, and the teacher can make checks on it for reinforcers. In a token economy, it is important to have effective back-up reinforcers that will appeal to all children in the class. To set up a token economy, the following is suggested:

1. Set goals or determine behaviors that are the target for the token economy system. The goals can be academic or behavioral.
2. Determine what will be used for tokens. They should be easy to dispense, since feedback should be immediate, and should be difficult to copy or counterfeit.
3. Determine back-up reinforcers. This will require determining the number of tokens needed for each reinforcer as well as the reinforcers themselves.
4. Determine when tokens will be exchanged, e.g., hourly, daily, or weekly, and how they will be exchanged.
5. Remember to include variety in the system, i.e., changing reinforcers and keeping the system motivating for the students.

GROUP REWARD STRATEGIES

Group reward strategies or group contingencies is a reward structure that reinforces behavior or achievement based on the performance of the group as a whole. The individuals in the group are responsible for the reward (or punishment) of the entire group. In this way, students may learn to cooperate and even to help each other by joining forces to ensure the group reward. A cooperative learning group is a popular method used to help students who are low achievers. In a meta-analysis of the research in this area, Johnson, et al. (5) concluded that cooperative learning was superior to competitive and individualistic strategies in terms of promoting achievement and productivity. Group contingencies have had wide application and have been successful in increasing academic achievement and decreasing disruptive behaviors.

Group Contingencies and Teams

A group contingency can be used to increase academic achievement by combining the achievement of the individuals. A thermometer-type meter can be used to monitor the progress of the entire class in completing the number of spelling words learned or the number of problems completed. As each individual child completes his/her list, he/she can add it to the group's thermometer to increase the "temperature" toward a certain goal. This type of monitoring is often used for community fund-raisers such as United Way, to show the amount of progress toward a group goal. Individuals can see their contribution toward the common goal, while the entire group reaps the reward.

The classroom also can be divided into teams where individuals earn rewards for their team rather than for the whole classroom. The team approach can be helpful for larger classes; it also can be used to reward groups of students who are performing well, while providing motivation for other groups. For a classwide management system, it can be easier to reinforce a team or group, rather than naming all the individuals in that team. Teams also can be used for individual learning groups for projects.

Token Economies

Token economies can be utilized for a group as well as for an individual performance. The group can collectively earn tokens toward a reinforcer. Individuals also can earn tokens for the group. In this manner, the teacher may have a jar in front of the room in which he/she drops tokens when either the group as a whole or an individual earns a reinforcer. The reward for the token can be determined by the class. For example, once the jar is full, the students can have a party.

Premack Principle

Premack Principle is the concept of using a high-rate activity as a reinforcer for a low-rate activity. In other words, you have to complete an undesired task (a low-rate activity) in order to get to do a desired activity. For example, you have to eat your vegetables *before* you can have dessert. Eating vegetables is a low-rate activity, or the less desired of the two choices. In the classroom, this principle can be used as a group contingency. For example, all students must have their work turned in before going to the assembly or going outside. Behaviors also can be used for a group contingency: "All children must be quiet before we can leave the classroom for lunch."

CREATIVE REINFORCERS

Since variety is one of the key factors in making reinforcers more effective, it is helpful to have unique reinforcers that can provide children either with unique opportunities or with a surprise component to the reinforcement. Listed below are some unique reinforcers that can add to the teacher's repertoire of standard tokens, stars, and praise. Remember that reinforcers are unique to individuals. What is reinforcing to one child may not be so to another.

Spinners

A spinner can be easily constructed by using either an old spinner from a game or by making one out of construction paper. A spinner adds an element of the unknown that can be a motivating quality to the reward. Children spin for their reward. Differing sizes of wedges on the spinner can make highly valued items, such as skipping an assignment, difficult to obtain. Children love the anticipation of spinning and not knowing what the reward will be.

Grab Bags

A grab bag works under the same principle as the spinner; however, with a grab bag, the child reaches into a bag to pull out a reinforcer. While material reinforcers are more easily suited for a grab bag, the bag also could contain slips of paper with activity reinforcers.

Reinforcement Maze

A reinforcement maze is another way to add an unknown component to a reward. A maze is drawn, using boxes or squares in a random fashion to make the maze design. "Magic pens" are used to write hidden rewards inside the squares. Magic pen sets are magic markers that include a clear marker that erases the colored markers. They also can be used in reverse order, that is, the clear marker is used to write a message and the colored marker makes it appear. This type of reinforcer was used as a reward in a peer-tutoring project and proved to be extremely reinforcing (7). Children never knew which reinforcer was in each square. They chose a square and colored over it to reveal the reward.

Reinforcement Pin or Ribbon

A pin or ribbon can be used to designate a special child who has achieved a goal. The child gets to wear the pin or ribbon for a designated amount of time. The pin or ribbon allows others to reinforce the child, especially if it says something such as "I did a good job" or "I got my work done." Other teachers or classroom visitors can comment and give additional reinforcement. Peers also may reinforce the person wearing the pin or ribbon by giving additional attention to him/her.

Dot-to-Dot Maze

A dot-to-dot picture can be used as a reward as well. As children achieve goals, they get to connect one more dot. A reward can be distributed when the picture is completed. The "magic pens" also can be used to add small rewards along the way as well as to add a mystery component. The clear pen can be used to make an X over one of the dots. When the colored pen is used to color over the dot, the X appears.

Unique Sensory Reinforcers

It is important to remember all five senses when trying to determine reinforcers. While most of us can name edible reinforcers (sense of taste), we usually do not remember to use our other senses. Listed below is a brief list of possible reinforcers to use based on the other four senses. Remember to be creative!

1. *Smell:* A smelling box can contain any number of smells, a few of which are listed here. Different scents are collected, and the child can earn either a certain amount of time with the box or a certain number of choices in the smelling box. This can be particularly reinforcing for young children. Possible scents are perfume; extracts such as orange, almond, or cherry; spices such as cinnamon, allspice, or clove; licorice; or incense such as pine or floral, which smells without having to burn them.
2. *Hearing:* Children can earn time listening to records or tapes of music or stories. Headsets for individuals or allowing the group to have music can be used as a reward and also can be educational.

3. *Touch:* Any number of items can be used to stimulate the sense of touch. Children enjoy putting on lotion, powder, or oils. They may enjoy a vibrator rubbed on their cheek or arm. A blow dryer feels nice and warm. Earning time walking in the sandbox barefoot or playing in a water table also are enjoyable. A touching or feeling box can be used that is similar to the smelling box. The box can either be open or closed, where children try to guess what they are feeling. Different shapes and textures enhance the quality of the experience.
4. *Sight:* While children use their sight daily, there are certain experiences that are unique and can be used as reinforcers. Earning time in a closet with a flashlight or glow-in-the-dark toy can be exciting; looking into a kaleidoscope is always fun, or wearing sunglasses or colored glasses also can be a fun reinforcer.

Unique Activity Reinforcers

Privileges and activities are inexpensive reinforcers that can stretch the budget dollar. Young children enjoy helping their teacher, and any number of helping activities can be used. Using this special relationship with the teacher, other privileges include getting to sit in the teacher's chair, holding the teacher's keys when leaving the room (being careful to keep an eye on them!), or using the teacher's pen during writing. Peer influence is strong, and peers can be used to help recognize a student's achievement. The students can all sing a song to the rewarded student, applaud, or shake hands with the student. As a reinforcer, the student may get to choose his/her seat for a day or a period. Less unique reinforcers include access to games or toys, being a line leader, skipping an assignment, or earning free time.

REFERENCES

1. Ayllon, Teodoro; Layman, Dale; and Kandel, Henry J. "A

Behavioral-Educational Alternative to Drug Control of Hyperactive Children." *Journal of Applied Behavior Analysis* 8 (1975):137–46.

2. Bernhardt, Alan, and Forehand, Rex. "The Effects of Labeled and Unlabeled Praise Upon Lower and Middle Class Children." *Journal of Experimental Child Psychology* 19 (1975):536–43.
3. Hallahan, Daniel; Lloyd, John W.; Kneedler, Rebecca D.; and Marshall, Kathleen J. "A Comparison of the Effects of Self- Versus Teacher-Assessment of On-Task Behavior." *Behavior Therapy* 13 (1982):715–23.
4. Hannafin, Michael J. "Effects of Teacher and Students Goal Setting and Evaluations on Mathematics Achievement and Student Attitudes." *Journal of Educational Research* 74 (1981):321–26.
5. Johnson, David W.; Maruyama, Geoffrey; Johnson, Roger; Nelson, Deborah; and Skon, Linda. "Effects of Cooperative, Competitive, and Individualistic Goal Structures on Achievement: A Meta-Analysis." *Psychological Bulletin* 89 (1981):47–62.
6. Kelley, Marylou L., and Stokes, Trevor F. "Student-Teacher Contracting for Maintenance." *Behavior Modification* 8 (1984):223–44.
7. Malm, Karen W. "Combining Tutor and Tutee Roles for Low-Achieving Students in a Peer-Tutoring Project." Ph.D. diss., University of Utah, Salt Lake City, 1989.
8. Merriam, G. & C. Co. *The Merriam-Webster Dictionary.* New York: Pocket Books, 1974.
9. Rosenberg, Michael S. "Maximizing the Effectiveness of Structured Classroom Management Programs: Implementing a Rule-Review Procedure with Disruptive and Distractible Boys." *Behavioral Disorders* 11 (1981):239–48.
10. Scott, John, and Bushell, Don. "The Length of Teacher Contacts and Students' Off-Task Behavior." *Journal of Applied Behavior Analysis* 7 (1974):39–44.

RESOURCES

Positive Reinforcement

1. Sprick, Randall. "Effective Reinforcement." In *The Solution Book: A Guide to Classroom Discipline,* edited by Randall Sprick. Palo Alto, Calif.: Science Research Associates, 1981.

Unique Reinforcers

1. Jenson, William R.; Neville, Melanie; Sloane, Howard; and Morgan, Daniel. "Spinners and Chartmoves: A Contingency Management System for Home and School." *Child and Family Therapy* 4 (1982):81–85.

Chapter 6

PARENTAL INVOLVEMENT

To maximize the effects of an effective behavior management system, it is beneficial to have not only the support of parents but also their active involvement as well. Parental involvement is listed as one of the highest levels of intervention for several reasons. First, the classroom teacher must have the classroom environment under control, must have the scheduling concerns and roles established, and must have an effective reinforcement system in place. Second, this level depends on someone other than the teacher to be invested in behavior management. It involves relying on others, which is always more difficult than doing something oneself. Furthermore, not all parents are interested in becoming involved in their child's education. For any number of reasons, parents may find any additional work that they have to do more than they can handle. On the other hand, some parents who want to help go beyond helpful or even go overboard in their efforts. Finding a delicate balance can be an art—enlisting parents' support while keeping them in line with the teacher's program. Finally, we need to balance our expectations of what we want from parents and what parents can realistically provide. Getting involved with a child's home situation can get us more emotionally involved with families than we really need to be or want to be. For example, if we begin a home-note system in a family and a child returns bruised after bringing home a poor note, we feel responsible for that child's punishment. While it is not the teacher's fault, we must somehow address the inappropriateness of the parents' actions. In other words, when we involve parents, we must be prepared for any consequences that action might make.

Research has suggested a positive view about involving parents in that adding a home component to a school intervention program can increase its effectiveness. Broden,

Beasely, and Hall (2) used parents as tutors to improve academic subjects. They taught parents how to review spelling word lists, how to use a standardized correction procedure, and how to give verbal praise. Tutoring occurred three nights per week. The results of the tutoring demonstrated an increase in average weekly spelling test scores from 41 percent to 94 percent. Gang and Poche (3) trained parents to be tutors for a reading program that was carried out over the seven-week summer vacation. Results demonstrated that parents could learn to be effective tutors, with the children reaching 100 percent accuracy across seven reading skill areas assessed. Swinson (6) used a less-structured reading program in which parents were instructed to listen to their children read each night. Specific correction procedures were taught when a child did not know a word or made an error. Parents also were advised about appropriate settings for after-school reading and about appropriate listening. Reading gains made by the children over the two terms the project was in force ranged from six to twenty months.

Using parents and home as reinforcement for school performance has been effective. Trovato and Bucher (7) used a home-based reinforcement system to nearly double the achievement gains made with a peer-tutoring project. Parents can sometimes offer more potent reinforcers than can be offered at school, such as TV privileges or staying up later. Home notes can be sent by the teacher; thus, parents can consequate academic or behavior changes at home. Studies have demonstrated improvements in academics, with the use of home notes raising math scores from the 47 percent to 77 percent correct range to 91 percent to 100 percent correct (5), and improving in-seat completion of reading assignments from 46 percent to 84 percent (4). Behavioral changes in the classroom also have occurred following use of a home-note system to consequate behaviors. One study demonstrated a 90 percent decrease in disruptive classroom behavior following implementation of a home-note system (1). Parents play an important role in helping students to improve academically and behaviorally.

USING PARENTS AS REINFORCERS

To use parents to consequate behaviors involves setting up a home-note system. Home notes should be simple and direct. Long complex notes that explain behaviors or academic changes are too time-consuming for both the teacher and the parents. If goals are set for the day or for the week, then a simple "yes/no" will be an easy and clear home note. The teacher must gain the parents' support and cooperation for the home-note system to work. A face-to-face meeting is helpful to outline the objective of the home-note system and to get the parents' input on what goals they would like their child to work on. Explaining the positive aspect of the home-note system is helpful since many parents hear only when their children are bad at school. The home note allows parents to hear about their children's accomplishments as well as about their problems.

When building-in the system of consequences at home, it is helpful to give parents suggestions about the kind of reinforcers to use. Parents might think that reinforcers are material goods and that this system will cost them money. Using privileges as reinforcers is an appropriate way to reward children at home. It also is important to build in mild consequences if the child does not bring home a good note. Having to go to bed early or missing some TV time are examples of consequences that can be used at home. There also should be consequences for coming home without a note. No excuses should be accepted for "forgetting" the note. Children can be creative with their excuses, and it is important to keep the child from sabotaging the program by conveniently "losing" the home note.

To set up a home-note system:

1. Contact the child's parents to determine whether they are interested in working with you in a home-note program. Explain what a home-note system entails, that you will monitor a goal at school, a note will be sent home on a regular basis so that the parents can consequate the goal, and the note must be signed and

returned to school so that the teacher knows the parents saw the note. If the parents are agreeable to participating, set an appointment for a face-to-face meeting.

2. Design a home-note system before the meeting. For young children, daily home notes are more reinforcing because young children have difficulty with delayed gratification. A daily home-note system can include the entire week or can be a simple daily note. The note should state the goal or goals and whether the goal was met that day. Figure 6–1 shows two examples of home notes. Some teachers have used a simplified system of red/green notes. The child brings home a red or a green note to denote whether it was a good day (green) or a bad day (red). The parents keep a data sheet at home, usually a calendar, where the daily notes can be tallied across a week. The drawback with this simple system is that there is a minimum of communication between the parent and teacher. Other notes can allow for a few comments.
3. List the behaviors and goals you would like the student to work on and be prepared to bargain with the parents and the child about items on the list. For young children, one to three goals is enough to work on.
4. Explain to the parents and the child at the parent meeting, how the home-note system will work. Talk about how often notes will be sent home, how the parents will dispense consequences and how often, what the consequence will be for not bringing a note home, and how parent and teacher will keep in touch. It is helpful to set up the parent reinforcement component at that meeting because it is too easy for the parents to delay getting started. Ask the child what might be appropriate reinforcers—what he/she is willing to work for. Also, discuss the consequences

Figure 6-1
Examples of Home Notes

Goal	M	T	W	TH	F
1. Do five math problems daily.					
2. Keep hands to myself.					

Daily note for: Debbie Smith

Goal: I will write my letters ten times without interrupting the teacher.

Date: ______________

Teacher's Signature: ______________________________

Parent's Initials: ______________________________

with the child. Sometimes children think of more punishing consequences than we would!

5. Bargain for goals and what the parents, the child, and you would like to work on. Write clear, concise, measurable goals.
6. Decide on a start date. Discuss how the home-note system will be faded and how to monitor whether the program is working. Remember that you must give

any new program at least two weeks to ascertain its effectiveness.

PARENTS AS TUTORS

Many parents ask if they can work with their children at home. While it is helpful to have parents provide extra help, the parameters of the instruction and the tutoring sessions should be outlined for the parent. Children can get confused if their parents teach them subtraction in a different way than the teacher does. It is important to train parents not only in the correct instruction strategies, but also it is helpful to teach them how to go about working with their child. It is not uncommon to find parents who spend hours a night tutoring their child—eliminating any playtime. To set up a tutoring program for parents, it is essential to spend some time training the parents.

Parameters of Tutoring

Set Time for Tutoring

When setting up a tutoring time at home, it is important for parents to set aside time in which there will be no interruptions, i.e., the same time each night (however, not necessarily every night), and at a time in which the child is relaxed but not tired. Tutoring immediately after school is generally not a good time, since the child deserves a break and some time to relax and have fun. After dinner is often a nice time to tutor because children are not hungry, they have had some play time, and yet they are not so tired that they are ready for bed. Schedule from ten minutes to half an hour. The younger the child, the shorter the session. Let the entire family know that this is a special time between the parent and child, and that there are to be no interruptions.

Relax

Parents should check on their own emotions before beginning tutoring. If they are feeling hassled, tense, or their minds are on their own work, then the session will be stressed. The child may sense the pressure and feel tense himself or herself. It is easier for a parent to be less patient when he/she is not relaxed. Before the tutoring session, parents should take a moment to relax, take a few deep breaths, and set aside the worries of the day. Rather than looking at the tutoring session as a chore or as something that takes time away from other duties, parents should view the session as a special individual time with their child. If the parents feel relaxed, then the session will be more positive and more enjoyable for both the parent and child.

Positive Reinforcers

Parents need to learn how to give praise and positive reinforcers. Using the same principles talked about in Chapter 5, explain to parents the best way to give verbal praise. Emphasize the use of verbal praise and that it should be given frequently and enthusiastically. Back-up reinforcers also are a possibility but should be used only if the child is resisting the tutoring sessions. It is better to use back-up reinforcers for the achievement gains made as a result of the tutoring.

Tutoring Procedures

Parents should be taught what to say during the tutoring session and how to teach. Training is essential, and most parents will be open to the teacher's suggestions—especially if the teacher explains that the child will get confused if the parents teach in a different technique than that used in school. Simple reading programs in which parents listen to their children read are effective, but parents still should be taught how to listen (without interrupting) and how to correct errors. Flash card drills also should have a standard procedure for training. Listed in Figure 6–2 are examples of standard training and correction procedures. Parents need to learn a correction procedure for when children make mistakes. Parents and the child can get frustrated if many errors are made. Having a standard correction procedure will take the pressure off both tutor and tutee since the procedure is preplanned and both will know what to expect. In the heat of the moment, when parents become frustrated, they might make a negative comment that they will regret later.

Troubleshooting

Parents should be told what to do if the session is not working or if things fall apart, for example, if the child starts to cry, the parent gets frustrated. Parents should know it is OK to call it quits at times, although the child should not be allowed to learn that negative behaviors get him/her out of the session. If the sessions continue to go poorly, it is helpful to have the parent come to school with the child. The teacher can sit with both the parent and child and review the tutoring session format. A contract also might be made to enlist the child's support for the tutoring. The teacher should check to make sure that parents are following the parameters of tutoring such as length of time, use of praise, and standard teaching procedures.

COMMUNICATING WITH PARENTS

Back-to-school-night conferences can be difficult for teachers and parents, especially if there is bad news. In general, teachers should have an outline of what they are going to talk to parents about. It is helpful to talk a little bit about the classroom curriculum, what the children are studying in school, what can be expected over the next few months, and other general class topics. The conversation then can focus in on their own child. Having examples of the child's work can highlight the discussion. Even though children may bring work home on a daily or weekly basis, having the teacher focus on specific work can help parents to understand more specifically what their child is doing in school. Highlight the positives of the child's performance and, if there are problems, allow the parents to feel that their child is doing well in something despite having problems in other areas. Finish the meeting by asking whether the parents have questions or concerns. If the parents have specific concerns, write them down.

Figure 6-2
Standard Tutoring and Correction Procedures

Flash Card Drills

Math

Tutor:	Two plus two equals how many?
Tutee:	Two plus two equals four.
Tutor:	Good job!

Correction Procedure

Tutee:	Two plus two equals five.
Tutor:	No, two plus two equals four. Try again.
Tutee:	Two plus two equals four.
Tutor:	That's better. Nice job!

Spelling

Tutor:	The word is "cat." You read it.
Tutee:	"Cat."
Tutor:	The word is "cat." Let's spell it together (while looking at flash card), c-a-t.
Tutee:	C-a-t.
Tutor:	(removing card) The word is "cat." Let's spell it together, c-a-t.
Tutor:	(card is removed) The word is "cat." Now you spell it by yourself.
Tutee:	C-a-t.
Tutor:	Good job!

Correction Procedure

Tutee:	C-o-t.
Tutor:	No, the word is "cat." It's spelled c-a-t. Now you try it.
Tutee:	C-a-t.
Tutor:	Good job!

Tutoring Procedures

Math

The tutor should have a standardized procedure for reviewing the math procedure as it is taught by the teacher. By using a standard script, the child then learns the process and can use the script independently. Following is an example of a standard script: "Okay, on to the next math problem. First, read the equation (child reads 'two plus two equals how many?'). Now, put down your slash marks. Good, now count your slashes. Good, now write down the number. Great. Read the whole problem now."

As the child gains competency, the parent can remove the prompts and remind the child, "What do we do next?" The child learns to rehearse, i.e., reads the problem, makes the slashes, counts my slashes, writes the answer, and rereads the problem. This provides for independent work habits. Train a standard correction procedure here as well.

"I think we made a mistake. Let's try this problem again. Remember to count your slashes carefully."

Reading

"Let's sound the word out together. R-r-u-u-n-n, run. Now you try it. Good Job!"

This lets the parents know that the teacher is really listening and plans some action regarding their concerns. It also helps the teacher to remember what was discussed during the meeting.

If the teacher has to relay bad news, it is helpful to begin with broad concerns and then focus on the more specific problems. Have some potential solutions available, for example, extra tutoring at home or home notes. If the child needs to be evaluated, give the parents the name of the resource teacher or the school psychologist who will be doing the evaluation. Highlight the positives such as that the testing will help us to understand how the child learns and that extra help will give the child the extra boost he/she needs now so that later on he/she will not be behind. Parents should be made to feel that they are a part of the educational team; therefore, ask their opinion of their child's problems. The case study presented below demonstrates how teachers can offer support and lessen the blow when a child is not performing well.

Overall, it is important to keep parents informed about what their child is doing in school. If a child misbehaves, the parents should be made aware of the problems and *solutions should be offered.* Parents get tired of the complaints only if they feel nothing is being done to alleviate the problems. Parents also may not know what to do when a child misbehaves. Teachers can offer input on what has helped other children in the past and can be supportive of parents in their efforts to control their child's behavior. It is important to convey the good news also. Parents will be more receptive to teachers who continually communicate with them through notes, newsletters, or phone calls. Keeping communication lines open makes it easier if a problem arises later.

CASE STUDY

Erik was having trouble learning his alphabet and, despite extra help in school, he still could not remember any letters. He also confused his numbers and had difficulty remembering the correct sequence of one to five for counting. Behaviorally, Erik had difficulty staying on-task and was bothering his peers who were working. Mrs. Coombs had tried spending extra time with Erik to help him learn. She had moved his desk away from the other children to try to get him more focused on his work. After two months with no academic progress and behavior deterioration, she realized that it might be helpful to have him evaluated to determine whether he had a learning problem. The following conversation took place:

Mrs. Coombs: Hello, Mr. and Mrs. Grant, I am so glad you could come in tonight. I have enjoyed having Erik in my class. He's such an enthusiastic child. He comes in to class every day with a smile on his face. He really enjoys the art projects we have done this year. Here is the pumpkin he made this week. He really worked hard on it. We have been working on learning the alphabet and counting to five. We spend time each day reviewing the letters we have learned and we use the letters in an art project, in our science discussion, and we rehearse them daily. Most of the children are picking up their letters, a few a week. Erik seems to have difficulty with his letters. We go over one letter and I think he has it, but the next day we have to start over. Have you noticed this at home? Do you ever tell him something one day and then he forgets it the next?

Mrs. Grant: Well, sometimes he forgets, but I think he is just being stubborn. He remembers the names of the characters on his favorite TV show. I can never get them straight!

Mrs. Coombs: Well, he seems to really be having a hard time with the alphabet. We also have been working in counting to five, and I have noticed that Erik forgets the counting day to day as well. He seems to want to learn. He enjoys sitting in a circle with the other children, but when it comes down to remembering one to five, he just forgets. Have you tried counting with him at home?

Mr. Grant: Yes, and I know he can't do it. He just runs off and plays. I can't seem to get him to focus on the counting long enough.

Mrs. Coombs: Yes, I know and it gets frustrating for you and Erik too, doesn't it? In class, he has a hard time focusing too. I have tried to work extra time with Erik and I even moved his desk so he wouldn't get so distracted, but it doesn't seem to have helped. I have tried all that I can. When I have a child who I just can't seem to get across to, I often ask for help from other people in the school who have more experience with kids like this. I would like to have them work with Erik a little bit to see if they can help us understand why he is having a hard time learning.

Mrs. Grant: You mean there might be something wrong with him? I think he is a good little kid. He's just not ready to learn yet.

Mrs. Coombs: I think Erik is a good kid too and I feel badly for him that he is having a hard time. He seems to want to learn, but just can't right now. If we can have some of our other people look at him and even test him, we might be able to help Erik better. As it is now, I have run out of tricks to help him. I would like to ask you if you would consider having him looked at so that we can do what's best for Erik.

Mr. Grant: I think we should do something now while he is young. It will be for the better to find out now if he needs extra help. Who do we talk to?

Mrs. Coombs: Here's the name of our school psychologist. She can answer any questions you have about the testing or what she will be looking at. I think Erik is really a sweet boy and he just needs a little extra help right now so he can learn and really enjoy school more fully.

REFERENCES

1. Allyon, Teodoro; Garber, Stephen; and Pisor, Kim. "Reducing Time Limits: A Means to Increase Behavior of Retardates." *Journal of Applied and Behavior Analysis* 9, no. 3 (1976):247–52.
2. Broden, Marcia; Beasely, Alva; and Hall, R. Vance. "In-Class Spelling Performance: Effects of Home Tutoring by a Parent." *Behavior Modification* 2, no. 4 (1978):511–30.
3. Gang, Deborah, and Poche, Cheryl E. "An Effective Program to Train Parents as Reading Tutors for Their Children." *Education and Treatment of Children* 5 (1982):211–32.
4. Imber, Steve C.; Imber, Ruth; and Rothstein, Cary. "Modifying Independent Work Habits: An Effective Teacher-Parent Communication Program." *Exceptional Children* 46, no. 3 (1979):218–21.
5. Karraker, R. J. "Increasing Academic Performance Through Home-Managed Contingency Programs." *Journal of School Psychology* 10, no. 2 (1972):173–79.
6. Swinson, Jeremy. "Encouraging Parents to Listen to Their Children Read." In *Parental Involvement in Children's Reading,* edited by Keith Topping and Sheila Wolfendale. New York: Nichols Publishing Co., 1985.
7. Trovato, Joseph, and Bucher, Bradley. "Peer Tutoring with or without Home-Based Reinforcement for Reading Comprehension." *Journal of Applied Behavior Analysis* 13 (1980):129–41.

RESOURCES

Helping Parents Understand Children's Behavior

1. Dinkmeyer, Don, and McKay, Gary D. *Systematic Training for Effective Parenting (STEP): Parent's Handbook.* Minneapolis, Minn.: American Guidance Services, 1976.

Discipline for Parents

1. Canter, Lee; Canter, Marlene; and Schadlow, Barbara. *Parent Resource Guide.* New York: Harper & Row, 1985.

Chapter 7

USING CONSEQUENCES TO AFFECT BEHAVIORS

While positive reinforcement involves affecting behavior through consequences in everyday language usage, most of us think of consequences in terms of punishers and reprimands. In our A–B–C model of behavior, we use positive reinforcement as a consequence to increase or maintain a behavior. Positives should be our first line of defense in promoting positive behaviors in the classroom. We should choose the behaviors we want to increase in order to promote the educational and social development of our students. However, teachers often have many behaviors they wish to decrease or eliminate. Using punishers is a typical response to changing these behaviors. While using negative consequences can be effective in changing behaviors, they should be used *only after other techniques such as changing the antecedents have been tried.* Negative consequences are too easy to use as the first attack on a problem. The reason that consequences are listed as one of the highest levels of intervention in this hierarchy is that you should be able to avoid many of the misbehaviors in your class through other means. Consequences are covered here in detail, not because they are a preferred approach, but because, since teachers use consequences, it is important to point out less restrictive alternatives and the correct use of consequences. The goal of effective behavior management is for the teacher to teach rather than to discipline all day.

When we work with consequences, we need to return to our assessment of behavior. First, remember the two basic reasons children misbehave: (a) there is a skill deficit, which we have talked about remediating through instruction, or (b) the child is being reinforced for the misbehavior. When we work with consequences, we are trying to change the consequence the child receives for the misbehavior. In other words, we want to eliminate the reinforcement the child receives for misbehaving. For example, if every time a child "clowns" in front of the class, the class laughs, then the child is being reinforced for clowning. However, if we take away the laughter, the behavior loses its reinforcing value. When we change the consequences of a behavior, the child will try harder to get that positive reinforcement until he or she learns that the reinforcement no longer occurs. It is important to remember this because a teacher may give up on an intervention plan before he/she has given it time to work. The behavior typically will get worse before it gets better. For this reason, any intervention tried should be used for at least two weeks. This gives us enough time to determine whether the intervention is having an effect on the child's behavior. Too many teachers give up when the behavior gets worse, thinking that the intervention is not working.

To relate to this phenomenon, we can think of examples from everyday life. Every day you use the same soda pop machine to buy a soda. You put the money in, and your soda comes out. (You are reinforced with a soda every time you put money in.) Then one day you put money in and a soda does not appear. You try again and again and again. (The behavior escalates as you try to get reinforced.) You might even resort to a little hitting on the machine to see if that works. (Frustration may lead to aggression.) Eventually you give up. You have learned that today you will not be reinforced for putting coins in the machine. If this happens for several days in a row, you will stop using that machine and perhaps will try another one; however, if one day you do get a soda, then you will try that machine again.

The same thing happens to little Sammy in your class. When Sammy burps in class, his classmates reinforce him by laughing. He burps, and the class laughs. You might try a punisher such as making him sit in a corner, but he has already gotten the reinforcement from his classmates and your punishment is not effective. To change the consequence, you must take away the laughter of the class. In order to do this, you have to offer the class some reinforcement for not laughing at Sammy. They are getting enjoyment out of Sammy's burping (and maybe even a little enjoyment out of seeing you become angry); therefore, you must offer something else. So, you chat with the class and explain to them that we must all work together to stop Sammy from burping. If they can ignore Sammy's burps and not laugh, they will earn ten points toward a party. If they can reach 200 points (which should give you enough time to stick through your intervention), then they can have a party. The first time Sammy burps and the class does not laugh, he waits, looks around, and waits for the laughter. He tries to burp again, and still no laughter. He may try to burp very loud and may even stomp his feet to try to get attention. Since you are reinforcing the class for every time they ignore Sammy's burps, "Nice job ignoring, class, you earned ten points toward the party," Sammy is not getting reinforced. He gives up for today. He will try again tomorrow, but if the class continues to ignore him, the behavior will slowly drop out. If, however, you have a substitute teacher one day who does not know the program and Sammy is reinforced, the behavior will strengthen again, just as yours did when you got a soda on one day. It is important to be consistent and to stick to the program. Intermittent reinforcement makes a behavior even stronger than if the behavior is reinforced every time.

POSITIVE CONSEQUENCES TO CHANGE BEHAVIOR

In addition to positive reinforcement, there are techniques other than negative consequences that can be used to alter behavior. After all other levels in the intervention system have been tried and you are ready to attempt something else, there are a few additional techniques to use before you try negative consequences. Although the following have high-sounding names, they are probably techniques you have already used, but perhaps in a less systematic manner. They still involve positive reinforcement but they attack it from a slightly different angle.

Extinction

Extinction, or ignoring (deliberate disregard), involves removing the positive reinforcement for the behavior, as in the above example of Sammy. The child has learned a chain of behavior in which, following a behavior, he/she gets reinforced. When we use extinction, we no longer allow the child to receive the reinforcement. As mentioned above, there is a burst of behavior responses, called an "extinction burst," that are used to try to get that reinforcement. Following this burst, the behavior generally tends to decrease as the child learns that reinforcement no longer follows the behavior. Extinction, in the form of ignoring, is often difficult to implement in the classroom, although it can be done. When you ignore, it is important to not give the child any reinforcement. You should avoid eye contact, not talk to the child, not laugh, and should try to completely ignore the student until the appropriate behavior occurs. Obviously, this is not the intervention of choice for aggressive or acting-out problems. However, it can be useful for many verbal behaviors. Figure 7–1 lists typical verbal behaviors and how ignoring can help.

Extinction also is helpful when you know that a child is behaving in order to get attention. Attention-getting behaviors can vary from offensive behaviors such as Sammy's burping to a child's crying every day to try to get comfort from the teacher. Children can be especially manipulative with parents by crying, acting ill, and otherwise trying to avoid school. When you are trying to understand a misbehavior, remember that attention often can be the reinforcement that the child is attempting to receive. By being aware that attention is a powerful reinforcer, you can alter the consequence by ignoring the inappropriate behavior.

Figure 7-1
Using Ignoring with Verbal Behaviors

Behavior	*Intervention*
1. Calling out	Ignore until the student raises his or her hand and is quiet.
2. Interrupting	Ignore until the student is quiet or until you are finished with your converstion.
3. Name-calling	Have offended child ignore the name-calling, perhaps add a reinforcement to ignore.

Differential Reinforcement of Other Behavior

Extinction can be combined with reinforcement to make an even more powerful technique. While ignoring the misbehavior, we can reinforce another behavior. Called "Differential Reinforcement of Other Behavior" (DRO), this technique draws on the positive approach of teaching a new skill to replace the misbehavior; thus, we ignore it when a student calls out your name, and we reinforce it as soon as he/she is quiet and raises his/her hand. Because we are teaching a new skill, we may need to prompt students or remind them of the appropriate behavior. As a child calls out, you might say, "I will call on students who are sitting quietly with their hands raised." This prompts the student to raise his/her hand and to be quiet. You also can use other students as examples of behaviors that are appropriate: "I like the way that Julie is sitting quietly and waiting to hear today's lesson. I like the way Bob and George are sitting quietly." Being noticed by the teacher is a very powerful reinforcer for young children and the class will often fall into line quickly. The disadvantage of ignoring problem behaviors is the same as with extinction, i.e., an extinction burst is still likely to occur. However, since the child is receiving other reinforcement, it is hoped that he/she will learn new behaviors more quickly than by extinction alone.

Differential Reinforcement of Incompatible Behaviors

In a slightly different twist, "Differential Reinforcement of Incompatible Behaviors" (DRI) reinforces behaviors that cannot occur at the same time as the misbehavior, thus eliminating the misbehavior. In other words, you cannot hit someone if your hands are in your pockets; thus, the hitting does not occur. Teachers use DRI when they have children walk through the halls with their arms folded. If arms are folded, then they cannot be used for pushing. If children are working, they cannot be fooling around. To use DRI, you must identify an appropriate behavior that you can reinforce that will compete with the misbehavior. Typical misbehaviors that involve the hands, such as pushing, shoving, hitting, pinching, thumb-sucking, nail-biting, and masturbating, are prime targets for DRI. During transitions, children may be instructed to carry papers or books with two hands to keep their hands busy. When sitting at their desks working, children can be instructed to keep one hand on their papers while writing. Keeping hands clasped while sitting at assemblies or holding an object such as the classroom key may keep hands busy.

USING NEGATIVE CONSEQUENCES

When we move into the use of negative consequences, we should proceed with caution. Negative consequences can be very reinforcing for the person using them because they can be so effective. An effective punishment, by definition, decreases a behavior. However, some schools have taken punishment to extreme and often violent means. Corporal punishment is still legal in thirty states, with at least one million school children getting paddled each year. Perhaps these schools find the punishment effective in terms of keeping children from misbehaving; but is the price in emotional and physical scarring worth it? Hardly! When we use negative consequences, it is important to use a hierarchy of consequences, just as we are using the overall hierarchy here. Once we get to negative consequences as an intervention, we should use the least restrictive alternative. As we move up the hierarchy, we should discuss the negative consequences with parents in order to seek their approval and to avoid any problems later on. Keep in mind that negative consequences should be used *only after* positive interventions have failed.

NEGATIVE CONSEQUENCES INTERVENTION HIERARCHY

Natural Consequences

The most natural and least restrictive intervention for consequences is to allow the natural consequence for the misbehavior to occur. We all are governed by natural consequences, and we want children to become governed by natural consequences as well. A natural consequence is whatever would naturally occur following a misbehavior if we did not intervene. For example, the natural consequence for not finishing your work is to have to complete it later, perhaps at recess or after school. The natural consequence for running in puddles outside is to have to wear wet shoes. Natural consequences should not be used when they endanger a child. For example, the natural consequence for shoving the class bully is to get hit, but this is not a practical or safe consequence.

Reprimands

Reprimands are the most common form of discipline in the classroom. A reprimand is a formal rebuke for a behavior, a scolding; it sends the message that the child has misbehaved. The average teacher uses some type of verbal reprimand every two minutes at the elementary school level (6). In fact, reprimands outnumber praise statements in every grade after the second grade (6)! While reprimands are effective under certain conditions, it is obvious that they can be overused as well as misused. A reprimand also can be stated as a request, for example, "It's time to get working." The message behind the reprimand stated in this instance is that the child is not performing appropriately and is being reminded of the expected appropriate behavior.

Just as there are methods of delivery that make delivering positives more effective, there are similar methods for making reprimands more effective. It is important to remember that in order to make reprimands effective in the long run, they must be reduced in frequency and should be combined with other classroom management techniques (5). The following is a list of techniques that make reprimands more effective.

Descriptive

A reprimand should be descriptive in terms of exactly what the child is doing that is inappropriate or what the child should be doing. In a teaching role, we need to identify what the child is doing that is incorrect and then state what is correct. The child can then learn what is appropriate behavior. Some examples follow:

1. Nonexample: "Johnny, get to work."
   Example: "Johnny, you are not working. You are talking to neighbors and are out of your seat. You need to get back to work."

2. Nonexample: "Boys, cut it out!"
   Example: "Tom and Joe, no running in the class. You need to get to your seats now."

3. Nonexample: "Girls, quiet down!"
   Example: "Sarah and Jean, no talking. You need to work now."

Personality and Eye Contact

Calling out to a general group of children is less effective than using names. When the reprimand is personalized, the child knows that you are talking to him/her. In addition, if you wait and make eye contact, the child and you both know that the message was received. Use the child's name, wait for eye contact, then deliver the reprimand.

Firm, Nonemotional, Soft Voice

A child learns quickly how to push your buttons, especially if you become emotional when you give a reprimand. If you are matter-of-fact and use a firm voice, you can disguise your emotions and be more effective in your delivery of your reprimand. Some children enjoy being able to make teachers angry. The punishment that follows an outburst is not nearly as punishing as watching the teacher get angry is reinforcing. Once you let children get under your skin, you have lost control. After you reprimand a child, you can go into your closet and scream into your coat; but do not let the children see you lose it! Research has shown that using a soft voice that is audible only to the child you are reprimanding is more effective than loud reprimands (4).

Planned Consequences and Follow-Through

Planned consequences are a technique that should be used along with controlling your temper. Mistakes are made in the middle of a rage when no consequences are planned. It is in the midst of anger that parents often say things such as, "I'll throw all your toys out!" or "You'll never play with Tommy again!" Teachers can get caught in the same trap. More likely they also forget to follow-through on reprimands because the class is so busy. If you reprimand a child or make a request, be sure to follow-through. Make certain that the child complies or use a planned consequence. Remember the precision requests discussed in Chapter 6. This is an excellent sequence to ensure follow-through. Once you begin to use precision commands, they will become more natural, and you will be able to follow-through more readily. When a consequence is added to the precision command sequence (following two requests), first, we label for the child the request he/she did not follow. Then we can either model the appropriate response if we feel that the child has a skill deficit, or we can apply a consequence if the child has the skill but is not complying. The sequence, then, sounds as follows:

> "Johnny, sit in your seat and start working, please." Wait three to five seconds. If the child complies, reinforce by saying, "Nice listening, Johnny. I like the way you are sitting and working." If the child does not comply, repeat the reprimand or request with "need," "Johnny, you need to sit in your seat and start working." Wait three to five seconds. If the child complies, reinforce by saying, "Good sitting and working Johnny." If the child does not comply, label the behavior and add a consequence, "No, Johnny, that's not sitting and working. Put your head down." Then, repeat the command sequence, starting at the beginning.

Using this command sequence ensures that you will follow-through on your commands. During the intermission that you are waiting for a response (three to five seconds), you can praise another child, give a request to another child or the class, or continue with your next instruction in your reading group. You would be surprised how long five seconds is! The consequence presented in the example is only one possible consequence. You can choose from any of the consequences we will discuss. If you do not follow-through with your command, the child learns that he or she does not have to comply because chances are there will be no consequence.

Distance

Just as positive statements are more effective if delivered from a close distance, so are reprimands. If possible, you should be within three feet of the child. However, class organization often makes this difficult. Following through will make your long-distance reprimands more effective. If you can, you should try to move about the room frequently. This will allow you to give your praise and reprimands from a close distance.

Praise Should Outnumber Reprimands

Overall, do not overuse reprimands. As discussed in differential reinforcement above, if you can praise children around the misbehaving child, that child often will shape up without your having to reprimand him/her. You can then follow-up with a praise statement to the child. If you are reprimanding constantly, eventually your audience tunes you out.

Reinforce the Next Appropriate Behavior

Once you have reprimanded a child, it is important to reinforce the next appropriate behavior. This moves the child back into positive responding. The child who has been constantly reinforced for negative behaviors will begin to respond to positive statements as well if you can teach him/her that it is more appropriate. Some children misbehave for attention; thus, if you can give them attention for positive behaviors, you can make a difference in the child. Some teachers might complain that a particular behavior-problem child has no positive behaviors to reinforce. You might really have to look hard, but it is essential to find something positive about the child, for example, whether he/she is sitting straight, holding a pencil well, or even breathing!

Overcorrection and Positive Practice

Along with reprimands, you can move to modeling the behavior for the child or having another child model the appropriate behavior. The offending child then must practice the behavior. For example, the class is being disruptive during independent seatwork. You reprimand the class, and remind them of the appropriate behavior. If the class does not respond to the reprimand, you can model the appropriate behavior. You point out a child who is behaving appropriately and have the class look at the child's appropriate behavior. The whole class then must practice the behavior. You request the class to show you the appropriate behavior. After they have practiced, then they continue working. This works with individuals as well. If Jeff is shouting at you for a paper, you have Randy model the appropriate response; then Jeff practices this response. You then can reinforce him for appropriate responding.

One step beyond modeling and practice is to have the child overcorrect the inappropriate response and/or to over-practice the appropriate response. For example, if a child misbehaves by coloring on a desk, he or she must "overcorrect" not only by washing his/her desk, but also by washing all of the desks. In positive practice, a child who runs to the desk might have to practice walking to the desk several times. The overcorrection and positive practice acts must be related directly to the misbehavior. There is a teaching component to the overcorrection in that the child is repeating the correct response many times.

Response Cost

In response cost, the child "pays" for his or her misbehavior by losing points or tokens. The child loses a specified number of reinforcers for the misbehavior. It is important that the points are specified, as in a planned consequence, so that children know what the consequence is. If children are randomly paying points, then the system will be perceived as unfair and unpredictable, as well as unrelated to their behavior. A response-cost system works only if children are receiving reinforcement points or tokens, and these have taken on a reinforcing value. If a child is not motivated by the token economy system, then he/she will not be deterred by response cost.

Contingent Work

We can have children "pay" for their misbehavior through work. If we use an act to overcorrect that is not related to the misbehavior, then we are using contingent work to punish the misbehavior. In contingent work, we make the offending child exert energy to "pay off" the misbehavior. For example, an offending child might have to write "I will not talk in class" 100 times, or might have to run laps in the gym for misbehaving. These consequences are not related to the misbehavior; thus, we lose the teaching component. Instead, we are punishing the misbehavior by making the child exert energy to "pay" for the misbehavior. Contingent work should be used cautiously. A child should not be expected to work to the point of pain or injury. Parental support is recommended for contingent work.

Loss of Privileges

Loss of privileges is another kind of response cost. It can be more punishing than losing points in a token economy because the child is losing something that he/she may consider a "right" or an unconditional privilege. For example, most children have recess, but a child may lose recess for a misbehavior. Children who misbehave when unsupervised often lose the privilege of going to the bathroom when they want to. They may be allowed to use the bathroom only when escorted and only at certain times of the day. Losing privileges can be very punishing for a child, especially when he/she can see others enjoying the privilege. Caution should be taken that loss of the privilege does not cause harm to the child, and that the child is not deprived of basic human needs such as water and food. School administration and parental approval is recommended when using loss of privileges as a punishment.

Time-Out

Time-out is defined as a procedure "in which positive reinforcement is withdrawn for a prespecified period of time following the performance of a misbehavior" (2, p. 71). This means that positive reinforcement is not given during a certain time period. Many teachers and parents believe that time-out means being shut into a room alone. There are many degrees of time-out that can be used effectively as a negative consequence for a misbehavior. When using a time-out procedure, the following sequence for implementation should be followed:

1. *Verbal reprimand:* Tell the child what he/she did that was inappropriate. Remember to use the child's name, establish eye contact, and label the misbehavior, e.g., "Johnny, that's not working quietly." "No, Billy, that's not walking."
2. *Give direction for the time-out:* Tell the child what he or she is to do for the time-out, e.g., "Johnny, head down." "Billy, you need to sit in the time-out chair."
3. *Monitor the time-out:* Ensure that the child does not receive reinforcement. Do not talk to him/her (except if a direction is needed such as, "You need to be quiet before you can go back to your seat"); do not allow others to talk to the child; and watch for reinforcing grins, looks, etc., from classmates.
4. *Release from time-out:* Do not berate for the behavior that got the child into time-out. Give the direction that time-out is over and where the child should go or what the child should be doing, e.g., "Johnny, you can get back to work now." "Billy, you may go back to your desk now."
5. *Reinforce the next appropriate response:* Catch the child being good the next possible moment. This ensures that the child will be receiving reinforcement for appropriate behaviors and is not just being reprimanded, e.g., "Johnny, nice working quietly." "Billy, nice sitting in your chair, your feet are on the floor, and you are sitting flat on your chair."

Several precautions should be considered when using time-out procedures:

1. Check with school officials regarding any policies dealing with exclusionary time-out procedures. It is wise to get parental and administrative support for the more restrictive forms of time-out.
2. Do *not* use time-out when you are angry and as an impulsive measure to "get rid of" the child. Time-out is a *planned* consequence. It should be used as a planned consequence for a misbehavior. Time-out is a punishment procedure and should be treated as such. It is *not* a convenience to get a child out of the room or out of an activity.
3. Do *not* raise your voice and verbally berate the child in time-out. Use a calm, firm voice. When a child is in time-out, do not talk to him/her or allow his/her tauntings to get you involved in a power struggle. Although the child may be calling you names or complaining how unfair you are, do not get "sucked" into a verbal confrontation. Simply remind the student that he/she needs to be quiet before he/she can rejoin the class. When the child comes out of time-out, move on; do not beat him/her up with his/her offense.
4. Reinforce the class for following your instructions and for not paying attention to the child in time-out. If the class is laughing at the child or paying attention to him/her, then the child may be getting reinforced. One difficulty with a disruptive child is that often the entire class is interrupted and is staring at that child. By increasing the reinforcement for ignoring, you can keep the rest of the class under control, for example, "Nice working, class. Joe is having a hard time today, but we are going to just go about our business and not pay attention to him." By acknowledging to the class that a child is having difficulty, it lets them know that you are dealing with Joe's problem and that it is not their concern.

5. Do *not* use extended time periods for time-out. For young children, minutes can seem like hours. Being removed from the class for one minute can be very punishing for a kindergarten student. Again, the length of time-out should be planned and any contingencies for removal from time-out, such as being quiet, should be planned as well.
6. The activity the child is missing must be a reinforcing one. If the child does not care about the activity, then the time-out is not effective because he/she is not missing receiving reinforcement. For example, why suspend a child from school who hates school? The child is escaping a negative place rather than missing a positive experience. Be careful that the child is not manipulating you by using time-out to avoid work or an activity. The child should finish the activity or command that was started before time-out started.
7. Do *not* overuse time-out. Remember that it is one of the most restrictive interventions and should be the last line of defense.

When using time-out, you should use the least restrictive intervention first. The following is a hierarchy for time-out procedures.

Quiet Time

A "quiet time" in which a child places his/her head down on the desk is a mild time-out. During this time, a child must sit quietly and cannot participate in class activities. This is a good procedure to use to get children quiet and refocused on the task at hand. A head down can be used for a short interval, either as an individual or whole-class procedure.

Partial Exclusion

You can grade the amount of removal the child has from the group. In a circle activity, the child may have to move a few feet away from the group. In this manner, the child can see the group but cannot participate. The child can turn around and face away from the group; he/she can hear what is going on and what is being missed, but cannot participate. You can move the child to the other side of the room where he/she can see the class, but, again, cannot participate.

Losing a Reinforcer

By definition, time-out means exclusion from reinforcement; however, you can use specific reinforcers that the child cannot receive or that he/she loses. For example, a child may be allowed to keep a prized possession on his or her desk as long as his/her behavior is appropriate. However, if the child misbehaves, the object is put in time-out, and the child cannot have access to it. The child also may lose access to a reinforcer or privilege. For example, if the child is throwing food at lunch, taking the lunch tray away for thirty seconds can be an effective time-out. Losing a minute of recess or having to wait until the other children have lined up also are brief time-outs. It is a time-out from receiving an expected reinforcer. Parental support is recommended when using this procedure.

Group Contingencies for Time-Out

The group can be enlisted as helpers in a time-out. If a child misbehaves, then the group times him/her out and does not give the child reinforcement. For example, if Dave hit a child during free play, he may need to play alone for five minutes. During this time, he is "timed-out" from the rest of the group. If Joanne has been screaming at her friends, the teacher may have her friends time Joanne out from their interactions by ignoring Joanne's taunts until she is appropriate. Caution should be used so that children are not ostracized by the class or abused by others. Instruct the class on what the time-out means. For example, "Dave hit his friend when they were playing. Dave needs to play alone for a few minutes so he can learn to play better. When Dave is playing alone, we are going to leave him alone and not talk to him or tease him. When he joins us again, we will be friendly and let him play." Parental and administration support is recommended when using this procedure.

Exclusionary Time-Out

Exclusionary time-out occurs when a child is removed from the classroom and is excluded from the group completely. The child may be removed to a partitioned part of the class, to the hall, to the principal's office, to the resource room, or to another area away from the group. Closets or bathrooms are not appropriate time-out rooms. Children should be safe and unable to destroy property or harm themselves. This is the most restrictive form of punishment and should be used cautiously and judiciously. Be sure to have preplanned procedures and time limits. Parental and administration support is essential.

Overall, remember that time-out is a *planned* consequence with specific parameters. It should be used *only* after all other interventions have failed.

TROUBLESHOOTING SPECIFIC BEHAVIOR PROBLEMS

Books have been written that present specific interventions for specific behavior problems. (See resource list at the end of the chapter for a few examples.) However, it is helpful to identify a few typical classroom problems that are usually handled with punishers to show how they can be dealt with in a more positive approach. By understanding why the behavior is occurring, rather than using a generic punishment for all misbehaviors, the intervention plan can directly address the child's needs.

Swearing

It is quite distressing for teachers to have a kindergarten student let out a string of four-letter words. Before you become angry and march the child to the principal, think for a minute about why he/she is swearing and what benefit he/she derives from swearing. For older children, swearing is often a malicious and conscious behavior, but for young children, swearing is different. First, young children do not know what the words mean and are merely modeling what they have heard elsewhere (often at home). They often use swear words in context; for example, if a child bangs his thumb with a hammer, he/she may let fly an expletive. He/she has probably seen daddy do this, so it seems appropriate. When children swear at you in anger, they are modeling what they have seen happen before. In these situations, it is better to deal with the content rather than to be sidetracked by the fact that the child is swearing. In other words, attend to the real issue. The child is angry and needs to be told how to show his/her anger appropriately. To illustrate, let us say you reprimand a child for a misbehavior. The child gets angry and begins to swear at you. You can label the feeling for him and teach the appropriate behavior. You say, "Sam, you are feeling mad right now. You can tell me you are mad. But remember, when we hit other children, it means we have to sit alone for a minute. When you are quiet, you may join us." In this way you are helping the child learn a new behavior.

If we attend to the swear words, we are teaching only the attention-getting nature of these words. Children learn quickly that swear words get adults' attention quickly. It also makes adults angry and can get them off the subject. Thus, if a child is told to pick up the crayons that were thrown across the room and he/she starts to swear, the teacher might attend to the swearing, get angry, and take the child to the principal's office. The child was successful in avoiding picking up the crayons as well as some class work. The consequence of going to the principal's office may be less aversive than staying in class. If a child gets no reinforcement for swearing in terms either of getting attention or getting the teacher angry, then the behavior will drop out—especially if we also teach new ways of expression. It is better to consequate talking-out behavior rather than specifically to pinpoint the swearing. The swearing will drop out faster if the child learns that it does not work in getting your attention. To intervene with swearing, identify the purpose of the swearing by: (a) attention-getting (intervention—ignore the swearing and consequate other behaviors associated with the swearing such as yelling or talking out), and (b) modeled "appropriate" swearing (intervention—label the feeling for the child and teach the appropriate response).

Fighting

Fighting is one of the more problematic behavior concerns in classroom management because it often takes the teacher away from the other students; if an injury occurs, then the parents of the offended child want justice. There are several situations that occur in the classroom that can develop into fights. Instead of having a generic response to fighting, we can use these situations to help us to determine interventions relating to the specific reason for the fight.

Difficulty Sharing

A fight often breaks out when children have difficulty sharing a toy either by taking turns or playing with the toy together. *Sharing* includes the "sharing of ideas," particularly in deciding what game to play, who gets to be "it," or who can play a game. The reason for the fighting in this instance is a skill deficit. The children do not possess the sharing and negotiation skills to effectively work out the problem. For intervention, a skills training program would be effective in helping children to learn how to share and how to negotiate. Children can role play what to do in specific situations and how to resolve conflicts. Social skills training materials often have ready-made teaching modules in how to share and negotiate.

Taunting/Teasing

Children can be mean to each other, and "name-calling" is a fact of life on elementary playgrounds. A fight often breaks out as a result of the taunting and teasing. Both the child doing the teasing and the one being teased should be involved in interventions.

For the teaser, a consequence for teasing behavior should be planned. The child may lose privileges or points following teasing behavior. A positive component should be included to reinforce appropriate behavior.

For the teased, a skill-building program designed to help the child to cope with and ignore teasing is helpful. Social skills programs can be helpful in teaching children how to ignore, to walk away from, and to cope with teasing. Offering a reinforcer for ignoring can be helpful. Training to help the child make new friends or to improve his/her appearance (if this is a source of teasing) also can be helpful.

The Aggressive Child

Once in awhile you will have a child in your class who has learned aggressive behaviors and finds aggression to work well in obtaining his/her wants and needs. Sometimes the child will come from an aggressive or even violent family, where hitting is accepted as a way of life. In this instance, the child will need social skills training to teach new and appropriate behaviors. You will need a behavior plan including both consequences for negative behaviors, and reinforcers for appropriate behaviors. Contracting can be helpful to monitor appropriate behavior and can include a penalty for fighting.

Talking-Out

An annoying behavior is "talk-outs," i.e., when children call out to get your attention, yell out responses to group questions, or talk to peers during seatwork. For young children, talk-outs are often due to a skill deficit and immature, impulsive responding. By using reinforcement of appropriate behaviors and teaching appropriate behaviors, you can reduce a lot of the talk-outs. Group contingencies also can be used to reduce class talk-outs. The "Good Behavior Game," used by Barrish, Saunders, and Wolf (1), is a group contingency where children are divided into teams and can earn reinforcers for having the fewest talk-outs and out-of-seat behaviors. Token economies also can be used effectively to reduce talk-outs in class by having children lose points for talk-outs and earn points for appropriate behaviors (3).

Examples of an intervention follow:

1. Teach appropriate behavior, e.g., hand-raising, waiting for a turn
2. Reinforce appropriate behavior
3. Reinforce others around the misbehaving child to model appropriate behavior
4. Use a group contingency to get class control
5. Use a token economy.

ETHICAL CONSIDERATIONS

When using any consequences in the classroom, it is important to consider the impact of those consequences on the individual child and on the classroom as a whole. The importance of using antecedents first cannot be stressed enough. We tend to jump to consequences first because they have worked in the past and there is no doubt that punishment is effective. However, we cannot just take away and extinguish behaviors. If a child disrupts the class because he or she needs attention, when we take away that attention by extinguishing the disruptive behavior, the child's needs are not met. Initially, we must meet the child's needs. To do that, we should give the child the skill he/she needs to gain attention appropriately. If the child learns to use appropriate social skills, then the need to attract attention by being disruptive decreases. *Always* try a proactive approach first.

When you consider using a consequence, first ask yourself whether you have examined all proactive levels of the hierarchy first. Have you asked yourself why the child is misbehaving? Have you changed the classroom environment by moving the child's desk? Have you considered how the child fits into the scheduling? Is it too long a period of time for him/her to sit? Does the child know the rules and routines? Have you examined the antecedents? Are you using effective reinforcers? Have you involved the parents? Now and only now are you ready for consequences. The least intrusive consequences should be used first. It is important not to leap to a tried-and-true consequence such as loss of privileges if a less-punishing technique will work. Each child must be dealt with individually, and we must be sure we are meeting the child's needs, not just our own.

REFERENCES

1. Barrish, Harriet H.; Saunders, Muriel; and Wolf, Montrose M. "Good Behavior Game: Effects of Individual Contingencies for Group Contingencies." *Journal of Applied Behavior Analysis* 2 (1969):119–24.
2. Foxx, Richard M. *Decreasing Behaviors of Severely Retarded and Autistic Persons.* Champaign, Ill.: Research Press, 1982.
3. McLaughlin, Thomas, and Malaby, John. "Reducing and Measuring Inappropriate Verbalizations in a Token Classroom." *Journal of Applied Behavior Analysis* 5 (1972):329–33.
4. O'Leary, K. Daniel; Kaufman, Kenneth F.; Kass, Ruth E.; and Drabman, Ronald S. "The Effects of Loud and Soft Reprimands on the Behavior of Disruptive Students." *Exceptional Children* 37 (1971):145–55.
5. Van Houten, Ron, and Doleys, Daniel. "Are Social Reprimands Effective?" In *The Effects of Punishment on Human Behavior,* edited by Saul Axelrod and Jack Apsche. New York: Academic Press, 1983.
6. White, Mary Alice. "Natural Rates of Teacher Approval and Disapproval in the Classroom." *Journal of Applied Behavior Analysis* 8 (1975):367–72.

RESOURCES

Intervention Handbooks for Behavior Problems

1. McIntyre, Thomas. *A Resource Book for Remediating Common Behavior and Learning Problems.* Boston: Allyn & Bacon, 1989.

2. Sparzo, Frank J., and Poteet, James A. *Classroom Behavior: Detecting and Correcting Special Problems.* Boston: Allyn & Bacon, 1989.
3. Wolfgang, Charles H., and Glickman, Carl D. *Solving Discipline Problems: Strategies for Classroom Teachers.* Boston: Allyn & Bacon, 1986.

Using Consequences

1. Sprick, Randall. "Effective Punishment." In *The Solution Book: A Guide to Classroom Discipline,* edited by Randall Sprick. Chicago: Science Research Associates, 1981.
2. ______. "Ignoring Misbehavior and Setting Goals for Student Behavior." In *The Solution Book: A Guide to Classroom Discipline,* edited by Randall Sprick. Chicago: Science Research Associates, 1981.
3. ______. "Establishing a Discipline Plan." In *The Solution Book: A Guide to Classroom Discipline,* edited by Randall Sprick. Chicago: Science Research Associates, 1981.

Chapter 8

CONCLUDING REMARKS

While no book on classroom and behavior management can cover every aspect of children's behavior and misbehavior, this publication attempts to cover the entire classroom system in a proactive approach. The hierarchy allows teachers to assess the classroom in a systematic way to determine whether the classroom system is working. If we deal with the potential for misbehaviors before the misbehavior occurs, then we can stay one step ahead of the game. The resources listed at the end of each chapter should provide a direction for teachers interested in further information or specific interventions for more severe behavior problems. Listed below is a checklist to help in assessing the classroom and for troubleshooting behavior problems. If an intervention fails at one level, move to the next higher level. If everything fails, you may want to reassess the problem and/or turn to help from the professionals in your school such as the school psychologist or the special education department.

1. What problems am I having in my classroom?
   a. List
   b. Prioritize problems
   c. Terminal objective (choose one problem, state the problem positively as something you want to attain)
2. Analyze the problem using A-B-C assessment.
   a. State the behavior
   b. What happens before the behavior occurs?
   c. What happens directly after the behavior?
   d. Why is the behavior occurring? Is the behavior reinforced? Is there a skill deficit?
   e. Do I understand why the behavior occurs and how it is being maintained?

      Yes: Go through hierarchy determining the least restrictive intervention to deal with the problem.

No: Brainstorm the problem.

(1) Have I clearly defined the real problem? Did I state the problem behavior clearly? Try rewriting the problem.

(2) Have I determined the antecedents? Have an observer watch the classroom to see if antecedents can be determined.

(3) Have I determined the consequences? Have observer watch for consequences. Brainstorm with other teachers about what consequences are occurring and what the result is.

(4) Is the behavior being maintained by reinforcement? How could the child or children be reinforced?

(5) Does the child possess the skill? Does the child know what is expected?

3. Classroom environment
   a. Desk and table arrangements appropriate for class?
   b. Environment: Distractions? Can everyone see the board?
   c. Classroom flow: Are there places where the traffic patterns cause behavior problems?
   d. Work stations: If used, are work stations in place and appropriate? Is the material self-starting?
4. Scheduling
   a. Does the schedule match the students' activity and attentional levels?
   b. Have I balanced the day with a variety of teaching methods and activities?
5. Antecedents: Rules and routines
   a. Are rules clearly defined and posted? Are the rules age appropriate and stated positively?
   b. Have routines and expectations been taught and practiced? Do children know what to do?
   c. Do I remember to be consistent and reinforce appropriate rule and routine behaviors?
   d. Have I tried to change behaviors by:
      (1) Shaping
      (2) Modeling

(3) Prompting
(4) Nonverbal signals
(5) Precision requests
(6) Skill training

6. Reinforcement strategies
   a. Are the reinforcers appropriate? Are they reinforcing?
   b. Do I use reinforcers appropriately?
      (1) Immediate
      (2) Frequently
      (3) Enthusiastically
      (4) Eye contact
      (5) Describe the behavior
      (6) Use variety
      (7) Close proximity
      (8) Personalize the reward
   c. Have I tried to change the behavior by:
      (1) Self-control/self-reinforcement
      (2) Contracting
      (3) Token economy
      (4) Group contingencies and teams
      (5) Premack Principle
      (6) Creative reinforcers
7. Parental involvement
   a. Have I tried to get the parents involved? Have I tried a parent/teacher conference?
   b. Have I tried to change the behavior by using the parents as:
      (1) Reinforcers using home notes
      (2) Tutors
8. Using consequences
   a. Has all else failed?
   b. Have I tried positive consequences?
      (1) Extinction
      (2) Differential reinforcement of other behavior (DRO)
      (3) Differential reinforcement of incompatible behaviors (DRI)
   c. After considering the ethical ramifications and after

contacting parents and school personnel, have I tried the least restrictive alternatives?

(1) Natural consequences
(2) Reprimands used appropriately
(3) Overcorrection and positive practice
(4) Response cost
(5) Contingent work
(6) Loss of privileges
(7) Time-out hierarchy

The Ops Officer's Manual

The Ops Officer's Manual

BY PETER T. DEUTERMANN, COMMANDER, U.S. NAVY

NAVAL INSTITUTE PRESS ANNAPOLIS, MARYLAND

Library of Congress Catalog Card Number: 79-89179
ISBN: 0-87021-505-1

Printed in the United States of America

To Vice Admiral H.T. Deutermann,
U.S. Navy, (Retired)

Chapter opening photographs:

Page 2. Fleet Operations: A destroyer returns to the formation.

Page 22. Planning session in the wardroom.

Page 50. Amphibious Operations: An LSD pulls alongside an LPH for refueling.

Page 78. Stateside Operations: Bridge watch team during a fleet exercise.

Page 96. Deployed Operations: U.S. Navy destroyers pierside in Athens, Greece.

Page 114. Eight o'clock reports: Planning the next day.

Page 126. Aftermath of a peacetime operational emergency—USS *Belknap* under tow.

Page 144. CIC: The nerve center.

Page 166. Inshore Operations: U.S. Navy Swift boats on patrol.

Contents

Preface

This book has been written for officers who are on their way to or serving in the billet of operations officer in a combatant ship of the U.S. Navy. It is a handbook on how to be a successful operations officer. It is based primarily on the author's experiences as an operations officer in both a conventional gun destroyer and an NTDS guided missile cruiser.

This book does not address tactics and doctrine, as these subjects are more properly the province of the U.S. Navy's Naval Warfare Publications series. It concentrates instead on the elements of managing the operations of a warship. The book describes the job of the ops officer, the fleet operations environment, both in home and deployed waters, and suggests techniques for planning, training, reporting, handling operational emergencies, running an efficient combat information center, and concludes with a discussion of combat operations.

In the chapter on training there is presented a somewhat innovative technique for constructing and managing a comprehensive shipboard training program, which has become a difficult task in the hectic environment of naval operations. The presentation assumes that the operations officer is also the training officer. While this may not be universally the case, the need for integration of the ship's training requirements, resources, and other shipboard activities makes it almost a necessity if the training program is to be more than just a paper exercise.

Allied with the concept on training is the idea of a centrally prepared master plan for the ship, presented in the chapter on planning. This too is an innovative proposal, and it requires the direct support and participation of the captain. If the reader agrees with the premise that the salient feature of the fleet operating environment is continuing change, then the value of having a long-range plan for the ship can be seen immediately—if only as a vehicle for coping with changes in a rational manner instead of having to react on a crash-program basis.

Being the operations officer in a warship is exciting. The tempo of the job is fast-paced. There is an enormous amount of personal satisfaction in seeing the operations department execute the many evolutions of fleet operations in a professional manner. Getting the ship's CIC, communications, and electronics maintenance divisions to work together effectively requires the personal leadership and interest of the operations officer.

The operations officer must be extremely flexible. Successful execution of an operations evolution requires the melding of several streams of activity, all of which have to come together at the right time and place to make the evolution work. There are many ways to achieve this in terms of the efficient use of the equipments and skills at hand, and the successful ops officer is the one who can put an evolution back on track when equipment breaks or people make mistakes.

If there is one thing which an operations officer must do, it is this: he must get ahead of the job, and stay ahead. There will always be more to do than time in which to do it. To get behind is a cardinal sin.

Many officers come to the job of operations officer with most of their experience in one of the other two principal line areas—engineering or weapons. They may be apprehensive because so much of the knowledge of how to do the job appears to be obtainable only through experience. This book attempts to describe much of that "insider's" lore in order that the officer new to operations can know what to look for to see if his department is doing the job correctly. There will be many differences among ship types and command philosophies. The aspects of operations described in this book are broad enough to accommodate these differences, dealing as they do with management elements rather than specific procedures. As with any of the department head jobs in a warship, effective management is the key to success.

The reader should understand that this book attempts to cover all the facets of an operations officer's job. In different ships, his job may include all of these or only part. Depending also upon the wishes of the captain and executive officer, the scope of the operations officer's job may vary widely. If each of the operations department's junior officers is competent and interested in his job, the department head's job will get progressively easier. The reader should not get discouraged at the scope of the job described in the following pages, for often he will find that it is this wide diversity that keeps the job interesting.

The Ops Officer's Manual

1
The Operations Officer

The duties and responsibilities of the operations officer are described in several documents:

OPNAV Instruction 3120.32 "Standard Organization and Regulation Manual (SORM)" (Chapter 3)
Commander Naval Surface Forces (Atlantic/Pacific) supplement to the above SORM
U.S. Navy Regulations, 1973, Article 1107
Individual ship's directives/regulations
Individual ship's combat systems doctrine
Letters of appointment/designation from the captain

The operations officer also has collateral duties. Since a collateral duty in a small ship may well be a primary billet in a larger ship, the operations officer must check the above references for descriptions of the collateral duties as well. It is very instructive for a new ops officer to make a copy of the pages which describe his primary and collateral duties from each of the above references. The resulting job description gives a clear picture of the scope of his duties.

Procedures

In addition to the formally prescribed duties and responsibilities of the operations officer, there are often certain procedures in the ship for which the operations officer is also responsible. For instance, each department head is responsible for preparing material casualty reports for the captain to release. Because material casualty reports trigger reports on operational readiness, a responsibility of the ops officer, ships normally have a procedure whereby the operations officer is informed of each material casualty report before it goes to the captain for release. This procedure allows him to initiate readiness reports, when required, in a timely fashion.

A second example of a fairly standard procedure is that of submitting weather data, one of the collateral duties of the ops officer described in the Navy SORM. The SORM states that when a ship has a full-time meteorological officer on board, he works for the operations officer. Most ships, however, do not have a full-time weather officer, and yet the SORM requirement that the ship must submit synoptic weather observations on a periodic basis still exists. In most ships, the actual preparation of the weather data is done by the quartermaster of the watch, checked by the officer of the deck, released by him, and transmitted by the communications center. The operations officer is not involved at all in this process, despite what the SORM has to say about who submits weather data, but this procedure takes care of the collateral duty required by SORM.

There will often be other arrangements in the ship, some unique to the type of ship, which call for the operations officer to perform a function or duty not specifically identified in the SORM. The new operations officer needs to be alert for the key words "Ops takes care of that." It is a good idea for a new operations officer to make a list of all arrangements of this sort, and to add them to his collection of job descriptions.

Relationships

Like all department heads, the operations officer must achieve an effective relationship with the commanding officer, the executive officer, and his contemporaries in the ship. He also must establish effective relationships with other operations officers, with staff officers, and officers in the shore establishment.

Relationships with Officers in the Ship

The captain sets priorities for his command and sets in motion the planning needed to achieve those priorities. Because the operations officer is the captain's principal assistant for operational planning, he must at times attempt to think as the captain does and not just as the manager of the operations department. In other words, he actually plays two roles: he is the operational planner for the ship, and also the head of the operations department. The allocation of his time in each role will be directed in great part by the captain. The captain may at first do his own operational planning; as the operations officer becomes familiar with his job, he can take over more and more of the planning role.

The operations officer's relationship with the executive officer is as set forth in the *Organization and Regulations Manual.* As a head of department, the ops officer works for the executive officer. He has the traditional access to the captain given to all department heads, but he must keep the executive officer informed. This is especially important if the ship is operating at sea, when changes to the day's operating schedule may be frequent. Such changes will almost always have an impact on the day's routine, a factor very important to the executive officer. It is crucial that the operations officer see to it that the executive officer is one of the first to know when there are going to be changes that will upset the previously established plan of the day.

The relationship between the operations officer and the other department heads is also dual natured. As the operations officer, he will be one of the first to know about schedule changes and other operational information which will have an effect on the other departments. He has the responsibility to keep the other department heads informed in a timely manner, so that their planning can be based on solid assumptions. As one of the ship's department heads, the operations officer must participate in the daily give and take of shipboard management, whether it be competition for limited operating funds, assignment of food-service duties, or responsibility for the cleaning and maintenance of shared spaces in the ship.

It is likely that the operations officer will also be the training officer. This is a coordination and planning job, which involves cooperation between the training officer and the department heads. It is important to remember that the operations officer, in his capacity as training officer, does not direct the other department heads. He coordinates their efforts under the direction of the executive officer, to eliminate mutual interference and accomplish genuine training. (This subject will be addressed in detail in chapter three).

Relationships with the Unit Staff

In smaller ships, the embarkation of a unit commander and his staff poses special problems because of the limited office and living space. As the operations officer, you are more likely than the other department heads to have direct contact with both the staff and the unit commander himself. You must realize that these officers have a heavy workload and many ships to consider. You must foster a cooperative and positive attitude towards the staff and recognize the flagship's duty to support the embarked commander.

The operations officer's relationship with the unit commander's staff should be controlled in tone and substance by the captain. This relationship should be fully discussed when you take over the job of operations officer, in order to establish clearly between you and the captain the limits of your authority in dealing with the ship's operational and administrative superiors. In any official dealings with the staff, the ops officer should be very circumspect when committing the ship to do or not do something.

As the operations officer, you will do much of your operational planning with your counterparts on the unit commander's staff, even if they are not embarked on your ship. If the staff operations officer calls and asks you to come over to the flagship to discuss the operating schedule, for example, you must inform the executive officer and the captain and obtain guidance from both of them before going to the flagship. If other topics come up during the discussion, you should make no commitments until you have had time to confer with the captain. If the staff operations officer gives you advance information on some upcoming event, that word must get back to the executive officer and the captain—and to the other department heads if pertinent to them. When one of the unit commander staff officers calls for information, it is a good idea to get him an answer on a priority basis. One general prudential rule for operations officers: captains deal more effectively with unit commanders than do department heads.

Relationships with Officers in Other Ships

Information is the coin of the realm in the world of fleet operations. One of the best ways to find out what is going on in the fleet around the ship is to talk to other operations officers, particularly those in similar types of ships or ships in the same squadron. If you are new at the job, you should not be reluctant to ask a more experienced operations officer how a particular matter is handled. If he does not have time to explain in detail, he can at least give you the appropriate reference in which to look it up. It is better to ask questions of other operations officers than to be continually badgering the staff operations officer with questions on procedure. In other words, ask another operations officer, then check the appropriate reference, and then confirm with the staff operations officer that this is how it is done in the squadron.

It is good to remember that almost everything the ship will do has been done before by another ship. When the ship is faced with an upcoming evolution that it has not done before—at least in the collective memory of the present wardroom—it is a good idea to consult the employment schedule to see if another ship in the area has done that evolution recently. If this is the case, you would be well advised to take an hour to talk to your counterpart on the other ship and discuss it with him. If there is a lot that is new or different about the evolution, it might be a good idea to recommend to the executive officer that you arrange a conference with the department heads of the two ships to get your ship's officers briefed on the lessons learned by the other ship.

Relationships with Officers in the Shore Establishment

Another very important relationship is with the home-port training coordinators. In each of the Navy's major home ports, there are formal procedures by which ships obtain either individual school quotas or team training time at the fleet training center. There are also informal procedures which can be used to very good advantage by the operations officer.

There is usually one officer or senior chief petty officer at the local fleet training center who administers the scheduling of all the courses offered at the school. He will know what openings there are at any given time. As a new operations officer, you should find out who this person is and call on him, in order to find out firsthand how his office works and what the proper procedures are for a ship to get training quotas.

You should tell the coordinator that your ship is interested in training opportunities, and you should establish a "call me" relationship with the coordinator's office. Then when another ship cancels out at the last minute, for instance, on an ASW team training session, the coordinator can give you a call. The ship may not be able to take advantage of that particular quota; on the other hand, it may be a badly needed training opportunity. The coordinator wants to get full use out of his facilities; as the operations officer, in your capacity as training officer, you want to know about all the training opportunities that come along, so the two of you have a mutual interest. You should consult weekly with the planning board for training to see what the ship's most pressing training needs are that are not included in the regularly scheduled training. You can then relay these needs to the training coordinators and find out what might be available soon. Such a relationship is a valuable complement to the established procedures for requesting training on a scheduled basis.

Most fleet training centers initiate a weekly message, usually on the same day each week, listing unscheduled or unfilled training quotas that will be available the next week. After you have learned what your ship's most pressing training needs are at the weekly planning board, you can call the center the day before this weekly message is published to see if any of these quotas are going to be listed. If they are, you can then acquire them before they are advertised to all the ships in port. Another technique is to call the training center on Monday morning to find out about no-shows.

Relationships with the Ship's Schedulers

One of the most important relationships you will establish as the operations officer is the one with the ship's schedulers, those officers in the chain of command who directly influence the ship's employment schedule. Depending upon the type of administrative organization the ship is in—be it division, squadron, group, or even one of a kind—the first flag officer in the chain of command has the most influence on changing the ship's operational employment schedule. If the ship is in a squadron, the squadron operations officer manages the ship's schedule, but the decision authority rests with the group commander's operations officer.

If the captain wants to change the ship's schedule, he has the operations officer propose the change to the squadron operations officer, who in turn checks it out with the group operations officer. The group operations officer might even check with the ship's type commander or the fleet commander's operations section. If there are no objections to the change, the ship then submits a formal request, by message, to the squadron commander, who in turn routes it through the chain of command until approval is received and a schedule change authorized by the fleet commander. This change will then appear in the fleet employment schedule.

Changes in schedules, however, are more often initiated by operational requirements than by the ships themselves; that is, a ship may be scheduled to fulfill a particular requirement, but for some reason has to cancel out. The requirement does not just go away; therefore, the fleet commander must find a replacement. The process described above would work in reverse in this case. The fleet commander would contact his group commanders, who in turn would suggest some ships as candidates, and then contact their squadron commanders. The squadron staffs, being most familiar with their ships' daily activities, would pick a candidate to meet the requirement and officially notify the captain or the operations officer of that ship.

If the proper relationship with the staff scheduler has been established, however, he will first informally call either the ship's operations officer or the captain and advise him that his ship is being considered for a commitment. Then, if there are late-developing problems which may prevent the ship from meeting the commitment, there is time to work them out or find another ship before a formal change in schedule is made.

To establish an effective relationship with the ship's scheduling authorities, the operations officer first must know and understand the captain's philosophy about such subjects as the proportion of sea time to in-port time, training priorities, maintaining a balanced schedule for the crew, and at what point he will balk at revising the ship's schedule in order to meet some unscheduled commitment. For example, the captain might have a policy which values at-sea operating time above all else. The number of at-sea operating days for all ships is governed by budgetary constraints which are balanced against the need to maintain readiness. The constraints are often expressed as "operating-days-per-quarter." The number of days at sea the ship actually gets may well be determined by how aggressively the captain wants to pursue at-sea time when it becomes available due to changes in the fleet employment schedule.

Once the operations officer is confident that he understands the captain's policy on the operating schedule, he will be much better prepared to deal with the scheduling authorities. The ops officer cannot make any commitments for the ship. If he knows, however, that the captain wants to get out to sea at every opportunity–if this is indeed the case–he can so inform the staff officers who do the scheduling. If the operations officer has established a close and cooperative relationship with the schedulers, no surprises should occur in the ship's schedule.

To summarize the ops officer's relationships, the new operations officer must develop his relationships with other officers both on and off the ship, since they have a direct influence over the ship's day-to-day activities. Some rules to remember:

1. Determine the captain's policy;
2. Do the informal liaison and leg work to see what evolutions are scheduled;
3. Report these evolutions to the executive officer and the captain and find out which ones they want to do;
4. Proceed with the formal request process;
5. Confirm that what has been set in motion remains workable and on track; and
6. Keep the other department heads informed.

Being an Operations Officer

Good operations officers have certain common attributes. First and foremost, they must know what major evolutions are planned for their ship in the future, and they also must know what the ship is going to be doing before that evolution. They are constantly on the lookout for information from a variety of sources and must see to it that the captain, executive officer, and the other department heads are kept informed.

Good operations officers get things done. They cannot afford to put things off. The ops officer should keep a list of his ten "hottest" projects and work on that list each day. If he procrastinates, the entire ship might be embarrassed by being unprepared to execute an evolution. He should make it a personal policy to complete any reports for which he is responsible one day early, unless they are specifically keyed to an "as-of" time.

Necessary Study

The best operations officers know a little bit about everything, and a lot about the doctrine and procedures of their own unit. To achieve this level of knowledge, the ops officer must make a conscientious study of all the naval warfare publications which apply to the mission of the unit. This reading cannot be done overnight or in a week's time; it is best to set aside some time each day for it.

The operations officer should also study the various applicable operations orders. The objective is not to memorize them, but rather to learn where all the procedures are written down so that when he needs some information, he knows where to look for it.

Flexibility

The operations officer must be personally and professionally flexible, because in his environment he must cope with many changes. He not only must be able to deal with change at his own level, but he must also be able to suggest alternative actions to the captain when things do not go as planned. If an incoming message asks a question about the ship's current fuel state and the ops officer gets the first call about the action message, he should call the chief engineer, get the fuel state, draft a reply to the action message, and take both the request and the answer to the captain. This cannot be done for every action message which comes in, but for the simple ones which are truly operational matters, this should be the procedure.

Delegation of Duties

There is more work for the ops officer to do in a day than there are hours in which to do it. He must learn to delegate those duties that are routine. For instance, before a week at sea, he should see to it that the CIC officer and the communications officer collaborate on the ship's communications plan as a matter of routine. The drafting of certain repetitive messages in Navy format can be assigned to one of the department's officers as a matter of routine. The operations officer should convert as many as possible of his routine functions into permanent tasks for the departmental officers and then train them to do those routine matters in a timely manner without any prompting from the department head.

Operations at Sea

When the ship is operating at sea, the ops officer should be either on the bridge or in CIC when something is going on that involves the entire ship. This objective has to be balanced against watch requirements and his own professional qualification program requirements, but it is a good rule. If he is on watch, the problem is solved. If he is off watch, and it is the middle of the normal working day, and something starts happening in CIC, he should check to see what is developing. If he is doing paper work in his stateroom when the ship is supposed to be in a routine transit, and there is a sudden burst of maneuvers, he should find out what is going on.

With experience, the operations officer will develop a second sense as to when his presence is required. He can train his departmental officers to call him at night if an emergency appears to be developing or if there is advance notice of a schedule change. If a major evolution is going to break loose in the middle of the night, it is better for the operations officer to have been called up to CIC by one of the watch officers a few minutes ahead of time than to be roused out of bed in the middle of a crisis.

When the ship is scheduled to conduct an exercise or even a real evolution that involves the combat information center, it is a good idea for the operations officer to see for himself that CIC is ready to do the job. This is primarily the responsibility of the CIC watch officer, or TAO if there is one posted, but the operations officer should also check. He should not rely upon a phone call, but rather go up to CIC and see for himself that the watch team is prepared for the evolution and that the watch officers are reasonably confident that they know what is supposed to happen. Nothing beats personal reconnaissance.

Planning Ahead

It is very important to develop the ability to plan ahead while getting the job at hand done. Although the ship might be in the middle of an exercise, the operations officer should be thinking ahead to what is scheduled next, as well as be thinking about his postexercise report.

The ops officer must always be aware of the requirements of the governing operations order, both for preexercise planning and for postexercise reporting. He must keep track of all the reporting requirements incidental to operations. The captain and the executive officer will both have ways to remind themselves of upcoming events, including operational requirements. It may aggravate the ops officer to receive a steady stream of notes from both of them asking if the ship will be ready for this evolution or that exercise, but their objective is not to harass him; it is, rather, to ensure that he does not overlook something in the press of current business.

Op-orders

The operations officer must become an expert in working with operations orders, commonly called op-orders. Op-orders are written according to a prescribed format and are written for every facet of a ship's operations in port and at sea. A ship which is in the refit phase between deployments is governed by the provisions of the home fleet's standing op-order. If the ship is under the operational control (op-con) of the type commander, the provisions of the type commander's standing op-order apply. En route to one of the deployed fleets, the ship is temporarily governed by a transit op-order, published by the senior officer in the ships deploying. Once change of operational control (chop) has been made to the deployed fleet commander, his op-order governs.

The ship can operate under several op-orders at the same time. She might be under the overall control of the Second Fleet commander while working up for a coming deployment. If assigned to work in the local operating areas conducting various fleet training exercises, she will operate in accordance with the local area commander's op-order, which lists procedures and schedules for use of the training areas. If involved in a major fleet exercise in those same operating areas, the ship will be governed by the op-orders of the fleet, the fleet exercise commander, and the area coordinator, depending upon what she is doing from day to day.

Although the operations officer cannot memorize op-orders, he should become very familiar with some of their details. And it is a good idea to index them at the same time, so that information and procedures can be found rapidly by any officer who needs them. Op-orders are therefore best perused with a set of index tabs in hand. If the orders are tabbed and indexed, however informally, they are much more useful to both the operations officer and the watch officers. The most rudimentary index is better than none. The index should be taken to the lowest level of detail that is functionally useful, alphabetized, and then inserted in the back of the operations order. An index will pay large dividends for operations and watch officers alike.

Prior to any operation, the ops officer will be expected to brief the wardroom and possibly key enlisted personnel on the overall plan of the operation and the highlights of the applicable op-order. Op-orders tend to be cumbersome documents—large, classified, and filled with minute details. They are unsuitable for briefing in their entirety; it is much better to break them down into sections which fit the ship's organization (communications, CIC procedures, engineering and logistics, etc.) and have the cognizant officers brief their sections on the op-order. This ensures that they have read and know their portions. The briefings should indicate which areas are most important to the principal watch officers. If there is a separate section in the op-order on reporting, this should be the subject of a separate brief, and at the briefs, it is a good

Briefing: A principal job for the operations officer.

idea to identify which officers are responsible for making the required reports.

One problem with operations orders is that they change, and sometimes the changes come fast and furiously by message. The operations officer must establish an effective system by which all copies of an op-order in use can be kept current, with changes entered legibly and a record of the changes kept at the beginning of the order. An op-order which is not up to date will often get the ship in trouble; it also does no good to keep only one master copy of the order current, because inevitably someone will pick up and use the out-of-date copy.

When taking over the job of operations officer, the ops officer should check the op-orders to ensure that they are current. If they are not, he should assign, through the CIC officer, a senior operations specialist whose primary administrative task is to keep the op-orders up to date. The operations specialist will understand better than anyone else the changes being made and will also appreciate the trouble which can arise from using an op-order which is out of date. The operations officer should spot-check the op-order collection from time to time and compare notes with other ships to make sure that his collection is current.

Message Writing

One very important facet of the operations officer's job is message writing. It is a fine art, which requires a great deal of practice and a great deal of care. Every message from the ship becomes part of the written legal record of the ship's activities. Every message transmitted is done so in the name of the commanding officer. It is crucial that great care be taken by those who draft, check, and release naval messages.

Two of the most important attributes of a good naval message are clarity and accuracy. Brevity is also important, but not at the expense of the first two qualities. If the message is a reply to another message, the reply should in fact answer the question. If the subject is being raised in a message by the ship, it should be written so that the addressee can quickly comprehend what is being requested or directed.

When writing a message, the drafter should ask himself, "What am I trying to achieve by sending this message?" When the message is finished, the drafter should ask that question again to be sure that what appears to be a good message satisfies the original objective. Messages should be factual and to the point. They should display no visible emotion. When preparing naval messages, do not criticize other commands directly. Unusual abbreviations should not be used, nor is humor normally appropriate. Message writers should be very sparing in the use of adjectives and adverbs. Finally, the drafter should read the message out loud to someone not involved in writing it to see if it makes complete sense to him.

After the operations officer (or any department head) has drafted a message, he will have to "chop" it, which means that he will take it to the executive officer for review. The exec may very well make changes to the draft in both format and content. If the drafter does not understand the reason for the changes, he should ask; this is a basic way to learn how to write better messages. The executive officer has had more experience with message writing than the department heads, and he can help them hone their skills. The executive officer also will know the captain's style and how the captain expresses himself. Often, by marking up the draft, the XO is not only making changes in style, he is also making the message more acceptable to the captain. The drafter should state the objective of the message to the executive officer so that he can judge if that objective has been achieved.

After the executive officer has "chopped" the message, the operations officer brings it to the captain for release. If the executive officer has marked the draft up considerably in his chop process, it should be rewritten so that the captain need not tread through the editorial work. Once again, the drafter should explain the objective of the message to the captain. There may well be more changes made, and, once again, the drafter should ask why in order to learn.

A new operations officer will find that there are subtle ways of getting his command's message through to the addressees without openly embarrassing another command, even if that command has made an error. If the captain's objective is to put another command on report, he will let the drafter know this. More often, however, the objective will be to rectify a bad situation, and if that is the case, telling tales about another command will not help the situation.

If the message is to be in a special format—and many of the operations officer's messages are—it is the drafter's responsibility to produce the correct format. The captain should not have to worry about this. The way to make sure that formats are correct is to check them; such things as paragraph numbering, classification, subject lines, etc., are all the drafter's responsibility. Some of the Navy's formats are designed for computer processing, and thus messages of this type require an extraordinary amount of checking. If the executive officer or the captain has to spend his time correcting errors, he will never get to the content of the message. The drafter should not fall into the trap of "let radio do it"; the radiomen should only be charged to type it, and nothing more.

Summary

The success of an operations officer is dependent upon his establishing and maintaining productive relationships with his shipmates, the executive officer, the captain, staff officers, shore organizations, and schedulers. The operations officer must know the captain's policies and objectives before he can represent the command effectively. He must keep in mind that he will often be the first to get word of an impending change and that he has a responsibility to inform all the key individuals affected by that change.

Secondly, the operations officer must concentrate on developing the skills and professional knowledge pertinent to his job. To do this he must:

- Undertake a conscientious reading program;
- Develop a fine sense of timeliness;
- React quickly to changes by proposing a new course of action;
- Maintain an interest in all major evolutions in the ship and personally supervise those of the operations department;
- Develop expertise in handling op-orders; and
- Be able to write effective messages.

The remainder of this book explores in detail many of the techniques mentioned in passing in the foregoing sections. While presented separately, these techniques should be applied in all aspects of the operations officer's job.

The operations officer will soon find that the activity which takes most of his time is planning, the subject of the next chapter.

2 Planning

How is planning at the shipboard level done? The basic elements are as follows:

1. Identify the objectives of the ship during a set period of time, e.g., a fiscal year. (This is done by the captain.)
2. Identify the resources needed, in terms of time, material, personnel, and assistance from outside the command, to accomplish each of the objectives. (This is done by each of the department heads for his area of responsibility.)
3. Lay out against the backdrop of the annual employment schedule the dates by which the objectives are to be achieved. (This is done in a CO/XO/department head joint session.)
4. Work back from each objective date or milestone and lay out the resources needed to achieve the objective at the desired point. (This is also done in a joint session.)
5. Provide some mechanism in the resulting plan which allows for making changes without having to scrap the whole plan.

The purpose of this effort is to create an annual master plan for the ship, a plan which will give the captain and the rest of the wardroom some measurable idea of the progress being made in keeping the ship at a high state of readiness. Before such a plan can be developed, the environment in which ships operate must be explained.

Cycles of Employment

Ships in the U.S. Navy operate in cycles whose time span varies with each class of ship. In general, a ship begins her life at the time of her construction and introduction into the active inventory of warships. There follows a phase wherein the ship fits out, begins basic shipboard training, advances to more complex levels of training, demonstrates proficiency through major fleet inspections, and is then certified as operationally ready for fleet operations. The ship is then deployed to one of the overseas fleets, or she enters a period of extended operations within the home fleet. There follows a cycle of being operationally ready, and then reentry into the "refit" phase, and so forth, until the ship enters her first regular overhaul. Following an overhaul, the whole process is begun anew. This process is called the employment cycle.

To find out where your ship is in this employment cycle, you need only look at the annual fleet employment schedule (described below). Your ship will either be in overhaul, in the refit phase, or in the operational phase. You will not find these precise terms in the employment schedule, but it will be obvious which phase your ship is in or about to be in.

The annual fleet employment schedule is the backdrop against which all operational planning within a ship takes place. It sets forth what the fleet commander has directed your ship to do for the fiscal year. The schedule is subject to changes. Those changes normally affect the minor employments, or perhaps make adjustments to the dates of the major employments, rather than introduce whole-scale major employment changes.

Annual Fleet Employment Schedules

The Atlantic and Pacific Fleets handle the fleet employment schedules differently. In the Atlantic Fleet, the first employment schedule published in a fiscal year contains both the annual schedule and the detailed schedule for the first quarter of the year. The remaining Atlantic Fleet schedules will be quarterly schedules. The Pacific Fleet publishes four quarterly schedules, but not a single annual schedule. Instead, there are pages in the quarterly schedule which describe major events throughout the year, such as group transits, major exercises, deployments, and so forth.

In both fleets, the quarterly schedules contain a great deal of information for the operations officer. Every day of the quarter is depicted, and the concept of minor employments is introduced. Minor employments are evolutions which the ship will do in conjunction with or in support of major employments. As an example, a major employment would be the period of time before an overseas deployment, which is known as POM (Preparation for Overseas Movement). Minor employments would consist of the many inspections, assist visits, and other preparatory evolutions which go to make up POM. Your ship cannot normally affect the scheduling of the POM period in the annual schedule, but it can make an input as to the day-to-day scheduling of the minor employments *if* a good case can be made for doing so.

Fleet Scheduling Conferences

Fleet employment schedules are finalized at the fleet scheduling conferences, held periodically throughout the year. These conferences are attended by representatives of the fleet commanders, the type commanders, and other organizations. Individual ships are not represented at such conferences; they are, instead, the resources which are used to meet the demands of operational commitments levied by higher headquarters.

Each quarterly scheduling conference precipitates a solicitation for inputs from the ships down at the squadron level. This normally takes the form of a message which calls for the ship's requirements for the next quarter. It should be understood that the ship can have very little real impact on the employment schedule because so much of it is determined by the type commander, who in turn is responding to the fleet commander. The squadron commander, however, often solicits the ships desires as to exercise requirements, maintenance availability, and training requirements. These inputs are consolidated and forwarded to group commanders, who in turn work with the type commander and fleet schedulers. You should not be surprised if your ship's "desired schedule" does not come out in the quarterly book with the same employments you asked for, because the type commander is usually facing more requirements than he has ships to fill them with. The process described above is only half of the picture, however. The other half has to do with schedule changes.

Changes in the Schedule

Once the annual and the first quarterly schedule have been published (and even before they are published!), the changes begin. Each evolution in the annual schedule is described as a commitment, with ships being committed by name to participate. When for any reason at all a ship cannot make a commitment, a schedule change is made in order to assign another operating unit to fill that commitment, particularly if it is a major employment such as a deployment to one of the overseas fleets. A change of this nature in turn precipitates a ripple effect through many other areas of the operating schedule, which brings us back to the matter of your relationship, as operations officer, with the officer who is your ship's scheduler.

Schedule changes are usually worked out informally among the staffs and the units involved before they are published formally by message as a schedule change. The fleet commander's operations office will contact the group commander's operations people and inform them of a need for a ship, usually of a particular type, to fill a commitment. The group commander's staff officers will in turn check with the squadron staff operations officer, usually with a proposal to modify the schedules of one or more ships. The squadron commander, being the most familiar with the day-to-day status of each of his ships, will make a tentative nomination, normally after talking with the captain of the ship being nominated. If you have established a proper relationship with your scheduler, the captain will be ready to address the matter with a prepared position, because he will have had some prior notice as to the possibility of the schedule change. This prior notice is achieved when the squadron operations officer gives you an informal call and tells you that a ship is needed to fill a commitment and that your ship is under consideration.

The Ship's Master Plan

When the annual fleet employment schedule arrives on board, you, the operations officer, should extract all of the information available in the schedule for your ship and chart it. The chart should show the year by months, with the major employments—such as fleet exercises, Preparation for Overseas Movement (POM) periods, deployments, or the beginning of an overhaul, etc.—depicted along a time line. The chart can be prepared on a large scale as a wall chart. You must be careful to extract from the annual schedule all of the evolutions scheduled for your ship. They are not all found on the page that lists your ship.

For purposes of illustration, let us suppose that your ship has finished an overhaul, certification trials, and refresher training, and is ready to enter the long part of the refit phase, which will end one year from now with a deployment. This situation will be used throughout this chapter to illustrate how the master plan is drawn up, and how the daily operational planning is done.

The employment schedule will show a mixture of in-port and at-sea time for your ship. Over the course of the year—which we will have correspond with a fiscal year for convenience—the in-port time will be spent in upkeep periods, maintenance, in-port fleet training center sessions, major inspections, and finally, a POM period. The at-sea periods will be a progression of individual-ship, multiship, and finally fleet-level underway exercises.

Priorities and Objectives

At the start of the employment year, the captain should set forth his priorities and objectives for the year. He will want the ship to be at a peak of readiness by the end of that POM period. Since it is the beginning of the fiscal year, he may also declare that the ship will do all of the training-readiness exercises competitively in order to qualify for a Battle Efficiency "E" award at the end of the year. He will probably direct that the ship strive for high grades in the major inspections—such as the Propulsion Examining Board, the Navy Technical Proficiency Inspection, and the annual Type Commander Inspections, such as 3M, Medical, or Retention. There may be some projects left over after the overhaul that he will want to get done before the deployment. There will be major training and qualification milestones for the officers to meet in order to have a full watch team for the extended operations. There will be a leave program, which will have to spread out over the year, and a schools program.

The captain will have had the experience to know what objectives can be attained in the course of a year, given the current status of the ship and crew. He will be as comprehensive as possible. This is very important, because adding new objectives after the plan is in effect will require a rearrangement of the available resources. The captain should also set priorities for these objectives, because inevitably they will outrun resources at least once during the year.

On a wall chart, you, as the operations officer, should then lay out the objectives along the time line of the annual employment schedule. The captain can help you with this part of the project, but the major milestones can be derived directly from the annual schedule. For example, suppose the ship is due to undergo the Propulsion Examining Board on a given date. The captain tells you that it will take as much as six months of material and training preparation to be ready for the exam. On the initial chart, you should put down the date of the exam, show a line that works back six months from that date, and then put down the date when the preparation should start.

"Ready" Dates

Similarly, with each of the major events on the schedule and on the captain's list, there should be a milestone showing a "ready" date and a line behind that milestone showing the best estimates of the other department heads, the executive officer, and the captain as to the time it will take to be ready by that date. If the objective is a continuing program, such as a continuing high degree of planned maintenance, the milestones involve quarterly squadron Planned Maintenance System (PMS) inspections interspersed with some PMS assist visits. A leave program, which attempts to grant everyone in the ship a set amount of leave in the year prior to deployment, is expressed on the yearly chart as a percentage of the ship's manpower not available. The milestones for being ready for a major fleet exercise include in-port team training, combat systems readiness reviews, presail conferences, qualification due-dates for such people as air controllers, the ordering of exercise weapons, etc. With the CO, XO, and the other department heads sitting around the table, there is a wealth of experience from which to draw when you lay out the resources for each major event and objective.

In this evolution the operations officer constructs the chart as the planning session progresses, and, of course, adds his inputs to the streams of activities. Such a session will take one to two days of uninterrupted planning in the wardroom and probably an entire bulkhead to display the chart. The plan which ensues, however, is very much worth the effort, because the top management of the ship gains a substantial appreciation for not only what lies ahead, but also for the problems of adjusting the priorities and resources in the ship throughout the year. A planning session which is conducted using a wall chart is also a good way to discuss conflicts and impossibilities in the annual schedule, or in the captain's objectives, or both. Neither the neatness or precision of the master plan chart is very important, nor is it possible to do an actual PERT (Program Evaluation and Review Technique) or other precise programming chart. The idea is to identify the major elements of the activities that will be required to reach each objective and to be ready for each major milestone in the annual employment schedule.

Outline of Master Plan

Having drawn up the master chart plan in a joint session, the operations officer should reduce the plan to outline form, again with the help of the department heads. The easy way to do this is to take each major event or objective and make a columnar list of the activities leading to the objective, with approximate dates for completion (as shown in chart 2-1). This effort gives all department heads broad guidelines against which they can check their own progress. The outlines can be circulated as far down the line as the department heads want, to give all hands an idea of what their divisions and work centers will be doing over the year ahead.

Allowing for Change and Uncertainty

When preparing any plan, it is important to allow for changes. This means that you must introduce margins for errors, unforeseen additions and deletions, and erroneous assumptions. You can do this three ways:

1. You can allow a margin of time. If an activity is thought now to require three months, you can add an arbitrary two additional weeks.
2. You can allow margins of resources. If each division is going to have to assign one four-man team to refurbish the fan rooms in the ship within the first two months of the

Program Event	Oct.	Nov.	Dec.	Jan.	Feb.
Admin Insp	CO Insp; READY				
IMAV	READY	Work Pkg In	SCREEN	RECLAMA; SHIP SHOP	READY
Team Training FTC	QUOTA	TEAM SET; TDY $	READY		
Leave Program		Watch bill set; READY	Xmas Period		
Medical Insp	INV	Assist visit		CLOSE GALLEY; Paint out MDX	XO INSP; READY
NGFS Quals	NGFS School	CIC Rehearsal	CIC Rehearsal	NGFS school; READY	
Etc.				FIRE DATES	
Deployment	(POM Milestones, from TYCOM Instruction)				
ROH	(Overhaul prep milestones from Fleet Instruction)				
REFTRA	(Preparation milestones from TRALANT/PAC Instruction)				

Figure 2-1. Master Plan (Milestones)

	Oct.	Nov.	Dec.	Jan.	Feb.	
In-port Employment At sea						
Inspections	RET Admin.	Supply PMS		NGFS	NTPI 3M MED	MTT
IMAV	AD 21				RSG	
FTC			ASW Attack Trainer		14A2	
Exer.		TYT SDIEGO Opareas		COMPTUEX 2-80		TYT
Leave	15%	10%	50%	10%	15%	10%
Etc.						

Figure 2-2. Master Plan (Schedule)

year, in preparation for a material inspection, you can add one additional four-man team, made up of one man from each of the departments, in case a division gets behind.

3. You can allow margins in the priorities. The captain may specify that five objectives have top priority, five more have second priority, and seven others have third priority. You can then have him identify one event in each of the three categories which he would consent, if necessary, to shift down one priority.

As a general rule, the greater the uncertainty of an objective, the more margins should be introduced. You cannot cover all of the eventualities, of course, but you and the other planners must make a conscious effort to identify the uncertain areas and make some provisions to deal with them. If you do not do this, the master plan will probably crumble within the first quarter. Remember, too, that someone sitting around that table will most likely have had experience with every objective and event on the chart.

A corollary rule when dealing with uncertainty is to try to identify those events or resources in each activity upon which the success of the whole activity might depend. Any subsequent changes involving these factors should be watched very carefully, because the whole plan is sensitive to those variables.

To keep the master chart plan realistic, there are some techniques which should be applied in the estimating process. The important ones are as follows:

1. Be realistic in estimating what people will be able to accomplish from week to week. Remember that daily PMS, corrective maintenance, and housekeeping will take up to 60-75 percent of the time of your work force.
2. Devote manpower and time to the captain's objectives according to his priorities.
3. Settle on an arbitrary uncertainty factor (fudge factor), and add that percentage of time to all of the activities.
4. Be comprehensive within the activities; that is, list every

item or event which anyone can think of that might be applicable toward achieving the objective.

5. Provide a reserve of people who will be available to take on crash projects when necessary.
6. Where uncertainty exists, allow for failures. (If, for example, a new piece of equipment is to be installed, followed by a sea trial, plan a back-up sea trial in case it doesn't work the first time.)
7. Do the whole thing in pencil, because you will change it.

Why does the operations officer do the charting in the joint session and produce the outline pages? Because he is the captain's principal planning assistant. By going through the mechanics of assembling the master plan, he will fix in his memory a knowledge of the events of the whole upcoming year.

It should be understood by all concerned that the master plan will probably not be executed as planned in that first session. Having it, however, gives the ship an enormous advantage when the squadron staff calls over and asks what the impact of a proposed schedule change will be. The CO, XO, and the department heads can unroll the wall chart and *see* what the impact will be and give a quantitative answer to the question. Further, if the schedule change comes to pass, it is far easier to rearrange the ship's activities when the overall affect of the change can be visually assessed.

Working with the Employment Schedule

The mechanics of how the fleet employment schedules are assembled were described earlier in this chapter. This section will discuss how the operations officer uses the employment schedules as a basis for operational planning.

The annual employment schedule is the master plan for the coming year. Once it has been drawn up, attention shifts to the four quarterly employment schedules, the first of which is published right after the annual schedule. This first quarterly schedule is a more precise statement of what the ship will

Second Quarter FY 1980 — Operations Opfiler

	Jan.	Feb.	Mar.
Ship A	UPKP SDIEGO; COMPTUEX 1-80; UPKP SDIEGO	UPKP SDIEGO (cont.); IMAV	STRL; POM SDIEGO
Ship B	UPKP SDIEGO; COMPTUEX 1-80; A	B; UPKP SDIEGO	C; POM SDIEGO
Ship C		ROH LBEACH	
Ship D		OPCON Seventh Flt	D; OPCON Third Flt

A: NCFS SCI B: PEB-OPPE MTT C: OPPE D: NTPI

Figure 2-3. Typical Operating Schedule

be doing day by day during the first quarter of the year. When the quarterly schedule comes in, the operations officer must make some quick checks.

The first check is to see what changes have been made from what was published in the annual schedule; if necessary, adjustments to the master plan must be made. The captain should be briefed upon receipt of the quarterly schedule, even if he is given nothing more than a quick overview.

Second, the operations officer should brief the next planning board for training on the contents and details of the quarterly schedule, and at that time hand out a memorandum to the XO and the department heads which outlines the operating and major-event schedule for the next three months, based on both the master plan and the quarterly schedule. It should be emphasized that the employment schedules are valid in inverse proportion to the amount of time remaining in the period covered. Some operations officers prefer to publish an outline plan for only one month if the quarterly schedule appears to be changing rapidly. These outline plans are used by the department heads for a variety of purposes, such as scheduling PMS, making requisitions of consumables, planning when to paint out the ship, and so forth.

A planning session should be held when the quarterly schedule differs significantly from the annual schedule. The master plan should be rolled out and scrutinized to see what the effects of the changes will be, and whether or not a request for a change in schedule can be or should be submitted. For instance, let us assume that the ship is to undergo a Propulsion Examining Board exam at the end of the first month of the current quarter. In preparation for this, there is a detailed sequence of activities laid out in the master plan, culminating in a ready date a few days before the examining board comes aboard.

The new quarterly schedule arrives, and it contains an entry which schedules the ship to be ASW school ship one week before the examining board arrives. The captain may feel very strongly that that would not be the time to have the ship operating out at sea, that it should be in port doing the intensive training and final maintenance to get the ship up to the peak of readiness expected for the examining board. He would order the operations officer to prepare a request for a schedule change.

Changing the Schedule

NWP-7 is the fleet reference that shows you how to submit a schedule change request. Before the message is written, however, there is some leg work to be done by the operations officer. Acting upon the captain's guidance, you should contact the staff operations officer and discuss the proposed change. You can make very good use of the master plan here, by showing him just how disruptive it would be to go out to sea one week before the propulsion exam. In some cases, the captain might actually present the problem to the unit commander, again using the master plan to show why the change is being proposed.

If the unit commander approves the proposal, your ship must then initiate the process of a schedule change in accordance with NWP-7. In some squadron organizations, the unit commander might begin the process, based upon the discussions described above. The squadron would submit the schedule change proposal up the operational chain of command to the ship's operational commander at the fleet or type-commander level. That level of command would either reject or approve the proposal by message, and signal its approval by publishing a schedule change. This change would then be entered in the schedules of every ship and staff in the fleet, and the problem would be taken care of.

It should be noted that every message from the fleet on a schedule change is published in serial form, and every published change must be entered in your ship's copies of both the annual and quarterly employment schedules. You are required to keep the entire document up to date, not just the

List items as they change	1980 Oct.	Nov.	Dec.	Jan.
Qtrly 3M insp	Failed; rescheduled for Nov. 30	ASSIST — XO INSP — CO INSP — READY		
Safety insp moved up two weeks				
Etc. ↓				

Figure 2-4. Master Plan (Changes)

sections which list your ship. Normally a ship will assign a senior petty officer to do this job of entering all schedule changes; he must do it scrupulously, and you should check on his progress periodically.

It should be apparent that the employment schedule is the basic document upon which the ops officer bases his inputs to the ship's operational planning. Similarly, the ship's master plan for the year is the document upon which the ops officer, as a department head, bases his administrative planning. The unique feature of the operations job is that it is the ops officer's function to keep a close eye on any changes in the employment schedule that have the capacity to alter his ship's master plan. There is no problem in doing this for the big, obvious changes, but there are changes that occur which might not be so apparent. For instance, a change in schedule can occur which cancels the participation of an aircraft carrier in a fleet exercise. If your master plan depended upon getting extensive carrier air services during that exercise, then you now have to make some other plans, even though this particular schedule change did not list your ship as being affected.

Operations Planning

Operations planning is done predominantly by the operations sections of staffs for underway operations. Since there are not always going to be staffs involved in every underway period for your ship, you as the operations officer will have to prepare and present operations plans for the captain's approval. There are concepts which apply to all operations planning.

Let us take the example of your having to plan for three days of underway training in the local operating areas with two other ships whose captains are junior to yours. Your captain has told you he wants an informal letter of instruction (LOI) published by message to the other two ships, showing in detail what all three ships will be doing for those three days. (See NWP-11 for format of an LOI.)

As always, you begin with objectives. You know what your ship wants to accomplish in the three days at sea, because it is in your master plan. You will have to sit down with operations officers of the other two ships to discuss their training needs. You may get some guidance from the unit commander's training and readiness officer on what the commodore wants all the ships to do. You will have made arrangements for training services (discussed in chapter four), as will the other ships. The three operations officers will draw up an integrated plan which allows each of the ships to get as much done as possible.

A primary consideration in this kind of planning is to allow enough time to do the evolutions, with some time built in to compensate for problems. For example, suppose that the three ships are scheduled to conduct gunnery exercises in both the morning and afternoon. Your plan should allow time to let the gun crews fix any equipment casualties which might have occurred during the morning shooting. If the morning period is set from 0800 to 1100, then plan for the afternoon period to run from 1400 instead of 1300. That extra hour might mean the difference between participating or not participating in the afternoon session.

A second consideration involves the time-distance factors. Your plan may call for a full day of exercises, which would get the most done in the time allotted. A review of the area coordinator's services schedule, however, may reveal that the gunnery exercises in the morning and the antisubmarine exercises in the afternoon are to be conducted one hundred miles apart! Thus, all operations planning should be done with a navigation chart and the ship's navigator or his representative present, in order to leave enough transit time between exercises.

Planning Board for Training

After the LOI is written, approved, and published, your ship must do its own internal planning. The forum for this is the

From: Engineer

To: Ops

1. I want to schedule following items of training for next week:

Time	Monday	Tuesday	Wednesday	Thursday	Friday
0800	6 men for FF school all day	M-DIV Safety lecture		R DIV P-250 TNG	M-B&R Supers 3M
1300			B DIV Valve maint		

2. Following major evolutions coming up:

Time	Monday	Tuesday	Wednesday	Thursday	Friday
0800			10-hand working party load eng. consumables		
1300	Load lube oil				In-port refuel

Figure 2-5. Planning Board for Training Inputs

planning board for training. This board is nominally made up of the XO, the department heads, the DCA (Damage Control Assistant), and one or more senior chief petty officers. In most ships it meets once a week, and while its name speaks to training, it is really the planning board for all of the next week's evolutions. This board is chaired by the executive officer, who is responsible for the overall training program in the ship. It is the most convenient forum for planning in the ship.

The objective of the planning board, after the LOI has been promulgated, is to assimilate the events of the LOI into a plan of the week. The executive officer coordinates the scheduling of the normal daily routine around the events in the LOI schedule, and each department head makes additions for training or other departmental evolutions. The ship's training plan is consulted, and items from it are inserted where possible in the next week's schedule.

There should be some contingency planning done, using the LOI schedule. If the ship is scheduled for gunnery drills at general quarters, and the exercise target aircraft does not show up, or the clouds overhead are thick enough to prevent firing, your plan should contain some contingency training events so that the time at sea is not wasted. As a general rule, these events should be ones which depend only upon the ship's own resources.

Tactical Operations Planning

In the operations planning cited above, you were presented with a situation in which you would have the time to sit down and do some careful planning in advance. The planning for tactical operations is done when the ship is already operating at sea, perhaps in a task group, and new orders come in to conduct an underway replenishment, change station in a large disposition, or otherwise do something that was not in the original plan.

Let us take an example: your ship is on station in a large disposition, and a signal comes in that directs you to take a new station forty miles away, and to refuel en route. The captain directs you to set up the plan.

The objectives are to get to the new station, after finding the oiler en route and refueling, and to determine approximately when your ship will complete the entire evolution. To do this, you need to know where the oiler is, what your fuel requirements are, about how long the replenishment will take, and on which course the ship will probably proceed while refueling. With this information, you and the navigator should be able to plan a track to get over to the new station.

Your ship can begin to respond to the signal before the whole plan has been made. You should recommend that the ship head towards the most likely position to intercept the replenishment ship; you should also tell radio to set up communications with the oiler in order to update the information on his position and intended movement and to pass him your fuel requirements. You should give the XO your best estimate of the time needed to arrive at the fueling rendezvous and the probable length of the evolution, so that he can rearrange the day's internal schedule of meal hours, etc., if necessary. The officer of the deck should contact the deck division and give them the word on the refueling, and the engineer should be alerted to prepare for the replenishment.

As a matter of training, the captain may have the tactical action officer do some or all of this planning. If you are not on watch at the time of the signal, however, you will certainly want to be involved, and it will probably be best if you simply take over the planning from the TAO while he resumes his watch over the local tactical situation. Having made up the plan, you should ask the executive officer to check it for mistakes and then brief the captain and the watch officer. When doing any sort of tactical operations planning, it is crucial that someone check your work, because in this type of situation even minor errors in arithmetic can be very costly.

The foregoing is a relatively simple situation. Other tactical situations can and will arise which have many more variables. When this happens, you should take one problem at a time while seeking more information on the other variables. Suppose, in the above example, you were told to join up with an aircraft carrier at some future time, but you were not told what the exact rendezvous position would be since the carrier did not know where the winds would take her. Add to this ambiguous situation a requirement to refuel whenever the fleet oiler gets within twenty miles of your ship. In this case, which is not unrealistic, you should take one problem at a time and concentrate on keeping track of the carrier throughout the day while staying within a range which permits a quick rendezvous. You should make general preparations to refuel, but until the oiler is actually nearing your position, that is as far as you should go with the refueling plan. In other words, in a tactical situation like this you must continually strive to refine the information, reduce the unknowns, and then act when you have confidence that you will be able to achieve the objectives.

Tactical planning is difficult but exciting. When this kind of planning works, it is one of the most satisfying aspects of the operations officer's job.

Resolution of Conflicts

An important aspect of planning in a ship is the resolution of conflicts. There are two basic ways to do this: you can apply priorities, or use a technique called sub-optimization.

Let us take another example. Suppose you as operations officer have scheduled five days of pierside training for the CIC, using one of the training vans from the local fleet training center. It has been arranged for weeks, and it will require that full watch teams be set up in CIC mornings and afternoons for each day of the week, as if the ship were at sea. When you sit down at the planning board for training, the supply officer announces that base supply has just told him that the sixty-day stores load-out, scheduled originally three weeks from now, must take place next week, during the CIC training, and that it will require a working party of all E-5s and below to get it on board. The stores are at the base depot. The van can come only next week or not at all. You have a conflict.

The executive officer could decide which evolution is more important and cancel the other. More likely, however, he will try to find some way to do both by making compromises. In this case, the load-out might be stretched to take three days instead of two, and the CIC training reduced to yield only two sessions per team instead of the three originally planned. This is sub-optimization; instead of one evolution being done exactly as planned, two evolutions are done, each somewhat less efficiently. It is fairly simple to manage a two-way conflict; three- and four-way conflicts are not uncommon when in port, and you will participate in a great deal of this kind of planning during your tour of duty. Sometimes the situations get so complex that the captain himself must be called in to resolve them. At such times it is a good idea to unroll the master plan so that you can gauge what the impact will be when resolving these conflicts.

Up-to-date Information a Necessity

Good planning is absolutely dependent upon having good information, and you must keep an eye on what is happening in the fleet to avoid being surprised. If the operations officer in another ship of your squadron mentions that his ship is scheduled to be the engineering school ship the following week but will not be able to make it, it might be a good idea to inform your captain. He may want you to make some casual inquiries at the squadron staff office as to what might be shaping up. You may find that your ship has become a substantial part of the staff's contingency plans.

You also have to keep an eye on what is going on in the fleet as well. If there is a major fleet exercise scheduled, and your ship is not to participate in it, but instead is scheduled to be in port for the same period, it would be a good idea for you to maintain a file on the planning traffic of the exercise. It often happens that one of the participants in the exercise must drop out and a substitute be found quickly. If your ship is nominated on short notice, it helps a great deal to be able to present a collection of the planning traffic of the exercise along with the schedule change. In other words, you should be aware of what is going on in the environment of fleet operations and be prepared for sudden changes.

Planning for Contingencies

A military contingency plan is one which is based on one central assumption, i.e., that some event will happen that requires action. If the event occurs, what will the ship's reaction be? Contingency plans range in scale from general war plans at the level of the Joint Chiefs of Staff down to an individual ship's operational emergency procedures (discussed in detail in chapter seven). Contingency planning in a ship is usually done at the direction of the captain. If he suspects that a certain event is likely to happen, he will then direct you to assume that it will in fact happen and to formulate a plan.

You may have a lot of information to go on or just a little. If it is only a little, you will have to make certain assumptions to support it. Make a list of all of these assumptions and have the captain assess their validity before proceeding.

Discuss the situation with the other department heads, and review the ship's procedures that are already written down—such as general bills—for possible courses of action. A contingency plan is usually only a sketch containing the major assumption (the "what if"), the supporting assumptions, and the recommended course of action. It should also contain a list of any resources that will be needed which the ship does not or probably won't have.

For example, the captain may tell you that he has a feeling the ship may be ordered on very short notice to enter a foreign port to evacuate American citizens. He directs you to make up a contingency plan. The major assumption is that you will have to do an evacuation on short notice. The supporting assumptions would deal with the geography of the port, the likelihood of opposition, the size of the party of evacuees, the availability of boats or piers, etc. Your ship has an evacuation bill in its SORM, and this should be used to do the actual evacuation. Some things that might be needed over and above what is in the ship could be extra medical supplies, bed linen, boats, etc. A general plan for the course of action can be set down in just a few pages and briefed to the ship's officers; the ship would then be better prepared to conduct an evacuation than if no contingency planning at all were done.

Whenever you do contingency planning, you must try to identify the sensitive variables. A sensitive variable is one in which a small change in the variable produces a big change in the plan. Using the above example, such a variable would be the ship's boats. If you had assumed that boats would be required and you knew your ship had only two small boats with which to do the evacuation, then your contingency plan would be very sensitive to the possibility of a casualty to one or both boats. You might not be able to do anything about this possibility, but the captain should be apprised that it exists. If a superior officer were later to ask him what assistance he would need to execute the contingency plan, the captain could then respond immediately and concentrate on the sensitive variables. If he has a plan for all contingencies, he will be miles ahead of the game.

Summary

Planning is probably the most important part of the operations officer's job. The fundamental concepts of planning remain the same regardless of the type of plan: you must state the objectives, identify the resources, integrate these factors, and address the matter of uncertainty.

The whole ship will benefit if the opening days of each fiscal year can be spent constructing a master plan for the year based on the annual employment schedule and the captain's priorities for his command. The master plan can then serve as a visual reference throughout the year and can aid substantially in dealing with the many changes that will come about during the year.

The best forum for doing major planning in the ship is the planning board for training, because it is made up of the managers in the ship, including the operations officer, who will inevitably have to execute the plans.

The next chapter deals with training. Since most of what a ship does in peacetime is training, the techniques of planning are closely related to the techniques of organizing a training program. The annual employment schedule is the basis for the ship's planning throughout the year. It is also the basis for constructing the ship's long-range training plan, because it provides the opportunities for the training. The coordination of the employment schedule, the ship's master plan for the year, and the long-range training plan is the job of the operations officer, acting in concert with the other department heads.

29
MARINE

3
Training

The purpose of training in the Navy is to ensure that the people who man the ships are able to do their jobs, both as individuals and as members of teams. Each ship will have its own unique set of training requirements, because the requirements are derived from the ship's assigned missions. The theory behind Navy training is that it requires a building-block approach. That is, first we train individuals, then teams made up of trained individuals, and then we have ships operated by trained teams. Because the ship's peacetime operations are so closely related to training requirements, the operations officer is very often the training officer as well. In this chapter, we will cover a general description of the kinds of training, the role of the training officer in constructing and managing a shipwide training program, for both officers and enlisted men, and how to integrate the training with the ship's other activities.

The Importance of Training

In peacetime the U.S. Navy operates under the general premise that it must achieve and maintain readiness for war. Overall readiness has two aspects: material readiness and training readiness. Because training must be a continuing process, it sometimes tends to fade into the background of day-to-day events aboard ship, particularly when some of the major material inspections are scheduled. It is easier to judge the readiness of a machine than the training readiness of an individual or a watch team, and thus, traditionally, the concentration has been on the material aspect of readiness.

The balance, however, is changing. Major inspection teams are now looking just as hard at the state of training as they are at the state of equipment readiness, preservation, and cleanliness. The Propulsion Examining Board (PEB), for example, inspects first for material readiness, and then conducts an examination of individual and watch-section performance. Another program has been introduced recently into the fleet, whereby the progress in ship-wide training of ships undergoing regular overhaul is assessed in order to plan for the scope and types of training to be conducted during the following refit phase.

More important than inspections and examinations, however, should be the realization that we are training ships and crews to fight. In the shock of battle, individuals tend to react and function only to the extent to which they have been trained. Without a solid foundation of training, individuals are more likely to be overcome by confusion, fear, and paralyzing uncertainty.

For a training program to work in a ship, all of the officers and senior petty officers, from the captain on down, must make a commitment to accomplish genuine training on a continuing basis. This means that when training is scheduled, it must be done. Therefore, the scheduling of training must be both realistic and systematic. There has to be a long-range training plan and a mechanism for translating the long-range plan into daily training evolutions. There also has to be a mechanism which allows the command to assess its progress in training and to make up any deficiencies.

The Progression of Shipboard Training

When a seaman recruit comes on board ship for the first time, his training progression begins. After he has been through the indoctrination division, he is assigned to his permanent division, and that division begins both his formal and informal training. He is trained both formally in organized training sessions, and informally on his own, by observation and word of mouth, with the proportion of each dependent upon the quality of the ship's training program. He is trained in the duties of his rate, as well as in his military duties, housekeeping and cleaning duties, watchstanding duties, painting and preservation, working parties, and general bills.

When the ship goes out to sea, the new man will receive more intensive watch-station training, which concentrates on the duties of his rating more than on the business of living in a ship. He will learn the underway routine and how to stand underway watches. When the ship exercises at general quarters, he will be exposed to combat systems training. When the

Training: A gun crew in USS *Coronado* (LPD-11) exercises the guns.

ship exercises the general bills, he will receive seamanship and safety training. He will work for a variety of supervisors and watch officers, from whom he will learn both good and bad habits. He will be trained either in the right way of doing things or the wrong way, depending upon the quality of the training he receives.

After the individual has been on board for a while, he will become an accepted member of the watch teams, no longer being the "new guy." As he gains experience, he will become a more important member of the various watch teams and in his work center. He may branch out via cross-training, learning another man's watch station so that the whole team gains some depth and redundancy, and also bettering his chances on the advancement exams. He will learn from his contemporaries and the old salts senior to him, and he will learn the tricks of the trade and the shortcuts of his rating.

He will also begin to participate in the personnel qualification system (PQS). He will progress through the theory, systems, and watch-station sections of various PQS standards, and perhaps he will have to go before an oral board for an examination. He will do PQS in his rate, for his watch station, and for the ship-wide requirements of damage control and material maintenance. As he grows in professional confidence, his training will be expanded to attendance at short courses at the local fleet training center. He will also participate in team training sessions when the ship sends over an entire team for formalized group training.

No longer the new man aboard ship after a year or so, he may become his division's representative at the human relations council, or become a member of the command training team for human relations. He may get the chance to go to the leadership and management school as he advances in paygrade to become a petty officer. He may become a retention counselor, a member of the welfare and recreation committee, and join in the ship's athletic events. All the while, he will be exposed to training in human relations, leadership, morale, petty-officer management, and perhaps even to training others himself. As he advances in rate and assumes a larger role in the enlisted structure of the ship, his influence on other people will grow.

The character and direction of his influence will be a direct function of whether or not the progression described above was the result of a consciously planned training program in the ship, one that was constructed and supported by the captain, the executive officer, the wardroom, and the senior petty officers of the ship.

Organizing the Training Program

In order for the ship to have a functioning training program, it must put together a training plan. The training plan must identify the requirements, schedule them, and then provide a way to handle changes in the schedule.

It is not too difficult to state the requirements and to handle the accounting of what does or does not get done. The problem area in the training program lies in the scheduling.

Many ships have what is called a long-range training plan, but it is often little more than a piece of paper, because its schedule is quickly overwhelmed by the cascade of changes in the ship's employment schedule, which defeat the accomplishment of planned training. Since surface warships are always going to face the problem of employment-schedule changes, the long-range training plan must have a built-in mechanism which allows the training to be done regardless of changes in the employment schedule.

One solution is to divide all of the ship's training requirements into three categories. This is not the only way that it can be done, but these categories do have the advantage of already having their own inherent schedule, and this feature provides a way out of the scheduling problem. The categories are as follows:

- operational training
- advancement training
- organizational training

Operational training is that which is done while preparing for and actually doing the type commander's required training and readiness exercises. *Advancement* training is that which fulfills and supports the individual advancement requirements for each rate and rating, in accordance with the Personnel Advancement Requirements (PAR) system. *Organizational* training is that which is done to enhance the ability of individuals and groups to perform well within the ship.

But dividing the training requirements into three categories is not the solution to scheduling problems if the ship sets up only one schedule for all three types of training. The solution is to write three schedules, one for each category.

Operational training is done on the basis of the (fiscal) competitive year. Advancement training is done on the basis of the advancement cycles established by the Naval Military Personnel Command. Organizational training is done on the basis of the Human Resources Management Support System cycle. Once the above categorization has been adopted, it is possible to construct a long-range training plan that is not so vulnerable to changes in the employment schedule.

Operational Training Plan

The elements of the training plan are similar to the ship's master plan discussed in the last chapter. There has to be a list of the training requirements (objectives), a schedule showing when the various training evolutions will be done in order to complete the requirements, and a means devised to keep track of what does and does not get accomplished, so that missed evolutions can be made up. In other words, we need a requirements list, a training schedule, and a make-up list. These three major parts to the ship's long-range training plan would appear as outlined in the following generalized examples.

Requirements List

All surface ships are required to perform a variety of missions, which can be broken down into primary and secondary missions. Each ship will have some unique missions as well as other missions which are common to all surface ships.

The type commander (Commander Naval Surface Forces Atlantic or Pacific) publishes a computerized printout for each surface ship assigned to his command. The printout lists all the missions for which that ship is responsible. It also has, in an accounting statement format, all of the training and readiness exercises which that ship is required to do in the course of a fiscal year, arrayed by mission, with an exercise frequency listed alongside. Figure 3-1 is a notional example of a printout.

COMNAVSURFLANT/PAC REPORT No.: ____________

SHIP/UNIT ____________

Overall Training Readiness Rating ________ As of ___(date)___

Exercise/Inspection Summary
Mission Area: *Mobility*

Required exercises:		frequency	rating	next due	remarks
Z-110-E	Economy trial	12 mos	C-2	6/8X	
Z-111-E	Full power trial	18 mos	C-1	9/8X	94.1 score
Z -40-E	Cas. Con drills	6 mos	C-2	7/8X	watch section
Z- 44-E	D/C drills U/W	6 mos	C-1	8/8X	

(and so on, listing every exercise in the mobility area which the ship is required by the type commander to do. The mobility area would be followed by the remaining mission/warfare areas in which the ship is assigned a mission. The actual report format and content is somewhat different from the above, and the report may also differ by ship type, or class within a type. When filled in, the report is classified because it shows the aggregate training readiness of a fleet unit.)

Figure 3-1. Operational Training and Readiness Report

For example, in the mission of *mobility*, the following exercises might be listed:

Full power trial–annually
Economy trial–twice per year
Engineering casualty control exercises
for all watch sections–twice per year

Every exercise required of your ship is listed by name, frequency, and fleet exercise publication number, with dates indicating when it was last done and when it must be done again in order to be current and "ready" in that exercise and mission.

This monthly printout is, in effect, the requirements list for your ship's operational training. It even contains a schedule of sorts, in that the regular recurrence of all the exercises is listed by date.

Training Schedule

In order to write the training schedule, however, the "due dates" of each of the exercises must be compared to the ship's annual employment schedule. This is best done in a chart format, somewhat like the ship's annual master plan, with the annual employment schedule depicted across the chart by weeks. Since the training and readiness credit balances do not just end at the end of each year, the dates at which every exercise must be completed to maintain current credit in the ship's training and readiness account should be marked in pencil along the time line. It will become clear very quickly if the schedule is possible as written.

Figure 3-2 shows a sample operational training schedule for the ship. Each of the ship's assigned warfare/mission areas are listed down the left side, and an employment schedule is drawn across the bottom. In the rows to the right are listed each of the required exercises for each mission area, taken from the type commander's printout. They appear on this schedule on the dates by which they must be done again to maintain C-1 credit. These are the same dates which will show

Warfare Areas	January	February	March	April	May	June	July	
Surface Warfare	Z-2-GM Z-10-AT Z-9-P	Z-40-E Z-6-S Z-7-S	Z-9-EW Z-44-GM Z-13-Y	Z-6-AW	Z-10-BA Z-14-BA	Z-24-T Z-23-G Z-17-AT	Z-6-AX Z-33-GM Z-40-E	
Anti-Air Warfare	Z-2-CI Z-1-GM	Z-14-AA Z-56-EW		Z-4E-EW Z-33-EW	Z-4-AA Z-40-GMA	Z-6-AA Z-9-AA Z-17-AA	Z-33-GM	
Operational Inspections			MTT 7W COURSE	OPPE	UNREP INSP AAW CIC CERT	NTPI	ORI	
Other Warfare Areas								
Employment	in port	at sea	in port	at sea	in port		at sea	in port
Schedule	home port	TYT	home port	COMPTUEX 1-8X	home port-UPK		transit-TYT	
Week	I II III IV	I II III IV	I II III IV	I II III IV	I II III IV	I II III IV	I II III IV	
Month	January	February	March	April	May	June	July	

Exercises are listed on the dates by which they must be done to either maintain current readiness ratings, or get back to the next higher rating.

Figure 3-2. Operational Training Schedule

up on the type commander's printout. Preprint the forms, and then pencil in the exercises. It will be clear at a glance that an ASW exercise cannot be done if it falls due on an in-port day or week; it will then have to be adjusted back to an at-sea period, or a schedule change will have to be requested to provide more at-sea time. You can have as many categories (mission areas) down the left as you want, to include major evolutions such as the Preparations for Overseas Movement (POM) events, as long as they relate to operational training.

If, for instance, in the training and readiness printout there is a requirement to conduct an air-gunnery firing exercise by May 15 in order to maintain readiness in that mission area element, but in the annual employment schedule there are no at-sea operations scheduled for the month of May, you will have to schedule the exercise back to an at-sea period. Since the annual employment schedule is based in part upon the training and readiness requirements of your ship, there should be enough opportunities in that operating schedule to perform all of the exercises and other required evolutions. It is up to the ship to ensure, by constructing a long-range training plan, that there are in fact enough opportunities. If there are not, the training schedule provides a good basis for justifying a schedule change at any time during the year.

There is no need to create a requirements list for operational training, since the type commander's printout has already done it for you, but you will need to draw up a schedule. (Since the printout also contains major operational readiness inspections, you will be using most of the operational training requirements list when constructing the ship's master plan, described in the chapter on planning.)

Make-up List

The make-up list begins each year as a blank piece of paper, and as the year progresses, it fills up with those exercises and inspections which have become past due. For example, in figure 3-3, the operations officer would lift from the monthly

Mission/Warfare Areas/Exercises	Frequency For C-1	Present Rating	Fell to present rating on (date)		Will drop again on	Tentative make-up
Mobility						
Z-111-E full power trial	18 mos	C-2	4/15/8X		9/15/8X	8/21/8X
Z-60-D in-port D/C drills	3 mos	C-2	4/22/8X		7/22/8X	6/15/8X
Anti-air warfare						
Z-9-AA gun exercise	6 mos	C-3	3/18/8X		9/18/8X	9/2/8X
Z-31G missile exercise	12 mos	C-2	3/21/8X		3/21/8Y	6/22/8X
Antisub warfare						

Figure 3-3. Operational Training—Make-up List

report any exercise whose rating showed as C-2 or lower, and write it in under the appropriate warfare-area section of the make-up list. This gives the captain and each of the department heads a quick reference that shows all the operational training evolutions which have to be done again to regain a C-1 (maximum readiness) rating. Each successive monthly printout is a good cross-check on your own make-up list, since it too will indicate past-due evolutions. The make-up list is not used for scheduling; it is simply a compilation of things which did not get done.

In summary, the operational training plan should consist of three sections: the *requirements list* (for which you can substitute the type commander's printout, supplemented by any additional training areas which the captain may wish to add); the *training schedule,* which is a graphic presentation of the entire fiscal year, with the employment schedule depicted, by weeks, along the bottom and the exercises/inspections listed across the top with the periodicity in the printout; and a *make-up list,* which shows, as the year progresses, the evolutions which have to be made up before the competitive year ends.

Advancement Training Plan

Writing the plan for advancement training is done in the same manner as for operational training, except that in this case you use the semiannual Navy-wide exam cycle as the basis for the plan. The key dates for each exam cycle are published twice a year in the Naval Military Personnel Command Notice 1418. If you are writing the training plan for a new fiscal year, one exam cycle would just be ending; therefore, the planning would begin with the cycle which ends in exams administered in the next month of March. It should be understood that the executive officer is in charge of advancement training, but the training officer is concerned with the scheduling of advancement training. As with the other kinds of training, if it is not scheduled, it will not get done.

Requirements List

The Personnel Advancement Requirements System (PARS) sets forth the requirements that a man must meet to be eligible to take the exam for the next rate or paygrade within his rating. These include demonstrating certain levels of practical knowledge, passing the appropriate military leadership exam, and passing the prerequisite correspondence course for his rating. In addition to completing the PARS, the man must be eligible under the criteria of time in service and time in his present rate. The training plan should include these requirements and it also should include the training needed by each individual to meet them. See figure 3-4. (The construction of an advancement training plan presupposes that the ship does, in fact, conduct an organized program to help its people advance, instead of making them do it entirely on their own.)

The requirements list should include such things as:

- the elements of the PARS common to all rates/ratings (courses, military leadership exams, time in rate, time in service certifications, and the recommendation for advancement certification).
- training sessions which support the military leadership exams, i.e., general military training programs.
- all-hands training requirements (damage control, and 3M).
- cross-rate training for some of the higher paygrades, such as personnel admin for CPO candidates.
- the program of augmenting correspondence courses for the technical ratings, such as basic electronics, basic electricity, etc.
- special programs, such as reading comprehension courses.

Advancement Training Schedule

The advancement training schedule is based upon the exam cycles for each of the paygrade groups—SN/FN, E-4, E-5, E-6, and CPO exams—with their attendant cut-off dates, terminal eligibility dates, time in service, time in rate, command recommendation certification dates, plus a mark in the schedule for

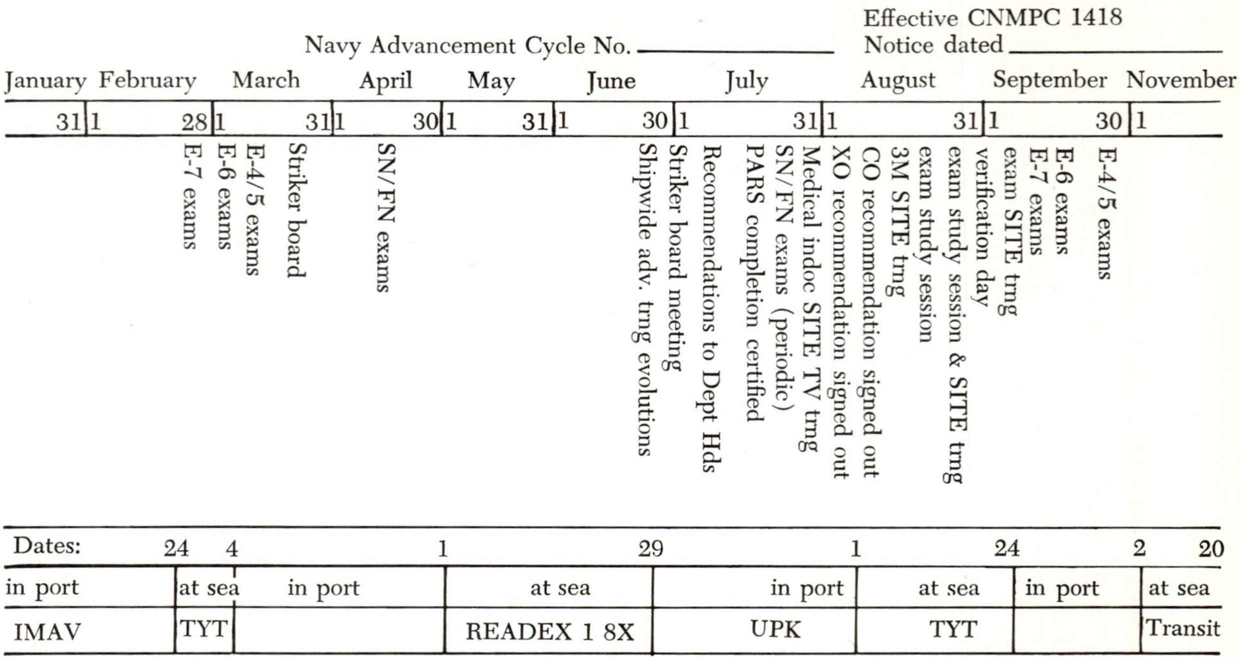

Effective CNMPC 1418

Navy Advancement Cycle No. ________ Notice dated ________

January	February	March	April	May	June	July	August	September	November
31	1 28	1 31	1 30	1 31	1 30	1 31	1 31	1 30	1

E-7 exams
E-6 exams
E-4/5 exams
Striker board
SN/FN exams
Shipwide adv. trng evolutions
Striker board meeting
Recommendations to Dept Hds
PARS completion certified
SN/FN exams (periodic)
Medical indoc SITE TV trng
XO recommendation signed out
CO recommendation signed out
3M SITE trng
exam study session
exam study session & SITE trng
verification day
exam SITE trng
E-7 exams
E-6 exams
E-4/5 exams

Dates:	24	4	1	29	1	24	2	20
in port	at sea	in port	at sea	in port	at sea	in port	at sea	
IMAV	TYT		READEX 1 8X	UPK	TYT		Transit	

Figure 3-4. Advancement Training Schedule

ordering the exams. Interspersed at regular intervals are the supporting exams for military leadership at all levels, normally at monthly intervals. Using a chart as before, you would lay out each of the exam groupings and construct the series of events in which each man must participate to qualify for advancement. Written along the bottom of the charts is the annual employment schedule, so that you can see where and when the various events will be possible. It becomes quickly apparent that there has to be a continuing program throughout the year in order to create the maximum opportunities for all hands to take advantage of the advancement program of the Navy. Figure 3-4 shows some of the more important milestones.

It helps a great deal to have as many of the events in the advancement program as possible occur at regular intervals to reduce the scheduling burden. For instance, SN/FN exams and the military leadership exams should be offered at least as frequently as regulations allow. Some ships use the technique of scheduling a two- or three-hour period each week, in which all divisions stop work and do nothing but advancement training.

It is very easy to adapt the general military training program to an "automatic" operation, using the following scheme. Make up a list of all the GMT topics in which the ship will require training. Assign a chief petty officer to become an expert in one topic and to be the "visiting professor" on that topic. Twice a week, schedule GMT at quarters. During these sessions, each division is visited by one of the experts and given a lecture on his topic. As the weeks progress, each division receives a class from every expert, and the GMT program gets full coverage by senior petty officers who really know their subject. The ship has full control over how fast all of the divisions are given the entire GMT package by the frequency at which GMT is scheduled. In terms of time, it only costs an extra fifteen minutes at divisional quarters.

Make-up List

The make-up list requires no special format and should be keyed to monthly events, because, of course, the Navy-wide exams cannot be made up except under very stringent circumstances, such as absence due to emergency leave or hospitalization. If, however, the periodic SN/FN exams were scheduled for the third Monday in the month, and a major underway replenishment took place on that day instead, these exams would become candidates for the make-up list at once.

Organizational Training

Requirements List

The requirements list for organizational training is an area in which the command can have a great deal of flexibility when constructing a program to suit the needs of the ship. It should include such things as:

1. leadership and management training, both on and off ship.
2. divisional training conducted by the ship's command training team in human relations, using the Navy-approved workshops on cultural expression, military rights and responsibilities, racism and counter-racism, and for some ships, women in the Navy.
3. regularly scheduled human relations council sessions.
4. ship-wide safety stand-downs.
5. legal-aid days once a quarter, wherein a JAG officer comes on board and makes himself available to the crew.
6. the Program for Afloat College Education (PACE), which is a program that provides college education level classes for the crews of deployed ships.
7. the achievement exam program (GED, CLEP, etc.).
8. retention education seminars.
9. any other "people-oriented" program which the ship desires to institute.

Training Schedule

Scheduling of these requirements is done in the same way as the other two elements of the long-range training program. A chart is constructed for the entire year, showing the annual employment schedule and a regular progression of the various programs listed above at a frequency chosen by the command. The Human Resources Availabilities (HRAV) can also be included when conflicting requirements are not a problem.

Make-up List

The make-up list for this section of the training plan works the same way as in the other two, although the command has more latitude in deciding what events it will try to make up. All of the scheduling and rescheduling can be done using the same notation as the 3M schedules: items which are missed are circled at the end of each week by the training officer and brought up at the planning board for training for the next week to see if rescheduling is possible.

Role of the Operations Officer in Training

The executive officer is responsible to the captain for overseeing the training program. Why then is the operations officer so often the training officer? The principal reason is that he is the command's principal planning officer, who is, next to the captain and possibly the XO, the most familiar with the entire year's schedule, having gone through the exercise of drawing up the ship's master plan. Secondly, he is conversant with the annual employment schedule as well as the schedule of the current quarter. Third, he has the task of operating the ship's readiness reporting system, in which all training accomplishments required for the year must be reported. For these three main reasons, in most ships the operations officer is made the training officer. Being designated as such does not mean that the operations officer actually directs training in the ship. The XO, through the planning board for training and through the line organization, does that. The operations officer manages the scheduling-accounting function—that is, the assembly and presentation of the requirements, and the accounting of what was achieved each week through the use of the make-up lists. The prime movers behind the three main divisions of training are the type commander for operational training, the Chief of Naval Personnel for advancement training, and the captain for the organizational training done in his ship. The operations officer can put together the operational training requirements list. He and the educational services officer and personnel officer can work up the advancement program list, and the captain, XO, and probably all of the department heads will join in the preparation of the organizational training list.

Scheduling the Training

Under the system outlined above, there is no need for semiannual, quarterly, or monthly training plans. Once the annual, long-range training program is constructed and approved by the captain, and explained to and understood by the planning board for training, the scheduling functions come down to the plan of the week. This is because the ship's schedule can be predicted with some degree of confidence up to a week in advance in almost all employment situations.

The forum for scheduling the training is, of course, the planning board for training, described earlier. The operations officer prepares for this important weekly session by accounting for what has gone on during the current week, and filling in missed evolutions on the make-up lists for each category of training. He should then prepare seven sheets of paper, one for each day of the week, and fill them in with the major employments of the command known for that coming week which are not really subject to change by the ship. He should copy them and distribute them to the XO and the department heads the day before the planning board. They in turn get to see what big events are coming up the next week, and can fill in the blank spaces with the things they would like to do. Each department head then arrives at the planning board with his version of next week's plan of the week.

The XO then directs the training officer to review the make-up lists to see what has been missed in the training program. After doing this, the ops officer should write in on a master copy of the plan of the week those items which are approved for rescheduling. Once this is done, items from the annual plan (arranged by weeks of the year) are included in the plan. Then the department heads can mention the items that will be going on in their departments the following week (perhaps from the sheets of the ship's master plan), and conflicts can be resolved by the XO. A review should then be made to see if any items in the following week's plan absolutely must be done that week, and a make-up time allotted in the plan in case a conflict crops up. At the end of this session, the operations officer hands over his marked-up copy of the plan of the week to the XO, who can then publish it in the next Monday's plan of the day, or when it suits him.

The plan of the week is used during the following week to actually schedule training (and other functions) into the ship's plan of the day. Division officers can perform the feedback in the program by reporting to their department heads what did or did not get done. The operations officer then only has to canvass the department heads once during the week to get inputs for his make-up lists. Each division is thereby spared the necessity of maintaining complex training records; under this system, they would record only what training was accomplished. (The make-up lists would be the ship's records of what evolutions did not get done.) Most surface ships' schedules are full to begin with, and not all training evolutions that are missed can be rescheduled. There is no point in keeping records of those things the command, at the planning board for training, decides it just will not do that year.

Training Opportunities

In most surface warships, imaginary snapshots of the ship at any moment during the working day would show many different things going on at the same time. Divisional housekeeping, maintenance, inspections, working parties, visitors, meetings, etc., are the daily fare in port. At sea, the daily schedule usually adheres to an operations plan devised for a group of ships. For the training program to work in the ship, time must be set aside to do the training. The events that appear in the plan of the week are automatically scheduled with time set aside for their accomplishment. Training for the divisions, work centers, or watch stations is more difficult to schedule. The way to do this is to allocate blocks of time in the plan of

Training: Midshipmen observe flight operations on USS *Forrestal* (CV-59).

the week in which the divisions have discretion over what training takes place. These need not be very long, nor scheduled very often. Each division should, however, get at least one, perhaps two, scheduled sessions each week wherein they can conduct whatever training the division officer feels is needed. This training will most likely be conducted in support of one of the scheduled training evolutions in the plan of the week. If, for instance, the condition-three watch team ONE is slated for a half day at the 14A2 ASW trainer on Friday, the CIC officer would probably use the divisional training hour on Thursday to review ASW procedures with his operations specialists. As a general rule, training will not take place, even when "scheduled," if there is not a block of time made available in the plan of the week for that training.

Officer Training

The thrust of the foregoing sections had been on training the enlisted men. Provisions must also be made for training the officers. Developments in the surface warfare officer qualification process in recent years make it possible to organize officer training into activities which lead to specific qualifications:

- surface warfare officer
- tactical action officer
- surface warfare command qualification

Surface warfare officer qualification is nominally a two-year, PQS-based program of progressive qualifications in an officer's first ship. All officers with an 1160 designator are given an initial three-year tour in order to allow the candidates two full years of qualification opportunity despite schedules which might include a one-year regular overhaul. Nevertheless, junior officers still need a training program that is administered by the command in order to make the qualification schedule.

Tactical action officer qualification is aimed at surface warfare department heads and second tour, 1110-qualified junior officers. It is a PQS-based program, and there are as yet no time limits set on achieving the qualification. Not coincidentally, the PQS program is an excellent preparation for the surface command qualification examinations.

Command qualification is not PQS-based, but rather requires completion of subqualifications which are PQS-based, such as engineering officer of the watch, officer of the deck, etc. The candidate must perform specific underway maneuvers, face an oral board, and then take a written examination which is prepared by the Surface Warfare Officer Schools Command in Newport, Rhode Island.

Surface Warfare Officer Qualification

The Surface Warfare Officer (SWO) qualification program requires the most organization of the three programs. It is a PQS-based program, with most of the theory section and some of the systems section being accomplished at the SWO basic course in Newport. The remainder of the qualification must be done aboard ship. In most surface ships, the senior watch officer is responsible for SWO training.

There are five qualification areas in the SWO PQS:

1. division officer
2. engineering
3. officer of the deck in port
4. officer of the deck/CIC watch officer under way
5. surface warfare

The training program in the ship must allow the SWO candidate the opportunity to complete all five sections within the two-year time frame, with exceptions made for nonoperational time.

Since junior officers will come to the ship at irregular intervals, the program must be tailored to each individual officer's needs, while providing an equal training opportunity to all of them. One way to monitor their progress is to prepare a notebook, which has sections for each candidate. In each section are five graphs, one for each qualification area. The vertical axis is labeled in PQS points, from zero at the origin

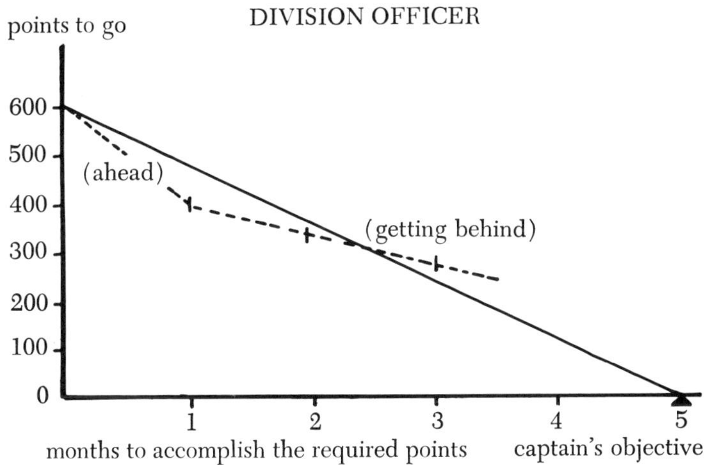

to the total number of points required for each area. The horizontal axis is measured in months.

The commanding officer should set forth his standards for the rate of progress to be made in each of the five sections. For instance, he might require that qualification for officer of the deck in port be accomplished within two months on board, and for division officer within six months, etc. Once these standards have been promulgated in the wardroom, each graph can be started by drawing in a progress line. The senior watch officer can then take a monthly look at each candidate's section and fill in his graph of PQS progress. He will readily be able to see when a candidate is falling behind or is ahead of the required rate of progress. This process takes care of the accounting; it also provides one objective factor with which to appraise the junior officer when filling out his fitness report on his progress towards SWO qualification.

Officer Underway Watch Bill

The officer underway watch bill is the means by which training opportunities are provided for the SWO candidates. The senior watch officer, using the graphs just mentioned, attempts to assign the junior officers to watch stations under way in order to keep the progress of PQS accomplishment even. The objective is to have the officer complete all of the PQS in the two years allotted.

In each ship, the requirements of the captain for levels of experience and qualification in the various watch stations have to be balanced with the requirements to give the SWO candidates a training opportunity. Thus, the watch bill becomes a matter for discussion among the senior watch officer, the executive officer, and the captain. The senior watch officer does his part by keeping the PQS accounts for each SWO candidate up to date.

In addition to the watch bill, there should be one or more officer-training sessions built into each week as a matter of routine: every Tuesday and Thursday at a specified time, or just every Tuesday and Thursday—with the times set in consonance with the plan of the week. The topics to be covered can be drawn from the major sections of the SWO PQS books, with presentations being given by department heads or the XO in their areas of management. The officer still has to do the PQS work, but he can count on a predictable schedule of lectures where he can ask questions and find out where the answers are.

Standards for Qualification

The ship should set up some system which provides a uniform and objective standard against which all SWO candidates can be measured for qualification. There are many methods. One good one is to have a series of written exams, one for each of the five sections. They can be closed-book exams with a mixture of objective and subjective questions. When an officer completes a section, he is given a written exam, which is graded by the senior watch officer or another department head. Areas of weakness are pointed out, and the officer is given two weeks to do some additional study. The SWO qualification board then holds an oral board after the board members have seen the candidate's exam. If the oral board thinks the officer knows the section, they recommend him for qualification in that section. He does each section this way, and when all are completed, he can be recommended for full SWO qualification or he can be given a general all-section oral board and then be recommended. Such a system allows the candidate to know in advance what is expected, and to know that everyone else has had to clear the same hurdles. It also provides a good basis for comparing the various junior officers at fitness report time.

The above system is one way to do it. The captain may want to do it another way. The important point is that there should be a systematic qualification process which applies equitably to all of the SWO candidates.

The operations officer has a good possibility of being the senior watch officer himself, and having to accomplish the functions described above. Even if he is not, he probably will be the training officer, and be administratively responsible to the executive officer for having (or possibly creating) an officer training program.

TAO and Command Qualification

The ops officer is very likely to be one of the ship's officers going through the TAO PQS. After graduating from the surface warfare officer department-head course, he has the theoretical knowledge to become a TAO. Once aboard his ship, however, he may find that the captain will require him to do the TAO PQS program as it applies to his ship. The PQS is a complete package, and the department head must work his way through it, probably within the first six months of his tour on board. He then would be striving toward the command qualification in the remaining eighteen months, with the command exam coming at the very end of his two-year tour. If the officer is not already a qualified engineering officer of the watch (EOOW), it will be very difficult for him to do the TAO and the command qualification in two years. The program must begin the first week the new operations officer is on board.

Summary

For the operations officer, the functions of planning and training are very closely related. Much of the planning that he will be doing in his job will have to do with training, as that is a prime mission of the ship in peacetime and is the basis for much of the employment schedule. The training objectives are a combination of those imposed by higher authority ashore and those set down by the captain as areas in which he wants the ship to concentrate. There has to be a long-range plan and a mechanism for translating that plan into weekly training. It is convenient to categorize all shipboard training into operational, advancement, and organizational training, because each of these categories has a clearly recognizable cyclic schedule. For every training requirement there must be a training opportunity written into the ship's weekly schedule of events. Officer training must also be the subject of a planned program, and should be oriented toward qualification.

In the next chapter, we shall describe what the operations officer does in the environment of fleet operations while based in the United States. It will become apparent that planning and training take up a great deal of his time.

STOP
1/3
2/3
FULL
FULL

4
Stateside Operations

As we have discussed, ships operate through a cycle which progresses from new construction or overhaul, to a refit phase, and then into an operational phase. What a ship actually does during stateside operations depends upon where she is in the cycle. For surface ships deploying to the overseas fleets, the preponderance of stateside operations have to do with the refit phase. These can range from individual ship exercises (ISE), type training with other ships of the same type (TYT), composite training unit exercises (COMPTUEXs), and fleet readiness exercises (READEXs).

These operations are usually conducted in designated fleet operating areas. The services used for training—which consist of aircraft, fleet tugs, drone-control units, other surface ships, as well as designated ranges, such as shore-bombardment ranges—are usually controlled by an area coordinator. Your ship might also be going out to sea for the underway portions of the propulsion examining board (PEB) or the board of inspection and survey's (INSURV) underway material inspection. If the ship has been under repair for an extended time, she may go out for a few days of sea trials. To best describe your job as the operations officer in stateside operations, an example will be used wherein your ship is scheduled for a week of independent steaming from Monday through Friday in the local fleet operating areas, and the captain has directed you to see that several items from the long-range training plan get done during that week.

Preparing for Week at Sea

The objectives for the week at sea are already contained in your long-range training plan, and also in the ship's master plan for the year. Preparations for that week must begin about a month ahead of time, so that your ship can get the training services she will need for her training evolutions. One good way to plan for this week is to ask the executive officer for a special planning-board session. The master plan and the long-range training plan can then be reviewed by all of the department heads. The captain may even attend this session in order to review the training status of the ship and to divulge his priorities for the week at sea.

For single ship operations, the training time in local fleet operating areas normally consists of morning, afternoon, and night exercise periods, to conform with the schedules of the various organizations that provide the services. To plan the week, the ship should try to schedule those exercises that require training services for the morning and afternoon periods. If the ship has not been to sea for a long time, it might be wise to spend the first day going through the exercise of general bills rather than jumping right into fleet exercise evolutions; this is a matter for the captain and the executive officer to decide.

Once the planning board has agreed on what exercises the ship will undertake—with and without the use of training services—you must then request the necessary services from the local area coordinator. This is done by message, in a format prescribed by the coordinator, and done early enough to meet his planning needs. The response will usually come back in a composite message, which lists all of the events and services allocated for that particular week to all ships and units requesting services. You can then piece together what the ship has actually been allotted in the way of services. This normally happens the week before you go to sea. Once the area coordinator's message has been analyzed, another planning board meeting is required to firm up the plan for the week at sea.

Second Planning Board

At the second planning board meeting, it is your job to brief the other members on what services have been allocated for that week. These services are usually something less in number than what was asked for, due to funding constraints and the requirements of other units. Once the services are scheduled by the area coordinator, the ship must arrange the next week's schedule around the availability of those services.

The resulting plan will leave gaps in the schedule, and these gaps should be filled with exercises which do not require any outside services. During the second planning board, it will also become apparent that on some days of the week it may be necessary for the executive officer to rearrange the ship's routine to conform to the services scheduled in the operating area.

The assignment of operating areas for the ship's exercises is handled in the same manner, and depending upon the area coordinator's rules, will be in the same message asking for the training services. The area coordinator will assign operating areas in his weekly schedule. The navigator should analyze these assigned areas to ensure that the ship is not scheduled to conduct back-to-back exercises in areas fifty miles apart. He should brief you on the time/distance aspects of the evolutions. If there are no problems, this can be stated at the second planning board session. If there are problems, the board must decide whether or not the ship can afford not to do one of the exercises, or an effort must be made to get the area assignments changed. Time/distance problems are not something you want to discover when en route to the exercise areas!

Preparing the Plan for the Week at Sea

After the second planning board session, it is possible to work up the plan for the week at sea. Since it is an underway period, the training events will be the driving factor in the schedule. It is a good idea to list, in parentheses, an alternative for each event in which training services are scheduled. This way, if the services cancel out for any reason, the training time is not wasted. It is not necessary to list alternatives for the internal exercises, because the resources needed for them are under the ship's control. The plan of the week is then published at the normal time, and it contains not only the scheduled training events (using event numbers from the area coordinator's message plan), but also the internal evolutions that have been scheduled for the ship, plus the routine evolutions that a ship does every week.

For one-week operations, there is often a tendency to fill up the week from dawn to dusk with training events. This is not always the best method. There should be time allotted for a briefing on the various exercises or for doing prefiring briefs when required. There should be time left open for daily maintenance and housekeeping. There should be a wrap-up session, possibly by extending eight-o'clock reports in the evening, wherein the day's activities can be discussed and weak areas noted for improvement. Transit times should be noted in the schedule, so that people know when time will be available. If the ship has not been operating for a while, it is a good idea to adjust the tempo from slow to fast as the week progresses and people get used to at-sea operations. There should be events for the night watches to do during the night steaming hours, such as CIC/Bridge voice-procedures drills or nonmaneuvering tactical exercises.

Preparing for Departure

Part of the ops officer's job is to arrange for the port services needed for departure from the piers. Once the captain sets the underway time, you should call the port services office and give them the underway time and the ship's need for tugs, a pilot, a crane to lift the brow, and electricians to unhook the shore power. You should also tell the port services office when you expect to return and what port services you expect to need at that time. These will be confirmed by a logistics requirements (LOGREQ) seventy-two hours prior to return time.

Communications Plans

The operations officer must check the communications plan for the week at sea against the planned exercises to ensure that all evolutions are covered. The CIC officer and the communications officer actually construct the plan by checking over the weekly operating area and service-assignment message upon which the plan of the week at sea is based. Operating frequencies for service aircraft and other units are listed in the schedule, with a frequency spread arranged by the area coordinator's office to prevent mutual interference. Your job is to check the communications plan to see that it is complete. It is also a good idea to add some back-up frequencies to the plan.

For example, the area coordinator's message might say that the aircraft providing services for your air-gunnery shoot at 1500 is also providing services to another ship in a nearby area at 1300. The latter exercise will normally be controlled on a different frequency from the one you will be using. It is a good idea to have one or more UHF radios channelized to cover the other ship's control frequencies, so that your ship can effect a smooth handoff of the aircraft from the other firing ship when her exercise is completed.

All communications plans must also include all of the air and surface distress frequencies, as well as all search-and-rescue frequencies used in that geographical operating area.

Readiness for Sea

If the ship is scheduled to get under way Monday morning for the hypothetical one-week operation, it is imperative that you and the other department heads make sure that you are ready to go to sea. You should see to it that your spaces are secured, and that the major equipments in CIC and in the communications spaces have been checked out and are in fact ready to go. One technique is to leave with the weekend duty officer for the operations department a list of items that you want checked. Alternatively, you can come in Sunday afternoon or night to see for yourself that the weekend duty section has in fact made everything ready for sea.

During the prior week, your division officers will have prepared new underway watch bills. It is a good idea to man the spaces with the individual sections the week before departure to see if there are any holes in the watch bill. You should also check the radar piloting detail to make sure that they are ready in case of low visibility.

Dealing with Changes when Under Way

Once under way, the ship will proceed into the local operating areas and begin the training exercises. Changes to the week's plan begin almost simultaneously.

USS *Hull* (DD-945) trains with the lightweight eight-inch gun off Southern California.

What changes? Many things can change, all of which can disrupt your careful planning efforts of the week before. The training service units—be they aircraft, drone units, target-towing ships, or torpedo retrievers—can develop problems which cause them to cancel out with little or no notice. The weather can interfere, either with fog or just plain bad conditions. Because Mondays seem to attract more than their share of these problems, it is a good idea to keep Monday morning open for internal warm-up exercises en route to the operating areas.

When you enter the operating areas, your CIC will be guarding the area coordinator's control net. This is the circuit upon which you will be told of cancellations. When they happen, you can drop back to the alternative exercise written into the plan of the week. This net will also be used to make services available. If another ship has a gunnery exercise laid on for 1400 and at 1200 she tells the area coordinator that she has equipment problems, an alert CIC can pick this up, check with you, the operations officer, who in turn will check with the captain. If he approves, you might go back to the area coordinator and see if that target-towing aircraft can be diverted into your area so that your ship can use its services. This would be particularly desirable if the weather had interfered with your ship's air-gunnery shoot the day before.

The area coordinator will also publish changes to his schedule by message all week long. These will be provoked by ships requesting changes, or by changes in the availability of services. You or the CIC officer must read each message and analyze it to see what changes affect the next day's schedule, and where there are training opportunities listed but not yet assigned.

Keeping up with the changes is a juggling act, and it is often frustrating to see an entire week's training plan be totally disrupted by them. It does happen, however, and it is the operations officer's job to get the best training possible out of the available schedule.

Daily Operations

As the operations officer, you will have many things to do during a week of operations in the local operating areas. You will be standing watches, either as an OOD or as the senior officer on watch in the CIC, and you will continue to perform your daily administrative functions in the operations department. Long-range planning functions do not stop because the ship is out at sea, and indeed, a week at sea is often a very good time to catch up on a lot of projects.

You will have to keep a close eye on the daily training schedule and the changes thereto published by the area coordinator. If the ship conducts a number of exercises at general quarters, you will be busy running your GQ station, normally the CIC. Between events, you should be looking ahead and making sure that the ship and any required services are on track for the next event. If the ship operates in condition three for training, as many do, either you, a tactical action officer (TAO) in CIC, or the OOD on the bridge if there is no TAO posted, will share the job with the officer who is running the watch team.

Stateside Operations: A guided missile destroyer conducts a full power trial.

For instance, suppose your ship is scheduled for a two-hour gunnery exercise at 0800; the ship will go to general quarters in time to be on station with the proper radio circuits up, waiting for the target services to arrive. During the gunnery exercise, you should be concentrating on your watch station duties to ensure a safe and effective exercise in your area of responsibility. Just as soon as the exercise concludes, however, you should begin setting up for the next event, whatever it might be. If it involves another exercise area and other services, you should be checking with the navigator to determine the track to the area of the next event. You should also be checking on the CIC officer to ensure that the proper circuits are being brought up and that all other necessary preparations are being made for the next event. You might also be checking your message traffic to ensure that the services for the afternoon events are still on track. In other words, as soon as one event concludes, you must turn your attention to the next one and keep a long-range eye on the ones that will come after that.

Safety

One of the duties of the operations officer during training evolutions which involve live ordnance firing is to be the CIC safety observer for the exercise. For example, let us assume that the ship is preparing for a gun-firing exercise using as a target a sleeve towed by an aircraft. The ship will have promulgated a preexercise message with specific instructions for the rendezvous of the ship and aircraft, and a delineation of the firing area—e.g., the ship should be on the southern boundary of the area, firing north. Prior to firing, the bridge and CIC will have scanned the area to ensure a clear range, and informed the area coordinator that the area was "going hot."

Once the firing runs begin, however, everyone involved in the exercise will tend to get absorbed with the fire- and gun-control problem, i.e., locking on to the target, maintaining track, and getting the rounds off. The ops officer, if he is the GQ tactical action officer (TAO), will have his part of this job to do as well, but he must also keep a continuing eye on safety. He must make sure that the people in the surface tracking area of CIC do not get wrapped up in the firing exercise to the point where they miss the small radar contact which is entering the fall-of-shot area. While many of the air trackers may have their scopes turned down to concentrate on short-range target acquisition, one air tracker must keep watching the long-range air picture to detect any aircraft that might enter the hot area. A well-run and seasoned CIC will do all of this as a matter of routine, but if your crew is inexperienced or "rusty," with many new hands, the matter of safety requires some close attention.

Off-watch

Where does the operations officer spend his time when not on watch as OOD or in the CIC? Like the other department heads, he will have plenty of administrative work to do. He should, however, be in and out of CIC on a regular basis all during the day and anytime he is up at night. The bridge and the CIC form the axis where information comes together and where operational decisions are made. If a quick schedule change comes in which deletes some services, and the captain decides to try for another exercise, the decision will probably be made in CIC or on the bridge. This is because the captain will want to look at a chart to visualize the time/distance factors, or maybe just look at the overall schedule of events to see which exercises might be possible to do.

The operations officer cannot afford to spend his whole day hanging around CIC or the bridge. He should, however, make it a practice to keep in touch with both so that he knows what is happening. Before securing for the night, he should make a last check in CIC to see that things are being set up for the next day's evolutions. He should read over the night orders to make sure that they conform to what he understands to be the schedule for the night. He should make a last stop by radio central to check his traffic for any last-minute schedule changes or changes in services which might undo the ship's planning for the next day.

In summary, the operations officer must adopt a proprietary attitude toward the ship's schedule for the near future, make sure that he understands it, and satisfy himself that his department is ready to execute their part in it.

Returning to Port

The operations department is normally charged with the responsibility of assembling the data for a logistics requirements (LOGREQ) report, which is the message sent to the port-control authorities stipulating your ship's logistic requirements upon return. The message should include the port and shore services needed and any other information that the port authorities should have to arrange for your ship's arrival. All departments have an input to the LOGREQ, and usually a junior officer in operations is given the task of walking a precut blank LOGREQ form around to get the data. Once he has all the requirements, he will ask the ops officer to check it over for form and content. Then the message will be checked by the executive officer and released by the captain. These messages should go out seventy-two hours in advance of your arrival to give the port authorities time to prepare for you.

Once the ship is back in and alongside the pier, the ops officer has the job of tabulating what was accomplished and sending in updates to the training and readiness files by message. There may be other postexercise reports required by other authorities, and these should be prepared and sent out before securing for the weekend. Once again, the operations officer must look ahead to Monday, and make sure that his department is getting ready for the next week's events.

In-port Operations

Strange as it may seem, the tempo of activity in the ship in port can sometimes be greater than when the ship is out at sea. The reason for this is that while the ship is at sea, she proceeds from evolution to evolution as an entity; for example, the whole ship gets involved in an underway replenishment, or in going to general quarters for an exercise. In port, the many and diverse organizations of the shore establishment interact with the ship's company within their areas of specialization, often with little coordination in their efforts.

A typical day alongside the pier may have your ship hosting the laundry assist team, touring fifty NJROTC cadets around deck, sending most of the chief petty officers over to another ship to conduct a PMS inspection, and participating in the weekly in-port training exercises, with a tender availability in progress all the while. A movie taken of the brow would show a steady stream of people going back and forth, many of whom are not part of the ship's company.

The net result is that you will find a large number of your people doing more things than had been planned for the current week. Examined separately, each of these unplanned evolutions is usually a legitimately necessary thing, but the overall result often seems to be the dissipation of both your and your people's time. After you have been exposed to the home port pierside environment for a while, you will appreciate the benefit of leaving the telephones behind on the pier when you sail!

Because of such unsettling yet necessary interference from the shore support activities when pierside, the planning board's deliberations each week must be as comprehensive as possible. The key is to identify every evolution which will be going on in the ship that affects more than just one division or work center. If evolutions can be incorporated into the plan of the week, then the amount of unexpected requirements can be reduced. They will never be eliminated, however; you might as well recognize that every day of the week will bring a phone call which gives the ship a task that was not in the plan.

The operations officer shares with the other department heads the job of providing people and time to handle the additional chores levied from above. In some home ports, there is a weekly berthing and training conference held by the senior commander at or near the piers to parcel out both training evolutions and the other tasks—such as providing line-handlers, inspection parties, hosting tour groups, etc. It is necessary for the ship to have a representative at such meetings, and the ops officer is a likely candidate. He works daily with the employment schedule of his ship and is conversant with what the ship is doing from week to week. And due to his familiarity with his ship's master plan for the year, he can also assess the impact of additional activities so that the higher authorities can at least understand what effect a new task will have on the ship's primary mission of maintenance or training. The ship's own planning board should not meet before the weekly conference, if one is held in your home port, because the ship's plan of the week may be radically altered at the conference.

The Operations Officer in Port

For the most part, when in port you will spend your time doing administrative work. The sheer volume of paperwork being processed in ships today may astonish you. In addition, you will be involved in planning, training, meetings, schools, inspections, and in the daily business of managing your people and the affairs of your department.

As a new operations officer, you will feel the need to do many things yourself in order to learn how to do them and to ensure that they do, in fact, get done. In order to keep up with the administrative load, you should delegate as many routine functions as possible to junior officers and senior petty officers, once you understand what the functions are and how they are to be done. You will not be stepping into a vacuum; your predecessor will have had some kind of an organization set up before you took over. See if it works, and do not change it all around just for the sake of putting your stamp on it. Look, rather, for weak areas within the department, and concentrate on fixing them. The executive officer can help you with this.

Another technique that is helpful to a department head is to set aside one time period during the day when your subordinates know that you are not to be disturbed. In just an hour a day, when the only people who bother you are department heads, the XO, or the captain, you can finish many of your daily chores. Conversely, it is a good idea to designate another time frame when your subordinates are encouraged to see you to discuss the innumerable details of the working day. Try very hard for that "do not disturb" hour, though; it is definitely necessary.

It is a good idea for the ops officer to come to work early enough to go through the night's collection of message traffic prior to morning quarters. That you have read the messages before the XO and the captain ask about them should become a matter of professional pride. Have your duty department head brief you on the message traffic each morning; it is good training for him, and it alerts you to the size and scope of any action messages that must be dealt with right away. It also helps when you can assign action projects to your departmental officers right after officers' call without having to chase them down a half hour later after they have begun their day.

In-Port Training

Much of your time will be spent coordinating and executing in-port training. Because of funding constraints, ships do not go to sea as much as in years past, and it has been found that a great deal of training can be done pierside just about as effectively as at sea. Communications and CIC exercises are particularly adaptable to pierside training, as are visual signaling drills, and even some seamanship evolutions.

Scheduling of the in-port training is becoming more centralized as staff organizations take over the coordination of training on the waterfront. In most ports, the weekly berthing and training conference coordinates the shifting of ship's berths among the piers and the intership pierside training. Some home-port areas have adopted the convention of having one day each week set aside for in-port pierside training exercises, a concept which really simplifies the planning.

Cross-decking

If for some reason your ship will not be able to participate in the full range of training exercises slated for a training day, give some thought to cross-decking. This means sending some of your people over to another ship to observe and participate in the exercises when your whole team cannot be present.

If your ship is slated to be in port for a relatively long period, you might give some thought to cross-decking petty officers and even junior officers to ships going out for short operations. This is a good technique for keeping air controllers qualified in live operations, and it is a very good way to let a junior officer see what an operation that might be unfamiliar to him looks like firsthand. Cross-decking can be worked out between operations officers once the executive officer clears the idea.

Team Trainers

When the ship is in port, the various team trainers at the fleet training center will be scheduled for use by the ship. The team trainers are very good devices which allow an entire watch section or GQ team to perform full-scale simulated evolutions, such as antisubmarine and antiair warfare and damage-control exercises. The trainers are sophisticated systems which can present very realistic exercise situations to your team within the confines of a building. There are some artificialities in equipment and watch stations, but the simulations are very realistic. Within the same building, many ships' teams can participate as if they were in company at sea. If you are not familiar with the facilities, call the training center and ask for a tour. They are usually more than happy to oblige.

Multi-ship Exercises at Sea

In addition to independent operations and in-port periods, stateside operations include multiship exercises such as the periodic composite training unit exercises (COMPTUEX) and the fleet readiness exercises (READEX).

COMPTUEX

A COMPTUEX is a regularly scheduled exercise at sea in which several surface ships conduct up to ten days of training operations in the fleet operating areas. There is normally a unit commander in charge. The objective is to make better use of available training services by providing them to multiship formations instead of to individual ships. For example, an air-gunnery target drone can be flown down the flank of a six-ship formation just as well as for one ship alone, providing simultaneous training opportunities for all six ships. COMPTUEXs normally do not use a war scenario, but rather a daily schedule of events in which ships are cycled through basic, intermediate, and then advanced operational exercises. COMPTUEXs are normally held a month or so before a major fleet exercise, and they present an excellent training opportunity for the ships involved. Not only does a group of ships have a higher priority in obtaining scarce services, they also present to shiphandlers the opportunity for task-group steaming experience. A COMPTUEX is a relatively simple planning evolution for the ships, because they simply follow the schedule of events or changes thereto from day to day, using a Letter of Instruction (LOI).

READEX

A fleet-level readiness exercise (READEX) is a much larger operation than a COMPTUEX. It is normally played within a wartime scenario, and involves simulated actions against U.S. Navy ships that are acting out the part of hostile naval vessels. Planning for a READEX is complex and involves a lot of study and briefings on the part of the department heads. Many READEXs are staged in phases, including an in-port training phase (in the trainers), a warm-up phase at sea, and then the wartime scenario. The READEX is the graduation exercise for a ship that is about to deploy to one of the overseas fleets. A deploying ship will normally be scheduled into a READEX in the quarter prior to deployment.

Summary

You will probably spend half of your tour as an operations officer in stateside operations, unless your ship happens to have an exceptional deployment cycle. These operations present an opportunity to train yourself in the job and to prepare both you and your people for the more rigorous tempo of deployed operations. Using the ship's master plan and the long-range training plan, the planning board views the time spent stateside as a big opportunity to upgrade material and training readiness.

The ship can participate in one of three exercise environments at sea—independent steaming, a COMPTUEX, or a fleet READEX. The ship will continue to conduct operations for training even when in port. From a readiness point of view, the time spent stateside is in effect an extended preparation period for deployed operations, the subject of the next chapter.

5
Deployed Operations

The thirty to forty-five days immediately prior to a deployment are listed in the annual schedule as the POM period, POM standing for Preparation for Overseas Movement. The ship will spend a lot more than a month getting ready for deployment, but the POM period is spent completing the final logistics, training, and material-readiness evolutions prior to leaving the country for six or seven months. It is also the time when the type commander and his intermediate unit commanders ensure themselves and the prospective fleet commander that the ship is ready for deployed operations.

Preparing for Deployment: POM

Logistics

Each department head is responsible for being logistically ready for the deployment. For the operations officer, this means that there is a lot of stocking up to do, because parts and consumables for the operations department are difficult to acquire overseas. Such things as teletype paper, teletype parts, message-printing paper, supplies for duplicating, signal flags and other bunting, halyard line, and routine electronics spare all must be stockpiled. The ship will receive a turnover letter from a ship that is about to come home from deployment, and for whom your ship is the numerical and type replacement. This letter will indicate what kinds of items are in tight supply on the mobile logistics ships. Operations will have to obligate a substantial amount of the current quarter's operating target (OPTAR) budget for deployment consumables.

Test Equipment

It is vital that a test equipment calibration program be conducted during the POM month or slightly before to bring as much equipment as possible up to calibration before departure. There are facilities for this in the deployed fleet areas, but the transportation to and from these facilities often "undoes" the calibration that has just been done. Do as much as you can in this area before departure.

Combat Systems Readiness Review (CSRR)

Prior to or during the POM period, a CSRR will be conducted on the ship if there are complex area-defense weapons on board. This is probably the single most helpful evolution for the material readiness of the operations department done during the POM period, and it is essential that the department's top talent be involved. Whether the ship is a complex combat systems platform, or one with just a few sensors and point-defense weapons, the CSRR will indicate whether or not the systems are ready to go.

Briefings

The POM period will be a time for a lot of operations briefings. These will include briefings on the deployed fleet's procedures, op-orders, manuals, and geography. There will be briefings on the group transit, if the ship is going over in a group sail. There will be briefings on the required reports in the deployed fleets, and on communications and other operations procedures which might be different from the way things are done in U.S. home waters.

A list of all the briefings requested by each department head, plus the ones that outside organizations will be conducting (overseas diplomacy, operational security, public affairs, overseas health programs, etc.) should be drawn up at a planning board for training before POM. It will be necessary to conduct a briefing of some sort just about every working day of the POM period, and these briefings should be scheduled early, so that the briefers and the attendees can plan ahead.

The briefings on operations orders are special cases. Op orders do not make for exciting reading, nor for exciting briefs. The object of op-order briefs is to tell people where to get guidance on various procedures, as opposed to describing those procedures in detail. Since the ops officer is the custodian of op-orders, it is expected that he will give many of the op-order briefs.

In addition to being briefed, many of the ship's officers have to read through the principle op-orders. One way to manage this is to have the operations officer and the executive officer prepare a matrix that lists all of the deployment op-orders and publications down one side, and the ship's officers and senior petty officers across the top, with an X indicating which publications have to be ready by whom. The matrix should be published at the beginning of the POM. The officers can then draw the publications from the cognizant custodian at their convenience. The reading list lets them know what the requirements are for planning their time during POM.

Returning Deployers

There will almost always be a ship in the home port that has just returned from the deployment area. By talking to the people in that ship, you can find out how things are done in the deployment area and what things need to be stockpiled before the deployment. The liaison can be done informally between the officers and senior petty officers of the two ships, or a half-day of briefings can be requested from captain to captain. You will find this additional information very helpful.

The schedule for the wardroom briefings should include a time shortly after each briefing for the officers to pass the information on to their divisions while it is still fresh. If the all-officer briefings are held at 1230, the divisions can be scheduled to muster in compartments at 1300. It is also a good idea to brief the chief petty officers and perhaps the first class petty officers on some of the general publications, such as the logistics manual or the fleet deployment manual. If the ship has a closed-circuit television system, senior petty officers can be assigned to make ten-minute "spots" on different aspects of preparing for the deployment. These can be run prior to the evening movie.

The Type Commander's Check-Off List

The surface forces commander on each coast publishes a predeployment instruction which lists all of the things that must be done prior to a ship's departure. This instruction is the requirements list for planning the POM period, and a quick look through it will quickly show you that some of the preparations for POM have to start literally months before the actual POM period begins. If there is a deployment in the ship's future when you first take over as operations officer, the POM instruction is one of the primary documents you should read. It also serves as a ready-made set of inputs for both the ship's master plan for the year and the requirements lists (see chapter 2) of the long-range training plan. If the ship does everything required by this instruction, she will in fact be ready for deployment. It will be clear, however, that there is more than a month's worth of work involved.

The solution to this problem is for the ship to complete some of the items on the POM check-list two to three months before departure. For instance, if an underwater hull inspection is required, it can be done two months before departure without measurably affecting the currency of the hull-inspection report. Some items should not be done early; for example, a requirement to have all of the ship's air controllers up to date in their certification might be done as late as possible in the POM period. (But because air controllers are often key senior petty officers who are very much in demand on board during POM, a trade-off must often be made.) The main point is to break out the predeployment check-off lists well in advance of POM to see what can be done ahead of time.

The Tempo of POM

The plan of the week during the POM period will often run to two pages, reflecting the many requirements the ship is trying to meet in the final month. It is a frenetic period, and one which will require very long working hours for department heads. Each week, the planning board will do its best to resolve conflicting requirements and to plan for all of the many evolutions. There will be conflicts, however, and some of the POM items will not get done.

At the beginning of the POM period, the ops officer should draw up a list of those activities in which the operations department is weak. The list should be limited to perhaps ten items. When conflicts arise during the POM, he can accept the cancellation of items on the POM check-list as long as it does not affect the items on the priority list. For example, there might be a weakness in teletype repair. The solution is to send the teletype repair man over to the local maintenance activity for a week to get some on-the-job training from the experts. Once deployed, the ship will become much more dependent upon the on-board talent and resources.

POM Reports

Each week of the POM period, the ship will have to prepare a report on the progress being made. The unit commander will take the inputs from each ship and forward a consolidated report up the line. This means that each week the department heads must be ready to inform the executive officer what was accomplished, or will be accomplished, during the week. Depending on the size of the ship's chain of command, this report may have to be transmitted on Wednesday, in order for the unit commander to get his report out Thursday, and for the group commander to get his report out Friday. In other words, the accounting period for the ship will run from mid-week to mid-week rather than from Friday to Friday. These reports take up time, but they contain information that is vital to the higher authorities.

Deployed Operations

The deployed fleets (the U.S. Sixth and Seventh Fleets) are predominantly made up of ships which have been certified as operationally ready by one of the two home fleets, the U.S. Second and Third Fleets. The deployed fleets are part of the global defense assets of the United States, positioned in support of both national and international commitments. For ships in the stateside environment, the emphasis is on achieving readiness. In the deployed fleets, the emphasis is on maintaining readiness.

"Birds away!" Surface-to-air missile launch—USS *Sampson* (DDG-10).

A great deal of training goes on all the time in the deployed fleets, but it is no longer basic training. Ships which deploy are expected to arrive with trained watch teams. Surface operations in the deployed fleets are aimed at polishing the stateside levels of training to a high degree of proficiency in all aspects of surface warfare. And except when ships are making their way to and from port, they almost always operate within a task group.

The Operations Job

When the ship is deployed, the ops officer assumes a seven-days-a-week, twenty-four-hour-a-day commitment to his job. He must learn quickly how to pace himself, and he must conscientiously train his departmental junior officers to do many of the jobs he did back in the States. When at sea, the ship is governed by the daily schedule of events published by the task group/unit commander; this schedule is often called the "tab," because it is officially a tab to an annex of the task-group commander's standing operations order. When the ship goes into port, either for a visit or an upkeep period, preparations for the next set of events begins.

When the ship is in port overseas, there is a semblance of the regular working day, but this semblance is colored by the knowledge that the ship may be called forth on short notice from upkeep or a port visit into a major operation. The ops officer should be paying a lot of attention to what is going on in his ship's theater of operations, always looking for indications that something may be brewing that may affect his ship.

He will be more involved in logistics than he was back in the States. Since most of the ship's supplies and repair parts will be coming via the mobile logistics force, he should be keeping an eye on where the replenishment ships are and where they are going to be. In the Sixth Fleet, the task groups converge monthly with the replenishment groups for major replenishments. In the Seventh Fleet, which is spread out more geographically, the replenishments often are done on an individual unit basis. In non-nuclear ships, the captain watches the ship's fuel levels very closely, and the operations department should be able to tell him at any time when and where the next replenishment will be done.

Intensity of Operations

When in the States, the ship usually goes through a sequence of operations while working up to higher levels of proficiency. A replenishment operation would be done with the ship first going alongside the replenishment ship and then perhaps standing off to receive a vertical replenishment once the fueling was done. In the deployed fleets, the helicopters bring the stores while the ship is alongside getting fuel, and the ship may have to stop the whole evolution on short notice and conduct an emergency break-away to pursue a sonar contact or to avoid a simulated enemy surface action group. It is also not unusual for a ship to continue doing her major CIC function, such as running an air-control and surveillance zone of the area, while she is conducting underway replenishments. Simultaneous operations require that departmental general bills be kept scrupulously up to date.

Rules of Engagement

The deployed fleet's rules of engagement (ROE) are normally very highly classified instructions which tell commanders what to do when presented with a set of circumstances involving ships, aircraft, or the territory of a foreign power. They are normally not very lengthy, but they are very important. Because of their classification, knowledge of these rules is restricted in most ships to the captain, the executive officer, and the tactical action officers or senior CIC watch officers. The operations officer normally maintains custody of the rules, and he must be fully conversant with them.

The Possibility of Conflict

Under routine circumstances, the possibility of a surprise attack in the local operating areas in the States is remote. In the deployed areas, the possibility of an attack is greater, and in some areas more than others. Rules of engagement cover many circumstances which are related to the ship's geographic position. Any time the ship enters a new area, the ops officer should review the rules of engagement, and prepare a refresher brief for those officers in the ship who are cleared for the material. Thereafter, when a ship or aircraft from a potentially hostile foreign power is detected, this contact must be evaluated from the point of view of its capability to launch a surprise attack. This does not necessarily mean calling the ship to general quarters, but it does mean that watch officers should be looking for warning signs which could be the precursors to surprise attack.

Operational Emergencies

When an operational emergency occurs in the deployed fleet, the ships and aircraft at the scene or close to it will be the first to react. A downed airplane in the local stateside fleet operating areas brings into play the national search-and-rescue organizations. The same situation in the Mediterranean or the Western Pacific means that the ships at hand are the search-and-rescue organization and must handle the problem without the help of prepositioned rescue forces. (This subject is addressed in detail in chapter seven).

Operations Orders

When the ship is operating in and out of U.S. ports, or working up for deployment, it is governed by the rules and regulations of the type commander, the local senior officer present afloat (SOPA), and the host naval station, as well as by the rules of the local fleet operating area coordinators. When the ship is deployed, it is governed almost exclusively by operations orders.

The basic operations order is the deployed fleet commander's standing op-order. It contains general information on the business of operating in the Sixth or Seventh Fleet. A second operations order, published by the task-force or task-group commander, covers in detail the facets of operating within specific task groups. Both of these operations orders are supplemented by some kind of operating guide or fleet deployment guide dealing with the administrative matters and situations encountered in the deployed fleet. For example, the basic operating orders current in the Sixth Fleet are as follows:

COMSIXTHFLEET OPORDER 4000 (basic reference)

COMMANDER TASK FORCE SIXTY OPORDER 4000 (operating reference)

COMSIXTHFLEET Deployment Manual (administrative reference)

COMSERVICEFORCESIXTHFLEET 4000 Series (logistics & maintenance).

The operations officer should keep copies of the basic references in CIC, in binders, with an index in each one for ready reference. This will allow quick access to them, not only to the operations officer, but also to the other department heads who may be standing watches as the TAO in the CIC.

Another feature of operating with the deployed fleets is that the ship may operate under many op-orders at the same time. If the ship comes out of port and heads for a rendezvous with one of the task groups, it is operating under the fleet and force op-orders. If on the next day, the group joins up with the replenishment forces for the monthly replenishment, it comes under the service force commander's op-order. If the ship then detaches to conduct surveillance, it would operate in accordance with the reconnaissance commander's op-order; if sent to join up with the amphibious task group or ready group, yet another op-order would govern.

Because operations orders are so important when the ship is deployed, the operations officer should periodically review each of the major commander's op-orders. That is also a good time to see if they are up to date and to make sure that message changes have not been taped to the inside back cover with the idea that they will "never" be used. If the ship is in

Replenishment Operations: Personnel transfer.

port with another type of ship—tied up near an amphibious ship, for example—it is a good idea for the operations officer to send one of his departmental officers over to the amphibious ship, with the amphibious group op-order in hand, to check on its currency with a ship who uses it every day.

Operating Techniques

The increased intensity of operations, coupled with the diversity of employment for deployed ships, can overwhelm the operations officer if he allows himself to get behind. He, as well as his contemporaries in the ship, must be looking ahead all the time. Each planning board for training should include a few minutes' discussion on the employment schedule for the next few months. Every evolution in the employment schedule will require some kind of advance planning, arrangements, or messages. Port visits require diplomatic clearances and logistics requirements, sometimes months in advance. A maintenance availability in a foreign shipyard may require that the work package be submitted to the fleet maintenance coordinator two months in advance. (If your first availability is one month after arrival, then the work package is due overseas before POM begins!) Each department head has to look into the future for his share of the responsibility for planning; as keeper of the master plan and the ship's schedule, however, the ops officer has the responsibility to remind his contemporaries of the requirement for advance planning.

Watching for Indicators

As the operations officer, you should make time during the day to go down to radio central and look through the broadcast rolls to see what is going on in the fleet. It is possible to get an indication of events that might affect your ship. If, for example, your ship is a destroyer and is preparing to leave port, and you see in the broadcasts that a carrier task-group commander is sending one of his planeguard destroyers into port because of engineering problems, you should alert the captain, executive officer, and the other department heads that the ship just might be getting a planeguard assignment on short notice.

Reporting Requirements

In a deployed ship, all of the ship's officers have to spend a great deal of time preparing reports for submission up the operational and administrative chain of command. However trivial and unnecessary a given report may seem to the officer submitting or preparing it, the requirement would not exist if higher authority did not need that information. The ship's reputation in the deployed fleet often depends on its performance in making reports. This requires some organization.

During the POM period and for the first month or so in the deployed fleet, the ship should take the view that reporting requirements are an operational evolution. The objective is to identify all of the required reports, get them listed on some kind of tickler system, and have action officers assigned to prepare the reports for the captain's release. The operations officer plays a big role in this process, because he has custody of the operations orders, wherein are found almost (but not all) reporting requirements.

One technique is to have operations departmental officers screen all of the major op-orders, looking for reporting requirements. The operations officer does the same thing, and compares notes with them to assemble a master list. The more officers involved in this process the better. Once the master list is assembled, it should be converted to a tickler system maintained by one central office. Sources for the report requirements include op-orders, deployment manuals, logistics instructions, and the set of standing fleet turn-over messages.

The Logistics Tracker

A logistic tracker is a senior petty officer whose function is to keep track of where all the fleet logistics ships are at any given time. It is a good idea to have such a tracker if the ship can afford the manpower required. To do this job, the petty officer is given daily access to the fleet employment schedule, from which he keeps a current listing of the replenishment ships assigned to the fleet. He can then tell the captain the location at any time of the nearest fuel, ammunition, or stores ship. This information is particularly helpful to ships that conduct a lot of independent operations.

Communications

The area of communications, particularly the tactical voice circuits, is another highly visible measure of a ship's performance, and this is true for deployed or stateside operations.

Once deployed, however, tactical communications become even more important because of the amount of time spent by the ship in task-group operations.

In smaller ships, the communications division belongs to the operations officer. Even though there is a communications officer assigned, the ops officer must pay close attention to the communications area because problems there affect all the other areas in the operations department.

The requirements for tactical radio communications circuits in a task group will often outnumber the pieces of equipment available in the ship. That is, an operations order may require twenty-five different UHF voice circuits, any of which the ship may be expected to come up on sometime during the course of operations. The communications officer solves this problem by using the channelized equipments to store all of the applicable frequencies listed in the op-order. If the ship has five UHF voice radios available, it will, of course, not be able to operate on any more than five at one time. But, as the ship progresses from exercise to exercise, or from a replenishment evolution to an AAW station, the CIC watch officer can set up a configuration of five new UHF frequencies to coincide with those required by whatever evolution is going on.

This management of the communications configuration is a technique which all TAOs and CIC watch officers will have to learn. (It is covered further in chapter 8). Before any evolution involving other ships occurs, the operations officer must make sure that CIC has set up the new communications configuration. The CIC watch officer/TAO should be responsible for this as a matter of routine, but if the communications do not work when the captain picks up the radio handset, he will probably call for the ops officer to look into the matter. It is worth some personal supervision until the watch officers get used to doing it.

Ships operating in task groups are faced with a wide variety of communications capabilities. Some ships have a relatively large capability, because they have many pieces of equipment. If they have problems, they just shift gear and patch in a new circuit. Smaller ships may not be able to do that and are reluctant to rearrange all of their equipments in an effort to restore just one circuit. When a communications circuit fails, it is best to assume that the problem lies with your ship and not the other ship. If you are on watch as TAO, you can take direct action. If you are not on watch, but happen into CIC and find a communications problem in progress, you should check to see that your ship is tackling the problem and not just waiting for the other ship to fix it.

Talking to Contemporaries

When you are coming into a foreign port with one or more U.S. Navy ships, make a point to confer with their operations officers. You may have some problems which have been defying solution for some time, and another operations officer may have had the same problem and come up with a solution. Deployed ships face the same kinds of problems regardless of type. Take a few hours after getting in port to talk to the other ops officers and compare notes.

Another technique is to have the ship's publications custodian get together with those from other ships in port to check on the currency of publications (other than the Communications Security Systems). Due to the vagaries of the mail system, the other ship may have received the two most recent changes to the deployment manual, while you were not even aware that they existed.

Summary

Being with the deployed fleet gives the entire ship the feeling of "doing it for real." The training that goes on is designed to sharpen proficiency, rather than just to achieve proficiency. Being ready for the deployment is the purpose behind all the months of in-port inspections and underway readiness exercises. Deployed operations will provide a great deal of personal and professional satisfaction when the ship and its departments and divisions work successfully together. Coming into port in the States usually means coming into home port; overseas, coming in means new places and new things to do and the challenge of conducting overseas diplomacy. In many ports your ship will be alone, and thereby will become a microcosm of the United States, responsible for the full spectrum of protocol, logistics, shore leave and liberty, transportation, currency exchanges, and foreign claims. When the ship deploys, the world narrows down to the lifelines; the ship and her entire crew becomes the entity they were designed to be.

Thus far we have covered the basics of the operations officer's job, and the fundamental techniques of planning and training which take up a large proportion of his time. We have described the two general environments of a ship's operations, stateside and deployed. We will now look at two more fundamental techniques, namely *reporting* and *handling operational emergencies,* and then proceed to describe the combat information center, and the special case of combat operations.

6 Reporting

Reports are the means by which ships and other Navy units provide information to higher authorities.

The officers and men in a ship direct their attention inward, to the ship. Higher authorities—by which is meant commanders of squadrons, groups, fleets, or even unified commanders—view ships as combat units, or as one ship among many. While officers in the ship may know that the boat-handling equipment does not work, there is no way for the ship's unit commander to know this unless a material casualty report is made. Until a report is submitted, the unit commander will assume that the boat-handling gear is working. This is a key concept. Commanders of groups of ships make assumptions about ships' readiness when they prepare their operations orders, contingency plans, or war plans. If the assumptions are wrong, then it is probable that the plans will not work. In order to assure themselves that their assumptions are valid, higher authorities require a continuous stream of reports from their assigned units.

Reporting Requirements

The national military command and control system is another generator of reporting requirements. A significant feature of the national defense strategy is that it is a forward strategy, which means that there have to be forces deployed at great distances from the continental United States. The object of this strategy is to see that the United States is able to deal with military problems at as great a distance from the American continent as is feasible. Feasible is the key word. It is not sufficient just to deploy large military forces around the world. The president, as commander in chief, must be able to command and control the deployed military forces.

In order for the commander in chief to do this, he and the other national command authorities must know what is happening in any situation which involves, or could involve, U.S. military forces. They must receive this information from great distances and from many kinds of military forces and units. The communications systems which make this possible are supported by automatic data-processing equipment. As a result, not only must they receive the actual information needed for long-range, operational decision making, but it must be sent in the proper format to satisfy the needs of the data-processing equipment.

There is a third factor at work in the making of operational reports. In addition to the requirements of national military command and control authorities, other government agencies and departments need to know about the kinds of situations that deployed forces confront from time to time. What may appear as a purely military situation to the forces on the scene may be part of a much larger strategic and political situation when viewed by other government agencies in Washington. The decision making which relates to the larger strategic picture normally proceeds at a more deliberate pace than purely tactical decision making, and because of this difference in pace, it is often necessary to duplicate the reports. A ship, for example, might make an operational report to elements of the military command system. A short time later, a request will come in by message asking that essentially the same information be sent to other addressees, with perhaps some amplification. What has happened is that the initial report has triggered the interest of another agency which needs more information in order to formulate decisions that may be completely outside the environment of military operations. Although a ship at the scene of action may consider this a redundant request, keep in mind that an operational unit may be the only source of information for both higher authorities.

Validity of Reporting Requirements

It is often remarked that the reporting requirements levied upon naval units are too numerous, duplicative, or perhaps just plain unnecessary. This may or may not be true, but to an operating unit, it is irrelevant. Any reporting requirement directed toward a unit by competent authority is an operational requirement and not subject to debate. While some reporting requirements may well be the result of overactive data-processing equipment, they come to the ship through the chain of command. As far as the operations officer is concerned, reporting becomes a *management* problem; he must know the requirements and respond to them.

Categorization of Reports

There are three kinds of reports that are usually made in a ship:

1. administrative reports
2. operational reports
3. emergency reports

Administrative reports are those which the operations officer makes, either by message or by correspondence, at the direction of the executive officer. Operational reports are those which the operations officer and the other department heads make, normally by message, in response to reporting requirements contained in operations orders, naval warfare publications, or in messages from superiors, which require operational reports to be made on a given subject. Emergency reports are those which are made normally by a watch officer, usually in an established format and by any means possible.

Administrative Reports

Each department in the ship is responsible for providing inputs to administrative reports. Normally, the ship's office maintains a master tickler file of required administrative reports. The ship's yeomen then send out memos to department heads reminding them that a report is due, and when it must be submitted for executive review.

The ops officer responds to this system, but he also should have a system of his own. When taking over the job, you should ask to see the operations department tickler file. If the system appears to work, leave it alone. Asking the executive officer is a good way to find out if the system has worked in the past. If there has been a lot of trouble getting the reports out of the ops department, a new system is needed.

New requirements for administrative reports usually arise when official correspondence is routed around the departments. Recent instructions and notices from the Naval Military Personnel Command, the type commander, subordinate unit commanders, the CNO, or the Ships Systems Commands, for example, may contain new reporting requirements or modifications to the present requirements. Some instructions will directly state reporting requirements in a "reports" paragraph; others will contain requirements in the action paragraph. The executive officer will spot the new requirements and direct the ship's office to make an addition to the tickler file, and perhaps make a note on the routing slip. Each department head, however, must review routed correspondence with an eye for new reporting requirements, either explicitly stated or implied.

Operational Reports

Operational reports have several things in common:

- They are keyed to events or to changes in the ship's status;
- They are almost always in format;
- They are almost always classified;
- They are time-sensitive, and thus reported by message.

Additionally, some operational reports are serialized, and require an accounting system to keep the serials straight.

The basic publication describing Navy operational reports is *Naval Warfare Publication* (*NWP*) 14-1. This book concentrates on the major types of operational reports and gives specific format and time-constraint information for some of them. Other sources of operational reporting requirements are the type commanders' instructions on readiness reporting, the fleet commanders' operations orders, and the local area commanders' requirements for making operational reports when, for example, the ship is operating in the fleet exercise areas. It is not possible to enumerate here all of the different operational reports with which the operations officer will come in contact; your predecessor should be able to turn over a list of the reports which are made regularly.

Operational reports have been more heavily influenced than any others by the growing use of automatic data-processing (ADP) equipment in the larger headquarters ashore and afloat. When a computer is used in operational reporting, the format of a report becomes as important as the actual content. This is because the ADP equipment in the headquarters is normally tied directly into a communications systems. If the format of an incoming report is not correct, the interlocked systems are likely to reject it. Rejection requires manual processing of the report, which in turn slows down the flow of data from a ship to the commander. The Navy's Readiness Reporting System is probably the best example of an operational report wherein the accuracy of its format is, for all practical purposes, as important as the accuracy of its data.

Operational reports are not the exclusive province of the ops officer. Each of the other department heads will also prepare and submit reports of this type. In those cases where the submission of one operational report may trigger the submission of a second report, such as an equipment casualty report (CASREP) triggering a change in the Readiness Reporting System, it is necessary for the ship or unit to have a procedure by which both reports are properly meshed.

Emergency Reports

Emergency reports are operational reports made under emergency conditions, and the element of speed is introduced. The emphasis in operational reports is on data and correct format. Ideally, emergency reporting stresses data, format, and speed; realistically, however, data and speed are the key elements.

The guidance for making emergency reports is contained in the OPNAV instruction 3100.6 Series, which is unclassified. Succeeding echelons of command within the fleet have published supporting instructions which amplify the CNO's requirements for addressees and formats. The objective of the CNO is to have all emergency situations reported using the formats and time criteria of his basic instruction. This document explains the mechanics of the reporting system, which are somewhat involved. The basic rule, however, is this: in an emergency situation, a voice report is submitted first, followed by a series of hard-copy messages.

Reporting Procedures

The executive officer is responsible for the overall management of reporting in the ship. The departmental officers actually prepare the great majority of reports, for the executive officer's review. The ops officer must set up a system that will set forth all of his reporting requirements, when they are due, and how they are done. In addition, he must set up a second system which will bring to his attention the operational reports being made by other departments in the ship, so that he can be sure that reports derived from other reports are made. Thirdly, the operations officer must set up a training program for all the watch officers to ensure that they are competent to work with the emergency reporting systems.

When you take over as operations officer, your predecessor will go over his current list or file of reports with you. He will probably have kept copies of previously submitted reports, perhaps in a file along with the document requiring the report in the first place. There are many ways to organize the reporting requirements—with file cards, lists, or file folders. Until you are completely familiar with the requirements of your department, it is a good idea to keep your predecessor's system intact. The preparation of the operations department's reports should not be a one-man job; each of the division officers should be taught how to prepare the reports that affect his area of responsibility. They should also be familiar with the requirements for the department as a whole against the day when they must stand in for the department head.

While administrative reporting is under the direct control of the executive officer, operational reporting is a major responsibility of the operations officer, both in making operational reports and coordinating reporting systems in the ship.

In most surface ships the operations officer is responsible for making those reports that are directed by the Navy Readiness Reporting System. The reference for this reporting system is the OPNAV instruction C3501.66 Series. This instruction is classified, and thus the details of this reporting system are beyond the scope of this manual. The important thing to remember is that when operational reports are made which change the ship's status or readiness, a parallel report is normally required by the Readiness Reporting System, which is why the operations officer must be informed when operational reports are filed by the other department heads.

Checking Process

One way to ensure a successful checking process is to establish the procedure that whenever an operational report is made, the operations officer gets to chop (initial) it. This procedure ensures that a second (and knowledgeable) person checks the report for errors in format. It ensures that the operations officer knows the report is going out. Another method is to serialize certain kinds of operational reports in the ship, with the operations (or Ops duty) officer maintaining the serial log. Before the message can go out, the drafter has to get a serial number from the operations officer, and again a check is made. Some operational reports require a serial number as part of their format, but there is no reason why a ship cannot serialize some of its operational reports, if only on drafter's copies.

Emergency Reporting

In chapter seven, we discuss how the ship organizes and trains to meet operational emergencies. One element of that training, which is done by the ops officer for the line watch officers, is making emergency reports.

It is not realistic to establish a procedure by which only the operations officer makes emergency reports. This is more properly a watch officer function, since emergencies by definition happen suddenly and not always while the operations officer is on watch. Training should include familiarization with the kinds of reports, their formats, the ship's emergency action folders, and a walk-through practice in each type of emergency report. The operations officer must first ensure that he knows how to make the reports, then train his division officers, and then train all the watch officers in sessions which have been set up by the senior watch officer or by the XO. Once he has gone through this training, the watch officer should be able to call radio central, identify the kind of report being prepared, and have the communications path set up automatically—by either patching in a voice circuit, or making a fill-in-the-blanks teletype message form available immediately.

If it should happen that an emergency situation arises for which there is no specific type of emergency report, a good rule to fall back on is the old scouting force report: what, who, where, when, why, and whither. Remember also the rule about fires: first tell the fire department, then go fight the fire. First tell the operational commanders that your ship is facing an emergency situation, then use all of your assets to cope with the situation. With sufficient training, the initial emergency report will go out automatically, correctly, and quickly without a big production.

Missed Reports

A report is missed usually because the officer who is responsible for preparing it is absent when the report is due. Another officer in the ship may be assigned to cover the absent officer's duties, but he might not know that a certain report is due. The tickler system would not necessarily pick up the discrepancy, because the tickler memorandum may not be addressed to the officer covering for the absentee. One solution to this problem is to have two names listed in the tickler file—one for the officer who normally prepares a report, a second for his likely alternate.

A report is more often late than completely missed or overlooked. This happens because the officer assigned to draft the report does not take into account the length of time needed for its review by the department head, the executive officer, and the captain. The result is a last-minute scramble to get the report out, often with errors which a more careful and deliberate review would have caught.

Complicating this problem is the process known as reporting for consolidation. This is a situation wherein a ship submits a report to the immediate superior in command (ISIC), who in turn consolidates the inputs from all of his ships into one report for the next level up. Consolidation always pushes back the due date for the ship's drafter, since the process takes time. If a report is normally due on 30 June, and the squadron commander calls for inputs for consolidation, the ship's drafter is going to have to back up as much as a week to meet the intermediate deadline.

The only way around the problem of late reports is to aim for early submission; allow a day for a message report to get to its addressee, another day for the addressee to do his consolidation work, and yet another day to get his message transmitted to the next echelon of command. Then add a day of grace, and your reports will always be on time.

Summary

Reporting is a major administrative and operational activity for all department heads. The operations officer has the added responsibility of preparing special reports which are themselves precipitated by reports. Before constructing an elaborate report-tracking system in the department, see if the current system is working. At the beginning of your tour as operations officer, you should:

- Find out what all the reporting requirements are;
- See if the operations department and the ship have adequate tickler systems;
- See if the tickler system lists both a primary and an alternate reporting officer;
- See if the tickler system effectively gets all reports out on time;
- Train the division officers in your department to make all the routine administrative and operational reports for which operations is responsible;
- Make sure that the ship's training program has adequate provisions for training watch officers in emergency reporting.

The next chapter deals with the problem of organizing for and coping with operational emergencies, including methods of accelerating the reporting process associated with these emergencies.

7
Operational Emergencies

This chapter will describe some characteristics of operational emergencies at sea, and will provide some techniques for dealing with such emergencies.

Considerations

Operational emergencies happen anytime and anywhere. Whether a collision, the eruption of a large fire, or the crash at sea of an aircraft, situations can and do develop in a random manner for which predictive rules cannot be written. A ship at sea or even in port must consider itself vulnerable to an emergency situation at all times.

A second characteristic of operational emergencies is that they occur with little or no warning. For example, an aircraft might be towing a target sleeve for your ship's air gunnery exercise. One minute the plane is making an outbound run to take position for the next firing run. The next minute it disappears off the radarscopes without any indication of trouble from the aircrew. Or, a helicopter might be hovering over the fantail lowering mailbags, and suddenly the engine quits and the aircraft pitches over into the wake, or worse, onto the fantail in a blistering crash.

The suddenness of operational emergencies tends to accentuate the very human reaction of disbelief, particularly if the emergency occurs during purely "routine" operations. This disbelief translates into momentary inaction at the very time when swift action is most needed. Since even the most routine operations carry at least the potential of becoming emergency situations, it is necessary that someone in the ship view every evolution with this in mind so that he will know what immediate actions will be needed if things suddenly go wrong.

A third characteristic of operational emergencies at sea is that an initially high level of activity is always necessary, which must be followed by activity at a more sustained level. For example, when an aircraft goes down in the middle of a task force, there is a flurry of activity when ships and helicopters move in to attempt recovery of the crew. If, however, that initial attempt is not successful, then some ships and aircraft will probably be detailed to begin a sustained search-and-rescue mission, which might go on for a day or so. Both the immeditate response and the transition to a sustained effort are subjects for planning and preparation. It should be noted that the sustained effort will ultimately have to be superimposed on the ship's other operational missions within the task group.

Another characteristic of operational emergencies at sea is the "everybody wants to help" syndrome. This is particularly true in search-and-rescue missions. Inevitably this creates a great deal of confusion at the outset of the emergency, exactly when you do not need it. For example, if an aircraft did crash in the middle of a busy fleet operating area, every ship in the operating area would begin to converge on the scene. This means that the ship which is at or near the scene must spend its initial efforts sorting out traffic rather than concentrating on setting up the vital initial search.

In the first phase of an operational emergency, tactical communications circuits quickly overload to the point of saturation. This is caused by two things: first, people tend to talk too much and too long when faced with a sudden emergency; second, the "everybody wants to help" syndrome comes into play, as every ship and aircraft in the vicinity comes up on the radio (invariably on the one circuit available) offering assistance. Whenever there is an operational emergency at sea, there will always be one (normally UHF) voice radio circuit, on which efforts to deal with the emergency will be initially coordinated, followed by the activation of other, specialized circuits as efforts to control the situation develop.

Finally, in the event of an operational emergency, there is a pressing need for someone to take charge right away. If there are two or three ships present when something happens, then the senior commanding officer becomes the on-scene commander. If your ship is operating independently, then your commanding officer will become the on-scene commander. If an accident or disaster on your ship *is* the operational emergency, and your ship has its hands full trying to control the situation, the first ship or aircraft to appear on the scene will take charge. It is a good rule of thumb that the captain of a ship which is involved in a major emergency on board should not be designated as on-scene commander, particularly after his ship has asked for assistance. There will be too much going on at the ship control stations on board to allow proper command, control, and coordination of all the units that might become involved in the assist efforts.

If, for example, a ship is controlling an ASW aircraft during an exercise when a major fire breaks out on board, and this is reported to the pilot or aircraft commander along with a request for assistance, then that aircraft commander will assume the duties of on-scene commander until the first assisting unit that is better equipped to coordinate the situation arrives on the scene. Above all, one unit must take charge right away and announce that fact to all units entering the picture, until that unit is properly relieved.

Preparation for Operational Emergencies

There is no lack of official guidance and procedures in the fleet for handling operational emergencies, particularly in the specialized cases of search and rescue or a lost submarine. An effective ship's emergency action bill is the means by which a ship will translate doctrine into action. The various type commanders have decreed the organization and titles of ship's bills in this area. There are general emergency bills, rescue and assistance (in port and at sea) bills, pilot rescue bills, etc. Your ship's organization and regulation manual will contain an entire section on operational and administrative bills.

There is, however, a problem with bills, and that is the problem of keeping them current and effective. Due to the high personnel turnover rate in today's fleet, *currency* becomes a problem. It often takes only a few months to have a significant number of the people assigned to a ship's bill transferred and replaced with new faces. By *effectiveness* is meant the ability of the people assigned to do what the bill is designed to do. Reliance upon an annual update of the emergency bills is a prescription for real trouble.

A regular and systematic exercise of the emergency bills is the only way to uncover personnel assignment problems and to determine the real state of training of the emergency teams. The best way to ensure that there are regular exercises is to have the planning board for training include emergency bill training in both the master plan and in the weekly training plans. Some bills are exercised daily, such as the in-port fire teams and rescue-and-assistance personnel. Other bills require more elaborate preparations and as much as a day of training time set aside to get a good look at the bill and the crew's ability to handle it. The Fleet Training Centers have recognized the need for emergency team training and offer one-day courses, the only requirement being that your ship send its entire team, as a team, to the Center for an uninterrupted day of training. These sessions are very worthwhile.

Handling Operational Emergencies

The operations officer has two distinct roles to play in handling operational emergencies:

1. Knowing the schedule for an up-coming week of operations at sea, the operations officer should try to identify those events which might produce an operational emergency; and
2. Having done that, he should make some arrangements which will make the ship more able to deal with an emergency should one occur.

Given a typical week of operating in the fleet operating areas, with training services assigned, what are the kinds of events which need special scrutiny? Some examples:

- Any exercise that involves operations with an aircraft;
- Any exercises that involve submarines;
- Firing with live weapons exercises.

As a general rule, operations which involve other units offer a greater chance for an operational emergency than independent operations. Having identified the evolutions which are more likely to produce emergencies, the ops officer can then begin his preparations.

For example, suppose the ship is scheduled to conduct a number of exercises with a submarine for an entire day. What is the worst thing that can happen? Something might go wrong with the submarine, which could cause potential maneuvering difficulties, or at worst, an inability to rise to the surface due to a rupture of the hull or other serious emergency. The pertinent operational procedures progress from operation SUBLOOK through operation SUBMISS to operation SUBSUNK. Besides the standard briefings given prior to conducting any exercises, an additional briefing must be given on what the ship should do if presented with indications of a SUBMISS/SUBSUNK situation. You would conduct operation SUBLOOK. A study of the applicable procedures will reveal that there are some things which can be done in advance.

For instance, the ship would already know the submarine's geographic location, or at least its assigned op-area, the submarine's name, the date, the water depth in the area, etc. A partial draft of the initial SUBLOOK/SUBMISS/SUBSUNK report could be made up before leaving port, along with pre-cut teletype tapes which would require only precise time and position data before being transmitted.

The week's communications plan should have provisions for the ship to come up on all of the predesignated local circuits which have been set aside for the SUBMISS/SUBSUNK contingency. The plan should also have a system of priorities for the circuits so that the radiomen know without being told which circuits have to come up first and which are apt to be dropped to make way for the emergency circuits. This can all be done before leaving port, and should be part of the week's exercise briefings.

Watch officers who will be in control when the exercises with the submarine take place will have to be briefed on the time-constraint rules for declaring an emergency and the special underwater signals which either the ship or the submarine might use in the event of emergency.

In other words, since the standard procedures for dealing with this particular situation are already known, and since the general situation—the participants, the location, etc.—is already known, then it makes sense to arrange as much as possible in advance. Then if something does happen, the ship is ready to deal with the emergency despite the distractions of the problems described at the beginning of this chapter.

Emergency Action Folder

One very useful way to assemble the emergency arrangements in CIC is to have an emergency action folder. Using a three-ring notebook and plastic page protectors, you can summarize all of the basic emergency procedures, arranged by category, on action check-off sheets. There would be a section on SUBMISS/SUBSUNK, on general search and rescue (SAR), on incident reporting, boarding and salvage, rescue and assistance, etc. Each section would contain a list of the appropriate references, an action check-off page or pages, a list of the primary communications arrangements, and fill-in-the-blanks samples of the first two or three required message reports, whether they be voice or record traffic. Having such a folder available, any watch officer can simply open to the right section and take the proper action. If your ship does not have such a folder in CIC, (and most do have some variant of this), it is a must to make one up. Preparation of the emergency action folder, done in company with the CIC and the communications officers, provides an excellent review for a new operations officer. The emergency action folder cannot be static. It must be updated to conform to the geographic location of the ship's operations.

The same kind of arrangements can be made for operating with aircraft, where the situation being anticipated is a search-and-rescue mission for a downed aircraft. There are procedures for SAR established for every geographical area in which U.S. Navy forces operate, both around the continental United States and overseas.

The preparations for aircraft SAR at sea are very similar to those for a submarine accident. SAR communications circuits are normally predesignated and would have to be put into the current CIC communications plan along with the SUBMISS/SUBSUNK circuits. Once again, the operating area is known, the time and date, which squadron will provide the aircraft, the aircraft base call sign, the type of aircraft, and even the number of people normally aboard such an aircraft for the type of mission being flown.

When it comes to aircraft SAR, the concept of planning ahead can be extended to the pilot rescue teams. If a ship is operating from its home port, the chances are that the aircraft squadron is also near the home port. The operations officer can call the safety officer or operations officer of the squadron which will provide the service aircraft, and arrange to have the entire pilot rescue team go to the naval air sta-

Search and Rescue Operations: Distress markers.

tion to inspect the aircraft first hand, and see what survival equipment is available on board to help them effect rescue of the aircrew.

The preparations for SAR, just like the actual ship's bills, must be tried out in training sessions to see if any problems arise. It is only necessary to man the CIC and communications center teams for an hour, announce the situation, and make a trial run of bringing up circuits and getting the initial messages set up. The combination of thoroughly checking out the ship's emergency bills by adding their exercises to the regular, planned training program, and making specific arrangements for upcoming operations will make your ship much better prepared for an actual emergency.

Warning Signs

When a ship or a group of ships assembles for an exercise, the emphasis is on having a smooth and successful operation. Because training services and underway time are scarce, everyone is concentrating on getting the most out of them. While this is, of course, the proper objective, it creates a frame of mind which tends to diminish a watch officer's awareness of an impending emergency. Officers experienced in fleet operations, however, can usually distinguish between the normal friction of a training evolution and an impending emergency, because there are some warning signs.

Let us take an example. A guided missile cruiser is at sea, and is conducting land-launch training for an embarked helicopter detachment. The flight operations bill has been set, the fire parties are in place, and communications are good between the landing signal officer, the helicopter, and CIC.

In the aircraft, there is one experienced pilot and one brand-new pilot who is making the approaches, landings, and takeoffs. The ship is steady on the flight operation's course and speed. The land-launch circuit has been patched to a speaker in CIC so that watch personnel can become familiar with the phraseology and procedure on that circuit. There is a normal flow of control signals as the aircraft comes in, touches down briefly, and then lifts off for another pass. Everything seems perfectly normal.

The operations officer happens to be in CIC, and although not on watch, he is listening to the land-launch circuit. He hears the new pilot complaining to the landing signal officer (LSO) that the airstream over the flight deck is getting more turbulent. The watch officer responds to the pilot, via the controller, that these are the best "winds" he is going to get, given present sea and wind conditions. Meanwhile the sound-powered phone talker in CIC makes the remark that the LSO said that this new pilot's landings were really sloppy. The copilot asks the LSO to relay to the maintenance chief that he wants the automatic stabilization equipment looked at when they finish the exercise, because it is cutting in and out. At this point, an experienced ops officer should be getting concerned. He has had three warning signs that a relatively routine training operation is starting to go wrong.

The situation described above does not call for stopping the evolution in panic, but it does mean that the evolution has progressed from a routine and relatively safe exercise to a situation where perhaps one more adverse factor could precipitate an operational emergency. In this case, the operations officer should notify the captain that the evolution is not going too well. The captain would then decide whether or not to continue the exercise.

The foregoing situation illustrates a case where the operations officer was sensitive to the subtle indications of possible trouble brewing in what had been a routine evolution aboard ship. Ideally, the tactical action officer (TAO) on watch should be alert to the same signs. The operations officer cannot be in CIC all the time; thus, it is important to include in the preparation and training for each major evolution a discussion of the possible warning signs.

Let us take a second example. Suppose the ship is operating in the fleet training areas and is scheduled for an air gunnery exercise in the early afternoon. The ops officer is in CIC checking to see that CIC is ready for the exercise and that a controller is up on the proper circuit and ready for the service aircraft. The aircraft's type and call sign are, of course, known.

The ship sounds general quarters, and all hands man their stations. The air controller reports no contact with the service aircraft on the scheduled frequency. This is a fairly routine occurrence, because service aircraft are often busy checking out their sleeve-towing equipment and other systems en route to the exercise area. They could also be late in getting off the field, or have the wrong frequency, or have a bad radio set. Or they could have crashed.

The weapons officer will be doing his final system checks, and the communications and CIC officer will be rotating radio equipment to ensure that the problem is not in the ship's communications. The operations officer, however, must be alert to the possibility that in this case it is not one of the routine problems, but possibly the beginnings of a SAR (Search and Rescue). There are several things he can do.

He can notify the local operating area coordinator that the scheduled rendezvous has been missed and ask him to call the field to double-check that the plane left. He can alert the radar operators to look carefully for distress displays and order the air controller to check all of the fleet operating area air-control frequencies to see if the aircraft is attempting to contact the ship on the wrong frequency.

In other words, the operations officer should not just sit back and wait for the plane to appear on station. He should

Search and Rescue Operations: Pickup training.

make every effort to make contact and to determine whether or not the plane did depart for the mission. Ninety-nine times out of a hundred it will be a routine problem. Until the ship knows this, however, she should take the preliminary steps to determine if an operational emergency is not in fact in progress. This becomes the operations officer's job, because he is normally the general quarters tactical action officer (TAO). If the ship is not at general quarters but is conducting a nonfiring exercise with manned aircraft, then the TAO would take these same steps. The operations officer's job then becomes one of ensuring that the TAOs are sensitive to all the possibilities when an aircraft fails to arrive when scheduled.

Reconstruction of Emergencies

A great deal can be learned after the fact about what caused an operational emergency, if there is enough data available to reconstruct what happened. As described previously, there are warning signs, but these sometimes are not recognized until later. The investigation which follows any major disaster in the fleet is very dependent upon retrieving accurate and factual information from units that were involved. Successful retrieval requires that a ship activate reconstruction aids almost as soon as she begins to deal with the emergency.

Reconstruction Team

If the people are available, it will greatly simplify the problem if a reconstruction team can be organized. The team can be made up of as few as three people, two of whom would be stationed in CIC and the third on the bridge with a camera. They would, of course, have to be trained, but basically their duties would be to record what is happening in the surface plot and decision areas of CIC and on the bridge during the ship's efforts to control an operational emergency. Maximum use should be made of portable cassette tape recorders, and team members should be taught the procedures of annotating the events as well as the times at which they occur.

For example, in the case of a Navy ship being dispatched to assist a burning merchant vessel, the ship would activate the rescue and assistance bill and begin coming up on the proper command and control circuits. At the same time, the reconstruction team would be posted, a time-check made over the 1MC, and the team members would begin to record the actions being taken at the control stations. The control station officers would thus be freed of any data-gathering responsibilities and be able to concentrate on the emergency. If the ship has automatic recording devices, such as a multichannel tape recorder for voice radio circuits, these would be activated right away, as would any automated data storage and retrieval equipment. The point is that there must be a reconstruction system/team organized that is ready to go into action when an emergency occurs.

If there is not sufficient manpower available in the ship to form a reconstruction team, then the principal control officers can make their own recordings. The simplest way to do this is for the TAO and surface watch officers to make a running commentary as to the progression of events, reports, and observations during the emergency. This is less than ideal because it tends to distract the watch officers from the job at hand. On the other hand, because those same officers will be required to reconstruct their actions and decisions after the emergency is over, they must have some system in effect to keep track of what happened. An open-microphone tape recorder can be energized at the TAO deck to achieve some recovery of data.

In addition to the above procedures, such things as dead-reckoning tracer plots, deck logs, circuit logs, and copies of all related message traffic will have to be collected as soon as the immediate emergency is over, and this is the responsibility of the operations department. The process of reconstruction will be much more effective if a mechanism for collecting data during the emergency has been set up beforehand. Each type of ship faces different manpower and equipment constraints; thus, the operations officer will have to tailor the design of his reconstruction team or system to his own ship. A photographer should be made a part of the bridge reconstruction team if possible.

Being the On-Scene Commander

It is standard Navy procedure to have one unit take charge of dealing with an operational emergency, and the senior officer or unit is called the on-scene commander. The rules for assuming this duty are governed somewhat by the situation. The first unit to arrive at the scene, be it aircraft or ship, will assume these duties until relieved by a senior unit or a unit better equipped to conduct control of the emergency.

The on-scene commander has a tough job, because he must not only apply himself to controlling the situation at hand, but he must also keep his commanders informed as to what is happening. On most ships, this means that the same officers who would be actively involved in the emergency would be at the same time preparing the required reports for higher authorities. Because of this, the reporting system in the ship must be prepared just like the reconstruction team was—before it is needed.

It should be obvious that the ship's preparations must include not only the assignment of responsibilities to officers for handling the emergency, but also for handling the job of on-scene commander. This is best done by two separate officers, and a common arrangement is for the captain to deal with commanding the recovery effort, while the operations officer handles the reporting and the control of assisting units.

As stated in the chapter on reporting, speed and accuracy are the main requirements of emergency reporting. The use of an emergency action folder simplifies the reporting to a fill-in-the blanks procedure, but it must be remembered that the captain ultimately has to decide what is going to be said in a report, and he will have to make that decision while commanding the efforts to control the operational emergency.

The operations officer's job in this circumstance is to act as the operations director of the effort, thus freeing the captain from the technical details of making reports.

The on-scene commander must also deal with the other units which will come into the area offering assistance. The basic rule for the on-scene commander is not to accept an offer of assistance unless his ship is ready to give the assisting unit something to do. The captain must decide whether or not to accept assistance, since units which hear about an emergency generally offer assistance without being asked. The problem is that they tend to do it on the same circuit being used by the on-scene commander to coordinate command and control of the situation. If your captain is on-scene commander and cannot immediately use the services of a second unit, the best procedure is to ask the second unit to stand by on a secondary circuit in an "on-call" status. To keep down the number of requests for information from units in the area, it is a good idea to broadcast a summary of the situation from the on-scene commander at periodic intervals. This keeps the primary control circuit free for control efforts.

Summary

Operational emergencies at sea require preplanning in order for a ship to respond effectively. The CIC is a natural place from which to direct the ship's efforts in handling an operational emergency. The operations officer's role in preplanning for operational emergencies is to assess an upcoming operating period for situations from which emergencies might arise. If the ship and its watch officers know in advance that a certain evolution might produce an emergency, they will be much more effective in reacting to it.

Preparations for operational emergencies consist of three main steps: organizational arrangements–i.e., effective and current ship's bills, the use of an emergency action folder as part of the CIC's standard operating procedures, and the prepositioning of initial emergency reports. These steps, when combined with proper briefings prior to each major evolution, can do a lot to overcome the initial surprise and consternation which normally ensue in an emergency. Some method of reconstructing the events leading up to an emergency, and then covering the ship's efforts to deal with that emergency, must be organized before the event.

When dealing with operational emergencies, the hardest part for the on-scene commander is that he must not only take immediate action, but also report his actions to his superior officers. The ship's preparations must always include measures which clearly spell out responsibilities within the ship for doing both.

8
The Combat Information Center

The combat information center is the heart of the operations officer's world aboard ship. While CIC is the direct responsibility of the CIC officer, its overall performance reflects the ability and professional knowledge of the operations officer.

The combat information center or the bridge is the place where the captain, or an embarked flag officer, will exercise command and control. The CIC is the only place where almost all of the ship's combat systems' sensors can be displayed simultaneously. It is the only place where a true-motion geographic plot of the ship's movements is maintained continuously, using a dead reckoning tracer (DRT). Significantly, it is the one place in the ship where operational reporting can be done in sight of a fairly complete tactical picture. And finally, CIC is the place where all of the ship's combat systems can be monitored and controlled by either the general quarters or a condition watch team.

Control Relationships

It is important for the new operations officer to know and understand the relationships between CIC and the bridge, hereafter referred to as control relationships. Some evolutions are controlled entirely from within CIC, others entirely from the bridge, with a large grey area of evolutions which fall within the watch responsibilities of both stations.

The commanding officer has the authority to release the ship's weapons systems for firing and to direct the ship's movements. Since he cannot be on the bridge or in CIC all the time, he delegates this authority to two principal control officers, the tactical action officer (TAO) and the officer of the deck (OOD). The relationship between these two officers, and the division of authority, is affected by several factors.

When the captain delegates his authority, he, and he alone, must specify in writing the limits of authority for both the TAO and the OOD, and in general, the circumstances in which the OOD becomes subordinate to the TAO and vice versa. This specification is normally found in the command and control section of the ship's combat systems doctrine.

The limits and division of authority are dependent upon two factors:

1. The capabilities of the combat information center and the bridge to exercise command and control, in terms of physical layout and equipment.
2. What the ship is doing at any given time, and in what environment.

The capability of the CIC in terms of physical layout and installed equipment will be a very important factor in determining the TAO's authority.

For instance, in a guided missile cruiser, equipped with the Naval Tactical Data System (NTDS) and a large array of communications and other electronics equipment, the TAO has at his disposal a much better tactical "picture" than the OOD on the bridge, even though the OOD can actually see much of a formation or force of which the ship is a part. If, on the other hand, the CIC is limited to a search radar repeater and DRT installation, with two or three radio circuit positions, the bridge and the CIC stations may be just about equally able to comprehend and display the tactical situation. The actual capabilities of your ship's CIC and bridge stations will determine much of the relationship between the TAO and OOD. It will always be in the context of what the ship is doing.

To illustrate, let us take two examples. In the first, the ship is participating in a peacetime antiair warfare tracking exercise, which requires that the ship detect, track, and report the exercise raiding aircraft, and, when possible, lock on to it with fire control radars to simulate a gun or missile engagement. This is the kind of evolution which is run entirely from CIC, and entirely under the control of the TAO. The OOD will participate only if the TAO directs a course change in order to unmask fire control directors or to clear launcher blind zones.

In a second example, the ship has been ordered to refuel at daybreak from a fleet replenishment ship. The captain has stated in his night orders that he wants the replenishment details on station and ready, with the ship in waiting station, at 0600. In this case, the bridge and CIC would work together to find the oiler during the night, with the bridge (OOD) having the principal role of getting reveille sounded, the personnel on stations, and the ship maneuvered, with CIC's assistance, into waiting station as the night orders direct. The actual approach alongside would be controlled entirely from the bridge. CIC would have no role at all in the final approach and conning once alongside.

The ambiguity in the relationship between the TAO and OOD arises because the TAO concept is a wartime, i.e., fighting concept. When the ship is under threat of attack twenty-four hours a day, there is little doubt as to the TAO's role, in that the ship's main business is fighting. In peacetime operations, the TAO's real job often becomes one of being an underway command duty officer responsible to the captain, as the senior line officer on watch, and of seeing to it that the events scheduled for the day are carried out. But that, of course, is also part of the OOD's job in a peacetime operation, and hence the ambiguity.

In some ships, the TAO is in charge of the watch team, which includes being in charge and superior to the bridge watch team, including the OOD. The OOD is responsible for ship control and for ensuring that maneuvers directed by the TAO are in fact safe maneuvers. The OOD is also responsible for implementing the plan of the day in regard to administrative matters, such as passing the word for scheduled meetings, payday, etc. In other ships, the OOD is in charge of the watch, with a TAO on watch in CIC with the sole function of watching for a potential surprise attack. If a surprise attack occurs, he has the authority to maneuver the ship, release weapons, activate electronic warfare equipments, and, in general, do everything the captain would do in the first critical moments until the captain arrives. The difference here is that his authority does not come into play until a specific contingency arises—in this case, a surprise attack in peacetime.

Because of the many different types of ships, missions, and capabilities, it cannot be specified here what the TAO/OOD relationship is going to be, other than to say that the operations officer must understand it, and that all of the line officer watchstanders must understand it. If the ship does not have this relationship clearly written down, it may become one of the ops officer's first projects to draft the necessary doctrine.

Organization of CIC

The organization of your ship's CIC watch will be set forth in the ship's combat systems doctrine and in the organization and regulation manual. The size and type of watch kept will be a function of the mission of the ship, the current condition of readiness, and the physical layout of the CIC itself.

The physical layout of CIC is a determining factor in organizing the watch. If the CIC is modular—that is, different rooms for different functions—then more people are required than if the CIC is contained in one room or space. This factor often results in the CIC people being in a higher condition of readiness than, for instance, the bridge watchstanders. The bridge might be in three sections, while the CIC teams are in port and starboard sections in order to keep all of the modules manned.

The normal watch organization in CIC has a watch officer in charge, either the TAO or simply a CIC watch officer, and one or more enlisted supervisors for each of the functions being performed (or each of the modules being manned). In a small CIC, there might be a CIC watch officer, a surface maneuvering supervisor, an electronics warfare supervisor, and a crew of three to six enlisted men to man the scopes, plot on the DRT, work maneuvering board problems, and act as radio net talkers.

In larger CICs, such as in a missile cruiser, there will be a TAO on watch. He might have a surface watch officer, a second officer acting as the weapons coordinator, an identification officer, and senior enlisted men as supervisors of the missile and gun systems, detection modules, electronic warfare, ASW weapons control, air controllers, and so forth.

As a department head, you, the operations officer, will probably be standing a TAO watch in the CIC watch organization. If your ship has a substantial weapons capability, you will discover that the combat information center is no longer a purely operations department space. The command and control equipments associated with long-range weapons systems are so closely integrated with the sensors and display equipments in CIC that weapons department personnel will man a significant portion of the stations within the CIC.

Depending upon how complex the combat systems are in your ship, the principle of command by negation, familiar to the practitioners of antiair warfare, will apply. That is, the TAO will order that a particular target be engaged, and the captain can negate that order, but otherwise he will say nothing more about the engagement as the CIC responds by tracking, designating, assigning and firing weapons, and analyzing the engagement to determine if a kill was made.

Condition Watches

Navy policies on manning ships are aimed at having the ships able to man the combat systems on a condition watch basis, normally condition three. Under condition three, some portion of all the weapons/combat systems are manned on a rotating basis of one watch in three. This results in the ship being nominally able to defend herself while operating in an environment where the threat is not well defined. The basic premise of condition three is that the ship will be able to begin self-defense and still have time to set up the general quarters team if a sustained attack develops.

Consider, however, the following situation: the ship is operating in a condition three state of readiness, with one defensive weapons system manned. A threatening situation develops suddenly, and the people in CIC become fully engrossed in using the condition three system to set up a defense against what looks like an imminent surprise attack.

The TAO, following the standard concepts of condition three, orders the bridge to sound general quarters. The entire division of operations specialists and the GQ weapons people come pouring into CIC, each with a dozen questions as to what is happening. In the midst of all this, the attack is launched against the ship. Who has control in CIC?

In modern naval warfare, engagements can develop so swiftly that the traditional response of automatically going to general quarters may be a fatal mistake under some circumstances. To change hands on the weapons and surveillance controls once an attack is inbound may very well deny the ship its best defense when it is most needed. Depending upon the circumstances, it may be much wiser to allow the condition three watch to conduct the first defense and counterattack, because they have the best picture of what is happening. The general quarters team is necessarily hitting the situation cold.

General Quarters

The advantage in going to general quarters is that it gives the ship the best material condition of readiness for resisting and combating battle damage, and also puts the most experienced people at the control stations. If the situation allows, it is best for the TAO to order general quarters, but he must understand that this course of action should not be automatic. The combat systems doctrine should address this problem and lay out guidelines as the captain directs. The corollary to the above discussion is that the condition three watch team in CIC must be trained and able, in fact, to carry the full load of an emergency engagement, from the TAO on down to the most junior enlisted man.

The combat systems doctrine must specify at which levels a threat of combat necessitates a shift to condition two or even to extended general quarters. The Captain will have set forth his policy in this regard, and the policy will reflect the ship's current employment. This means that the condition of readiness for CIC, and perhaps for other portions of the ship, will not be a static thing, but will vary as a function of the strategic, geographic, and tactical situation.

In practical terms, the foregoing means that CIC may have to operate in condition three or two, or even at general quarters if the situation dictates, while the rest of the ship is in a lesser condition of readiness. The criterion is that the CIC must be able to detect, evaluate, and make an initial defensive response to the level of threat that exists in the ship's operational environment. The operations officer, as the cognizant department head for the combat information center, must adapt the watch bill in CIC to the operational climate rather than just make an arbitrary division of the personnel available.

Operation of CIC

The operation of the CIC is the direct responsibility of the CIC officer, who is a subordinate of the operations officer. There is a natural tendency on the part of operations officers to take over the management of CIC completely, sometimes to the detriment of the CIC officer. This should be avoided, for obvious reasons. The operations officer should strive instead to be very conscious of the quality of the watchstanding done in CIC even when he is not on watch himself and try at all times to work through the CIC officer in squaring away deficiencies.

The operations officer will normally be the principal tactical action officer in the ship, and as such, will direct the operation of CIC during all evolutions which require general quarters. He will not be able to walk into the CIC on the first day and direct much of anything effectively. He will have to be trained by more experienced TAOs, and by the CIC officer.

Training the Condition Watch Team

Once he is secure in his competence in the CIC as a TAO, he will take over the training of the newer TAOs in the ship. The TAOs are normally the other line department heads, and sometimes even the executive officer. A TAO training program is necessary in order to make the condition watch team truly able to function by itself. In peacetime the ops officer ends up being the TAO for just about all firing exercises. (This is because firing exercises are conducted at general quarters, and he is the GQ tactical action officer.)

The secret of achieving real readiness with the condition three TAOs is to let them run firing evolutions using the GQ team as their watch team. Once each TAO has had the opportunity to run firing exercises using the GQ team, the next step would be to have them run the firing exercises with their own condition three watch team. The operations officer could take one section, the weapons officer another, and the engineer a third section. Then when the ship is scheduled for a gunnery exercise, she could station one of the TAOs and his watch team. Since the ship is at GQ, let the GQ team people be in attendance and supervise or train as necessary, but let the condition three team take a target from detection to firing. The objective should be to have each of the three teams confident and capable in their ability to defend the ship, because ultimately the ship will depend upon them to do just that.

CIC: Checking the communications plan to ensure coverage of all the circuit requirements.

As a general rule, the operations officer conducts the training for the TAOs, after he has become proficient himself. The CIC officer can conduct basic training for the watch-section personnel, but department heads will train more effectively with other department heads. Where you begin in this training program naturally depends on the current state of your own training and the training of the other TAOs.

The CIC Systems Notebook

One of the most important devices used to train personnel in the CIC is a systems notebook. If your ship does not have one, you and the CIC officer should make one up, and in the process you both will become experts in the CIC's physical setup.

The first thing to do is to make diagrams of the location of every piece of equipment, with one for each system. Begin with a layout diagram of the entire CIC complex, showing

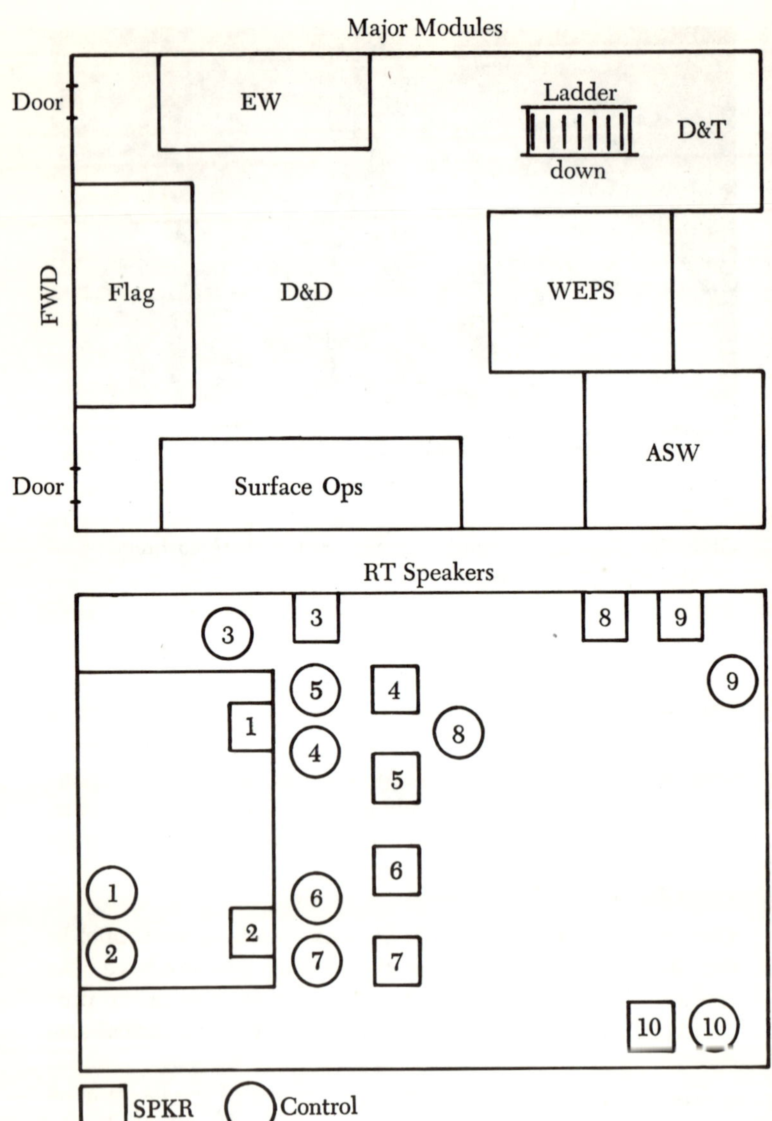

Figure 8-1. CIC Systems Book

major equipments, consoles, or scope positions. Then make up diagrams showing where all of the radio set controls are, all of the status boards and their controls, all of the telephone positions, all of the sound-powered phone connections, each of the patch panels, each of the NTDS consoles, etc., using one page for each system. For examples of pages from a typical notebook see figure 8-1.

Even for a small CIC, the systems notebook can be very complicated, and for a complex CIC, you might fill up several three-ring binders. The most complex portion will concern the communications equipment and how it is controlled and set up in the CIC. The notebook must contain diagrams of all the possible ways in which both UHF and HF communications equipments can be patched to the various positions in CIC, with the proper relationships shown among receivers, transmitters, antennas, couplers, radio set controls, remote selector switches, and remote-control channelization equipment.

The TAO and the CIC watch officer should be able to tell radio central what equipment capabilities they need (UHF/HF), what frequency or channels, which speakers they want for which radio circuits, which position they want for access to which equipment, and whether or not they want secure or clear radio voice communications. The ability to manage the communications systems becomes very important when equipment failures eliminate a vital circuit just when it is most needed. It is not sufficient for the TAO to tell radio that he has lost a particular circuit, because if all equipment is in use, radio has no idea which circuit the TAO can afford to give up in order to restore the one that was lost. Therefore the watch officers must know the systems and know how to restore circuits on the basis of operational priorities.

To complete the notebook, there should be a section on weapons control. This section should lay out the control modes and basic data flows for each weapons system, both for normal and casualty modes of operation. The best sources for this section will be the technical manuals for the systems, which normally begin with a block diagram of the overall system. The systems notebook weapons section should be kept as simple as possible, the objective being to present the control features rather than a large amount of technical data.

The systems notebook should be explicit enough to make it possible for an officer who is unfamiliar with the CIC to find each system and to be able to direct the physical implementation of the CIC communications plan for a given operation. Having such a document also overcomes the problem of the division becoming dependent upon the knowledge of one or two technicians who have been on board for some time.

Casualty Control in CIC

Engineers have long recognized the need for systematic recovery procedures in the event of various casualties involving the ship's propulsion systems. The same need exists in CIC.

A casualty to a UHF transceiver in the midst of an air-control exercise does not bring the ship dead in the water as does a main engine casualty. It does, however, cause the air-control exercise to be at best interrupted, and at worst, aborted entirely due to loss of communications. If an aircraft is being vectored out to investigate the source of a potentially hostile electronic emission, the casualty to the UHF transceiver may allow an enemy to get in a surprise attack while CIC is fumbling around trying to restore communications. Therefore, the CIC, as a control center heavily dependent upon electronic systems, needs to have a casualty control manual just as the engineering plant does. The systems notebook is the basis for this.

The most troublesome casualty, and the most common in CIC, is a failure in communications equipment. When this happens, the standard procedure is to substitute another equipment for the one that failed. This involves patching the new equipment to the position in use in CIC or on the bridge, and setting it on the same frequency that was in use on the equipment that failed. An electronics technician is then called in to diagnose the cause of the failure. As long as there are back-ups available, making the switch is not a big problem.

When, however, all of the operable equipment is in use, and one fails, the TAO or watch officer has to decide what to give up in order to restore the circuit. This means that there has to be a communications status board in CIC, which displays the equipment line-up, and some priorities for shuffling the equipments around when there are casualties. The TAO also has to know the patching and channelization scheme, as well as the physical layout of the equipment. All of this, of course, is in the systems notebook.

If a ship has only one dead reckoning tracer (DRT), and it fails in the middle of an ASW exercise, there is no alternative but to shift to manual plotting and call in the IC electricians to begin repairs. There should be a page in the CIC casualty control book, however, which shows how to operate the DRT in a reduced capability mode, if the casualty has not made the entire machine inoperable. Similarly, for other major equipments in CIC, there should be a page in the book which gives guidelines for action in the event of various individual equipment failures. The CIC casualty control manual need not be elaborate, and it should be written so that someone other than an operations specialist technician can restore failed equipment to operation in at least a reduced capability mode.

Electronics Supervisor

In large combatant ships which have complex CICs and sufficient numbers of electronics technicians, one innovative technique is to put the senior electronics technicians on watch in CIC as the electronics material supervisors in each watch section. This has several interesting advantages. The first is that the technician gains a genuine insight into what those "operators" are doing with his equipment. He learns why the watch officers are often very excited when they call in an electronics technician to fix a piece of communications equipment, particularly after he sees a few close-control intercepts done by the air controllers.

A second advantage is that there is no need for the operators to go through a middleman to get a technician. One is right there, and can see or hear the problem himself. If he is a communications technician, but the problem has to do with radar, he knows exactly who can handle the problem, and can probably make some initial repair efforts himself by following another technician's instructions over the phone.

Although the electronics supervisor works directly for the TAO or watch officer, he should be free to go to any of the electronics spaces to reset equipment or to make repairs. He is also knowledgeable in the patching systems of radio central, and can often detect a patching problem which an operator might consider an equipment problem. The whole arrangement works wonders; it sharpens the response of the ET gang to operational problems, and it also makes them feel as though they are part of the operations team rather than on-call repairmen.

Smaller ships might not be able to afford the luxury of an electronics supervisor because of heavy maintenance loads and the lack of qualified personnel. They can, however, use this technique in an exercise or on those occasions when the CIC is going to be operating at a very fast tempo during a period of intense operations.

If everything is working in CIC and the situation permits, the electronics supervisor can give the operators training on how to make constructive adjustments to communications and display equipments. Most of the equipment has a wide range of possible adjustments, and often it is adjusted improperly, which can lead to casualties. The electronics supervisor can show operators how to prevent these problems. The supervisor can himself be cross-trained in areas of CIC such as the reconstruction team.

Operating the CIC

An operations expert can walk into a CIC and tell by what he sees and hears whether or not it is being properly managed.

Combat information centers should be relatively dark and quiet. Darkness tends to keep the radarscope operators' attention fixed on their scopes. Quietness allows the entire watch team to detect changes in the tactical situation by the increase or decrease in the volume of tactical communications, or simply by being able to hear contact or other reports when they are first made. If communications circuits have been patched to speakers, the speakers should be just loud enough for the operator and his supervisor to hear. If the watch officer/TAO wants to listen to a circuit, he should have it patched to a speaker that is near his position.

The principal control officer, be it the TAO or CIC watch officer, should stay in one central location rather than wander all over CIC. This encourages the use of the CIC internal communications lines instead of having people shouting reports or questions. It also reduces lag time in properly evaluating a contact or other tactical data reports. If the ship was not built with a TAO console or station, consider building a temporary one, using a desk. MC systems, handsets, speakers, telephones, and sound-powered junctions can all be installed temporarily on or near a desk without making major ship alterations in the CIC, and having a central station for the TAO is well advised. If there is room enough, make the desk large enough for two people, and the captain can then get closer to the CIC action.

If the ship operates in formation on a continuing basis, it should be standard procedure for the surface watch to keep a continuous track of all the other ships in the formation. CIC should always be able to answer a question which begins with, "Where is ______?"

If there is an aircraft carrier within your ship's surface-search radar range, the carrier *must* be tracked at all times, no matter what she or your ship is doing.

The watch officer in CIC and his team must keep in mind that in a maneuvering situation they are there to support the officer of the deck and the conning officer on the bridge. While it is true that the officer of the deck is performing the same maneuvering board computations, he may be performing them under conditions of darkness, rain, two or more tactical radio circuits intermixed with conning orders, and the ever-present requirement to pay close visual attention to where the ship is heading. The surface-module team has the advantage of being able to operate out of the weather with a DRT, tables, chairs, lights, and an attentive watch officer who is being assisted by two or more operations specialists.

Whenever a tactical signal is given, the CIC should pass its meaning out to the bridge, along with recommendations for making the required maneuver. Once the maneuver is executed, the CIC should then pass out follow-up information and refined maneuvering solutions until the ship is almost on station. The officer of the deck and his team may appear to ignore the CIC recommendations for reasons visible to them but not to CIC. This does not change the requirement for a steady stream of supportive information moving from CIC to the bridge, and that stream should not require any prompting.

The passing of information between CIC and the bridge brings up the matter of phone talkers. Most ships have an operations specialist on the CIC end of the sound-powered maneuvering information circuit between CIC and the bridge. Because of manpower constraints, however, the bridge end of the circuit often has a deck seaman as talker, and this can cause serious problems in a tight maneuvering situation. If this is the case in your ship, the CIC officer must ensure that deck personnel who man this circuit get adequate training in the CIC, so that they understand what they are passing to the bridge watch team. If you know in advance that there is going to be a period of intense maneuvering during a given watch, it may be a good idea to replace the deck seaman with an operations specialist temporarily.

Almost all ships have an announcing system, called the 21MC system, which is a combined transmitter/receiver intercom unit. You may find that your ship has fallen into the habit of using the MC system instead of the phone talkers for passing maneuvering information. This is an indication that the CIC–bridge sound-powered phone circuit is a problem. While the 21MC does allow the watch officer to talk directly to the conning officer and officer of the deck, it also raises the noise levels in CIC and on the bridge. It also competes with radio circuits in both spaces.

The 21MC system should be reserved for emergency information, and the sound-powered phones used exclusively for the maneuvering information. Then when the CIC watch officer sees that the ship, in his estimation, is standing into real danger, his call-up on the MC system will indeed get everyone's attention and possibly avert a collision. Routine use of the MC system can often be an excuse for avoiding a proper training program for the phone talkers.

Lookouts

The CIC officer is charged with the responsibility of training the ship's lookouts, and this training is sometimes neglected. Part of the problem is that the men who stand lookout belong to a different department. Also, they usually rotate through all of the bridge watch stations; as a result, no one becomes a specialist at being a lookout.

The lookouts can do their job without any electronics support. Their station is connected via a sound-powered circuit with CIC and the bridge and they are an important source of information to the CIC people, who, of course, cannot see or hear anything from inside. The lookouts have to be trained continuously on how to use binoculars, how to make sighting reports, how to determine target angles, and how to recognize both U.S. Navy ships and aircraft and those of other navies.

As the operations officer, you must see that the CIC officer puts together an effective lookout training program, and that he gets the lookout watchstanders together for training on a regular basis. There are prepackaged lookout training and recognition kits available which are very good training aids. It is also useful to have the lookouts spend some time in CIC to see for themselves what CIC does with their inputs. There will always be some people who are not suitable to be lookouts, either because of visual or hearing acuity problems, or because they do not stand watches well when unsupervised. These people should be proscribed from assignment to duty as lookouts, just as those who can and do stand a good lookout watch should get entries in their service records qualifying them as such. Finally, on slow watches you can get the boatswain mate of the watch involved in lookout training by having him hold short daytime and nighttime sessions on recognition and identification of navigation aids.

CIC Training

While the CIC officer is charged with training and maintaining the qualifications of individuals within his own division as well as the lookouts, the operations officer should be responsible for the training of the combined weapons operations watch teams in CIC.

Like any other training program, the progression of team training is from the simple to the complex. The best way to acquaint new men with the physical layout of CIC and with the basic operation of electronics systems is to use the systems notebook discussed earlier in this chapter. Ideally a man would not be allowed to man any station in CIC, be he in the operations or weapons department, until he had mastered the basic qualifications for his watch station. The problem once again is lack of manpower, which often makes it necessary to put a man on one or two break-in watches, and then have him take a watch station while still not fully qualified.

The Personnel Qualification System (PQS), mentioned in the chapter on training, is the best compromise, because it allows on-watch training as part of eventual qualification. PQS, however, does not do much for organized team training, which remains a task for the operations officer.

Cross-training in the CIC team is also very important, because it permits watch-station rotation. It has been shown that an individual's performance on a radarscope deteriorates significantly after about a half-hour's time on the scope. This means that all the watch personnel must be rotated from station to station periodically on a four-hour watch. This can only be done if the CIC officer maintains a good cross-training program for his people, and it also means that the weapons department personnel must do the same for their equipments in CIC.

Brand new junior officers, who are just beginning their surface warfare officer (SWO) qualifications, are often started out on the watch bill as surface watch officers, (or CIC watch officers if there is a TAO on station). The theory is that the enlisted surface supervisor will in effect "carry" the new officer until he becomes more familiar with his duties and the systems in CIC. The operations officer must impress upon a junior officer that his real job in CIC is to supervise, i.e., he watches the watch. He will not be able to do this if there are functions performed in CIC which he does not understand; therefore, he must first be trained in the CIC functions. Then he must learn to stand back from the action and take a genuine supervisory role. His job is to ensure that a proper DRT plot is maintained, logs kept, maneuvering boards worked correctly, and if a maneuver is in progress, that it is going properly. Too often CIC watch officers do not make the transition from their training phase—where they actually do all of these things themselves to learn how—to the supervisory phase, where they see to it that the enlisted watch does its job. This is a transition which must be nurtured by the operations officer after he evaluates the junior officer's progress through the appropriate SWO PQS.

During a slow watch, officers who are new to CIC often succumb to the temptation to work on paperwork at a desk in CIC instead of standing a proper watch. If this situation occurs, it is instructive to shrink the CIC watch-officer sections by one in order to provide the offender with some more basic training. Better yet, the fleet exercise manuals are full of exercises which require only two CIC circuits and one radio circuit for those slow mid and morning watches. If there is not another ship around, let the bridge and the CIC act as two separate stations for radio and maneuvering board drills.

Summary

In summary, the combat information center is the focal point where command and control of combat systems and communications are exercised. A properly run CIC is quiet, relatively dark, with watch personnel at their stations doing their watch jobs and not drifting around doing other things. In a properly operated CIC:

- The control relationships between the watch officer in CIC and the watch officer on the bridge must be spelled out in a ship's combat systems doctrine.
- This doctrine must be a dynamic document which is updated as the ship's operational environment changes.
- The condition watch teams in CIC should train together in order to be effective.
- The operations officer, once qualified, has the overall responsibility to train both the watch teams in CIC and other department heads who are not yet qualified as tactical action officers.
- CIC needs to have a systems notebook which clearly and simply depicts the physical location and operating parameters of the major electronic systems.

- The CIC watch team must take the initiative in supporting the bridge watch team in maneuvering or other tactical situations, and do so making use of sound-powered rather than multichannel announcing systems.
- The CIC officer has the responsibility for training individuals and module teams; the operations officer has the responsibility for training entire CIC watch teams.

No CIC can be operated successfully if the officers who stand watches there are less competent in the operation of the CIC than the individuals they are supposed to supervise.

9
Combat Operations

Combat operations are surprisingly much like peacetime operations; in wartime, naval units spend most of their time doing what they have been doing all along in peacetime, with only a relatively small portion of their time devoted to actual engagements. Unlike land warfare, where contact with the enemy is made and held for long periods of time, naval forces tend to deploy into an area, make contact, fight, break off, and regroup. With the exception of amphibious operations, there are no tangible objectives to be taken on shore in engagements between naval forces; the other side's forces themselves are the objectives.

Because the forces involved are mobile, there can be no fighting until the forces come together, or come within range of each other's missiles or aircraft. This results in there being two kinds of time in combat operations, waiting time, and engagement time. Waiting time is caused by many factors. If our side has the initiative in a particular theater of operations, we might be waiting for new units to join up, waiting to amass logistical support, or waiting for a suitable target to present itself. If the other side has the initiative, we might be trying to remain undetected until our strength increases, or we might be conducting raids to reduce the other side's strength by attrition prior to a general engagement. The significance of waiting time is that ships will occupy themselves doing routine operations. The crew will stand watches, maintenance and diagnostics will be performed, training will go on, and logistical evolutions will be carried out.

Engagement time, on the other hand, has no real counterpart in peacetime operations. About the only evolution which comes close is a battle problem conducted by the fleet training groups. When the threat signals are real, however, and when the traditional "hit alfa" of the battle problem results in explosions, fire, smoke, and personnel casualties, everything changes. Time seems to pass at an incredible rate. People feel that they have been in action for hours when only minutes have passed. Because the emotions of fear and anger are stimulated by extreme danger, the shock of combat also induces people to act and react instinctively rather than rationally. It is the human reaction to the stress of combat which makes prior training so vitally important.

Training in Wartime

In peacetime, ships work up to a high state of operational readiness on a cyclical basis; that is, they get ready for a fleet exercise or a deployment, and then cycle down to a lesser level of readiness during in-port upkeep periods, holiday periods, or during time at sea devoted to scheduled type exercises. In wartime, ships not only have to achieve through training a high state of operational readiness, but they also must maintain that readiness for long periods of time. Crews entering a combat zone for the first time tend to be very much on edge, tense, and ready to shoot at the first provocation. The units which have been there for a while, in the manner of "old hands," appear to be a little looser and more casual about the environment. The real difference is that the new ship is operating at the peak of readiness, while the old hands are operating at a level of readiness which they can sustain.

There are several factors about a ship which must be assessed before conducting training in the environment of combat operations. The most important of these are:

Amphibious Operations: Landing the landing force.

- the condition watch plan
- the material condition of readiness

The Navy recognizes that a ship cannot steam at general quarters twenty-four hours a day. As a function of the threat, however, the ship has to organize condition watches which trade off readiness against crew fatigue.

The captain must assess his ship in terms of the capabilities of his people. There is never enough fully trained and experienced talent to go around, particularly when wartime comes and the fleet expands. It is not unreasonable to expect that a ship would go to and remain in a condition of readiness two—that is, port and starboard watches—while in the combat zone, in order to maintain systems and experienced people on the line. The captain will have to weigh the impact of physical fatigue against the requirements of being ready to fight. In World War II, it was traditional to have the ship go to general quarters at dawn and dusk, as these were considered the best times for an attack. In contemporary warfare there are no best times, and the ship has to be ready to engage supersonic missiles which come from submerged submarines and other launch platforms well beyond the horizon. Achieving this state of readiness is going to take more than condition three watches. In any event, a condition watch scheme will have to be designed which can adequately cope with the threat and be maintained for weeks on end.

The major advantage of general quarters, aside from having all hands at battle stations, is that the ship sets material condition zebra for maximum damage control protection. Just as a ship cannot steam around at general quarters for days, it cannot practically steam for an extended time at condition zebra either. Material condition yoke, on the other hand, even if properly set, does not afford that much protection. There is also the problem of having a damage-control party on station. There are repair parties on station at general quarters; there are not normally any parties on station during condition three watches. The ship may well have to work out a material condition of readiness somewhere between zebra and yoke, and may have to include the stationing of one or more repair parties in its condition watch plan to meet the threat over sustained periods. Each ship is different with respect to missions and capabilities. The point here is that sustained combat operations may require deviations from and modifications to the methods of operating that are used in peacetime.

Once both the condition watch plan and the material condition of readiness have been established, the ship is ready to conduct combat training. The fundamental principle is this: the ship has to conduct combat training as a fighting entity—that is, with the condition watch set and the material condition set.

When entering a combat area for the first time, the ship will normally be given briefings by unit commanders' staffs or other ships who have been on station for some time. These officers will indicate what the current threat is and in what areas the new ship will conduct training. If circumstances allow, there will initially be a period of time during which a ship can work in company with another unit which has been on station. This will not always be the case, however, and sometimes the ship must get the last-minute training done on its own. The best strategy is to use all of that waiting time described above to accomplish as many combat training exercises as possible.

Preparing for Engagements

From the point of view of the operations officer, preparing for engagements is not much different from preparing for all other kinds of operations. The difference is, of course, that in addition to weather, equipment failures, bad luck, and other adversities, there are enemy forces that are trying their best to make everything go wrong for your ship. In combat operations, it is very rare for things to go according to plan, and your preparations should include as many back-ups and contingencies as possible. All of the ship's watch officers must memorize the fighting instructions and procedures in the operations order—not just those of the TAO, executive officer, and captain. Briefings on an impending operation must be thorough and understood, with time for questions, because people must understand what the ship is supposed to be doing if there is going to be a fight. In contrast to peacetime operations, there is no lack of motivation for people to pay attention.

Operation orders written for combat operations tend to be smaller and more concise than the large, standing op-orders of the peacetime fleet. When standard operating procedures are contained in a combat op-order, they must be known and understood by all of the watch officers and senior CIC supervisors. The operations officer should satisfy himself in particular that the cognizant people do in fact know the procedures, because the unit commanders and task-group watch officers will assume that your ship knows the rules.

There will be new procedures in effect when your ship joins a combat force. These will have arisen out of new threats and unforeseen circumstances. Some will be improvements on old doctrine, others radically new. These procedures will have to be briefed to the condition watch teams, because the ship's internal procedures will probably have to be modified.

Flagship Procedures

If your ship enters a combat zone and becomes the flagship for a unit commander, there will have to be a clear understanding of the commander's procedures and needs. Time will not be available for the usual methodical period of acclimatization between flagship and staff. The people on the staff will have to be briefed on how your ship's combat systems work and how the CIC is organized and laid out. The staff operations officer will probably ask you to look over his operations order or plans to check for holes in the staff work. Many unit commanders believe that the best way to get a new ship broken in as part of a combat organization is to move on board. They can share their knowledge directly with the new ship's officers, as well as make a first-hand appraisal of the ship's state of training and overall readiness.

Intelligence

A vital part of preparing for combat operations concerns intelligence. It is a standard rule in staff intelligence work that a commander must evaluate the enemy's capabilities and not his intentions. This is true at the ship level as well. The operations officer, for whom the intelligence officer works in ships which do not have an intelligence specialist assigned, must prepare a threat analysis for the captain and the TAOs. This consists of a concise estimate of what the enemy units that are thought to be in the area are capable of doing. The standard naval warfare publications contain a wealth of parametric data; the threat analysis should list the maximum capabilities attributed to enemy platforms and make use of the task group's intelligence estimates as to which of those platforms are supposedly in the area. Most ships adopt the procedure of having a daily intelligence briefing when in a combat zone.

Combat Systems Doctrine

Finally, the combat systems doctrine must be reviewed for currency. By this is meant that the sections in which the captain delegates weapons-release authority have to be reviewed in order for the doctrine to be in compliance with the rules of engagement for the combat area. Some elements which have to be addressed are the following:

- definition of the enemy forces
- priority of threats
- conditions for opening fire without recourse to the commanding officer
- restrictions on the use of weapons and active electronic warfare equipments
- general policy on the use of electronic/acoustic emitters
- policy as to the material condition of readiness to be maintained
- policy as to the condition of combat systems readiness to be maintained.

It should be clear from the above that the combat systems doctrine is not a static document. The command and control section, which describes the TAO's authority, the OOD's authority, and the control relationships, has to be updated (normally by the operations officer) every time the ship's strategic environment changes. The captain can generally lay out his policy on all of the matters addressed above in a few sentences on each topic. The operations officer has to sit down with the captain, and preferably with the executive officer and the other TAOs as well, and write down this policy. The resulting pages are then entered into the front of the combat systems doctrine for all watch officers to read. Writing it down makes it easier for everybody concerned to get the correct word. Given the confusion attendant with combat operations, it is important to ensure that the ship's watch officers understand the rules.

Combat

After a combat engagement begins, things happen fast. The stream of information coming into CIC accelerates to the point where people can mainly just react, as opposed to making carefully considered decisions. When an electronic emission is detected, whose bearing correlates to that of an incoming radar target that behaves like a known enemy anti-ship missile, it provokes an immediate reaction from CIC to assign and release weapons. When more missiles are detected than the weapons systems can handle, the TAO has to set priorities. The importance of prior training becomes apparent in this situation. If the watchstanders are not trained to react as a team to information received on high-speed incoming threats, mass confusion will result.

Shore bombardment operations.

If the ship is at general quarters, the operations officer will normally be the TAO. The captain will more than likely be in CIC also, where he can get the best tactical picture. Before an engagement begins, the control relationship between the captain and the TAO must be understood. There are two ways it can work:

1. The TAO can receive evaluated data from the functional supervisors, and then make recommendations to the captain as to what has to be done next; or
2. The TAO can receive the same data, and make decisions and issue orders, which the captain will countermand if he does not agree—i.e., control by negation.

How it works in your ship is of course the captain's decision, but the watch team or GQ team should practice both methods to see if the one chosen actually works with the people involved.

The complexity of the engagement has a bearing on this matter. The captain may wish to use the first method in a situation where there is only one target being engaged, or where there is a "situation" which has not yet become a real engagement. Conversely, in a general all-out battle, such as a task group under large-scale air attack, there may not be time for piecemeal decision making. Whatever the arrangement, it should be clearly established before an engagement begins.

There are times when a tactical situation becomes too complicated for one TAO to handle. Consider the case where a task group is countering a large-scale air attack, and contact is made on a submarine in the operating area. The immediate problem is one of information display: the displays for the AAW problem require a coverage of hundreds of miles; the displays for the ASW problem require only about ten miles. The AAW action will be controlled in the air-warfare module, whereas the ASW action will be controlled in the surface-warfare module. One TAO cannot be in both places at once, nor can he effectively direct the ship's movements in a multiship

ASW action while sorting out an air defense picture. In this case, there will have to be a second TAO, and a division of labor made. Close coordination is still required, because a submarine presents a formidable AAW threat with its antiship missile systems. Once again, this is a subject for prior discussion, incorporation into the combat systems doctrine, and practice.

Losing the Picture

Most officers who have been in the TAO's position in a complex action have experienced the frightening sensation of losing the picture—that is, being overwhelmed with the sheer volume of tactical data to the point where they draw a blank and cannot act.

There is a technique for handling this situation, and it goes as follows: the TAO declares aloud that he has lost the picture. Immediately, the supervisors of the various sections of CIC, in a prescribed order, give him a verbal update as to what they face, what they recommend that the ship do about it, and what the TAO's last orders to their section were. The TAO must concur with their recommendation, or disagree and give them another order, or have them say it again. In this manner, the TAO automatically reenters the picture as he deals with each supervisor. The objective is to recover quickly by treating this situation as any other system casualty in CIC. If it happens more than once in a given situation, it is a good indication that a second TAO is needed to handle at least one of the warfare areas.

Noise in CIC

During an engagement, there tends to be an increase in the amount of noise and number of personnel in the CIC and on the bridge. If the control stations are normally operated in a quiet and calm manner, the increased noise level can be accepted. If the stations are noisy in peacetime operations, the excessive noise in combat will seriously hamper efficient operation.

Much of the noise is the result of people trying to relieve the stress of combat. They shout an order which they might normally speak. There is also a feeling of intense anxiety when human beings have to stand and watch while machines engage a target. Once a guided missile has been fired, the people in CIC have to wait. They then tend to ask unnecessary questions, give redundant orders, or otherwise get in the way of the controllers, simply because they want to do something about that incoming target. The TAO has to make a conscious effort to get people to be quiet and to stay at their stations in this situation. This is hard to do; the penalty for not doing it, however, is that the TAO and the captain may miss a vital report because of all the noise.

Reduced Capability Modes

When there is battle damage, the ship may lose all or part of its electronic equipments temporarily while the repair parties go to work. When this happens, the CIC must have back-up operations and not just sit down and quit. Visual data can still be plotted, and control of the weapons systems can be shifted to missile-and gun-plotting rooms, with only target-assignment functions remaining in CIC. The reduced capability modes of operation for the various systems and major equipments should have been identified and entered in the systems notebook. Navy combat systems equipment is always equipped with some kind of casualty mode, and sometimes with several alternative methods of operation. There should be a plan which details what each warfare module can do under the various casualty circumstances.

After Action

If possible, the reconstruction team discussed in chapter seven should be posted prior to any action wherein the ship initiates an engagement. After-action reports require a good bit of precise data, and the people who are busy controlling the action will not be able to take notes. If there cannot be a reconstruction team stationed, then the operations officer should make use of portable tape recorders at key stations to record the stream of orders and the traffic over the primary radio circuits used. When the action gets in close enough, the ship's photographer should be stationed at a good vantage point to take photographs of what is happening. Most interior communications (IC) rooms have the capability to tape the sound-powered phone circuits. Have the IC room tape the JA, JC, 1JS, and the 1JV circuits during combat training sessions and during live action. These tapes can be very helpful for pointing out weaknesses in the ship's battle organization.

Summary

In the combat environment the ship has to put to use all the prior months of peacetime training and organization. The similarities of the two environments are that the ship will fight as it has trained, and that even in wartime, the ship will continue to do many of the same evolutions done in peacetime cruising. Actual combat will take up a relatively small percentage of the ship's time, although preparations for an engagement will be more intense than preparations for a peacetime operation or exercise.

There is no way to predict how people will react to the shock, disorder, noise, and confusion of an engagement. A ship can reduce this uncertainty by continuing to train intensively when in the combat theater of operations. It may very well be necessary to modify the watch organization and the damage-control arrangements to suit the new situations encountered in wartime. The operations officer will be concerned with ensuring that the combat systems doctrine is current, and that control relationships are clearly spelled out before the ship goes into action.

Index